DRIVING ON THE SUNNY SIDE
WITH 10,000 STRANGERS

CELEBRATING THE LIVES OF MY UBER/LYFT RIDERS

DRIVING ON THE SUNNY SIDE WITH 10,000 STRANGERS

JEFF HOENIG
"THE SUNSHINE MAN"

PALMETTO
PUBLISHING
Charleston, SC
www.PalmettoPublishing.com

Driving On the Sunny Side With 10,000 Strangers
Copyright © 2023 by Jeff Hoenig "The Sunshine Man"

All rights reserved
No portion of this book may be reproduced, stored in a retrieval system, or transmitted in any form by any means–electronic, mechanical, photocopy, recording, or other– except for brief quotations in printed reviews, without prior permission of the author.

First Edition

ISBN: 979-8-8229-1505-3

Dedication

First: this book is dedicated to the thousands of people who needed a ride somewhere who I was lucky enough to drive. They entertained me, educated me, inspired me, and many of them generously tipped me. Thank you for making my life and the lives of my other riders better over the past five years.

Second: Uber was my wife's idea in the fall of 2017 in New Jersey. We had several conversations like this:

Monika: I want to sign up and drive for Uber.

Me: I don't understand. You want to sit in a parking lot waiting until a complete stranger contacts you? Then, you want to pick that person up and take them somewhere and you're going to make money doing that?

She was right as usual. She gave one ride in New Jersey to the airport, and it paid thirty dollars; that convinced us that it might be worthwhile.

We are celebrating our fortieth anniversary this year, and she is the love of my life. I've been very fortunate to have met some incredible people while driving, but the most amazing person in my life has always been my wife, Monika. She gave me three wonderful children and did everything else to make my life great. She's still my princess—thank you honey. The best day of my life: 8/28/1983.

TABLE OF CONTENTS

1. My Three Favorite Rides — 7
2. Occupations—What People Do — 13
3. What's in a Name? — 49
4. The Rest of My Top Fifty Rides — 65
5. Destinations from Everywhere — 119
6. Sports-Talk Uber — 155
7. Relationships are the Best — 185
8. Southern Hospitality is Real — 227
9. Driving in Charleston, South Carolina — 239
10. Motivation and Inspiration — 255
11. Words of Wisdom and Advice — 271
12. Fun Moments — 277
13. Great Quotes — 291
14. Rides From the Twilight Zone — 329
15. My First Uber Ride as a Rider and My Ten-Thousandth Ride — 341
16. Me, My Car, My Gift, and My Uber Song — 347
17. Comments and Compliments — 361
18. "And in the End" — 373

DRIVING ON THE SUNNY SIDE WITH 10,000 STRANGERS

How are you today? Thanks for picking up this book, but I must prepare you. This is not a normal book, because I'm not a normal kind of guy. I'm an Uber driver; I'm used to giving people rides, and right now, I want to give you a ride like you've never had. In 1989, thirty-four years ago, the movie *Honey, I Shrunk the Kids* was released. The actor, Rick Moranis, played an inventor who accidentally shrunk his kids and his neighbor's kids down to a quarter inch.

I want to intentionally shrink you down, so you are about three inches tall. Then, I want to put a lot of superglue on both your feet, and I want to stick you right on the dashboard of my car next to my cell phone. Play along with me on this and I promise you an Uber ride that no one else has ever experienced. I want you to enjoy the rides I have had without having to worry about driving or paying. You don't have to say a word, and you can enjoy this experience any way you want and as often as you like.

Why did I write this book? I've now given over ten thousand Uber and Lyft rides in five years, mostly on the weekend. This book is not about me; it's about you. Maybe this is about your parents, best friend, next-door neighbor, or someone you work with. I've driven the young and old from this country and from foreign countries who were living in or visiting Myrtle Beach or Charleston, South Carolina. Except for one New Year's Eve, I've mostly driven from 5:30 a.m. to 7 p.m. Very rarely have I had riders in my car who have had too much to drink; about 98 percent of my riders have not been drinking.

I've enjoyed having about fifteen thousand people in my two vehicles. Although they started out as strangers, in many cases, we wound up becoming friends. These are their stories: regular people with incredible jobs or no jobs, people who are wealthy or living paycheck to paycheck, some with no children and some with many. My rides were as short as a minute long or as long as six hours. My goal was to give them the best ride they'd ever had and to treat them as friends.

When my wife and I moved from New Jersey on December 26, 2017, I decided to write a blog, "Becoming a Southerner" (jeffbecomingasoutherner.blogspot.com). We arrived in Myrtle Beach, South Carolina, the next day. I wanted to keep my dad, my three kids, a few relatives, and a few friends up to date on our adventures. When I started driving for Uber and Lyft in July 2018, it was natural fit to write a blog at the end of each month about the riders I had met that month. The following year, I started writing two blog posts a month; one included a few stories about my favorite riders and the other included some of my favorite comments of the month.

At the end of 2019, my first full year of driving, I wanted to thank my riders for the things they educated me about, all the moments they made me laugh, and of course, their generosity in tipping me for the ride I gave them. How do you thank complete strangers by giving them a holiday gift that they will like and is inexpensive, so your wife is not mad at you?

In 2019, I started giving some of my riders a gift by putting together a list of my best comments of the year. The appreciation I received from them led me to give out my 2020, 2021, and 2022 lists for the entire year to some of my riders. Frequently, they would tell me that I should write a book. I wrote this book to document this wonderful experience I've had, mostly as an Uber driver. (I started driving for Lyft also, but after doing over 1,100 rides and getting a very nice jacket from them, they told me during the beginning of the pandemic that my car could no longer be used. I think they mixed up the different models of a Ford Transit van, but I could not convince them of that.)

On the front cover of this book, you can see my orange 2022 Ford Transit passenger van. I waited eleven months during the pandemic before I could get it and I have given more than 2,500 rides in this car. On the back cover is my gray 2017 Ford Transit passenger van that helped me give 7,500 rides. Of course, that is me on the front cover, welcoming you into my car and opening the door for you to let you out when you're finished on your journey with me.

I'm ready to go, but I'm going to give you some tips on how to read this book and get the most out of it. The stories and comments you are about to read are true. I absolutely believe you will enjoy many of them and I encourage you to share them with others. My business name is "The Sunshine Man," and it is my pleasure to be able to put a smile on your face, get some laughs, or just brighten up your day. I've been driving on the sunny side and my only regret in giving you this ride is that I won't be able to hear your story or your comments. Maybe someday…

How To Read This Book

I strongly suggest that you read this book however you want to read it! We all know that no one likes to be told what to do and how to do it, so it's up to you. This book is different, so here are some of my suggestions:

1. Chapter 1 is my top three rides. If you read only one story in this book, please read my third favorite ride, "The Man with the Great Life." There is a lot of humor in this book, but there isn't any in this story. I sincerely wish you were in my car for this one ride; it's the one ride I cannot adequately share.
2. You can read this book from the front to the back, or you can read the last chapter first. The next to last chapter, Chapter 16, has some info on me and how I became a driver as well as some rider comments about me, my car, the gift list I gave them, and my Uber song.
3. What kind of work are my riders involved in? Chapter 2 will list more than 150 occupations, some comments about them, and more. It is quite a collection.

4. If you have a unique name, you may want to read Chapter 3 first and read about other unique names that I've collected. You'll enjoy learning about how some parents picked their child's name.
5. The fourth chapter has stories on the other forty-seven of my favorite fifty rides. These are special people to me, and they are unforgettable. These stories have something for everyone, and you'll wish you really did have a chance to meet them.
6. Where do the riders come from? Where have they been? Do you like to travel? Chapter 5 is "Destinations from Everywhere," and here, you'll find comments and a few stories from all over the world.
7. If you love sports as I do, Chapter 6 is "Sports-Talk Uber." I never thought I'd have my own sports talk show, but I do now. As a New York fan, I have enjoyed hundreds of Boston/New England fans, and you have to read some of the stories they have told me. If you're a Pittsburgh Steeler fan, you must read the story on "The Immaculate Reception."
8. Friendships, families, dating couples, and married couples—all share some incredible stories and comments that will make you laugh and surprise you. Chapter 7 is one of my best chapters, and it's on relationships.
9. Southern hospitality is not a myth. When many of us move to the South, we have to adjust to some of the friendliest and nicest people we've ever met. Don't miss out on the two best southern hospitality stories you will ever hear and a whole bunch of entertaining comments in Chapter 8

10. If you live in Charleston, South Carolina, or went to school there, you might want to go straight to Chapter 9 and read about my adventures driving in Charleston. See the Ravenel Bridge as you never have and experience the College of Charleston with my riders. This book would not be the same without the people I've met in Charleston.

11. So many riders have inspired and motivated me during these ten thousand rides. Thirteen of them are in my top fifty favorite rides and have an asterisk next to their title. This book would not be complete without including another twenty-two riders who inspired me and a few who I inspired. Read these stories in Chapter 10.

12. Are you looking for some advice from people you don't know? When I put these all together, I was impressed by how good the advice was. In Chapter 11, "Words of Wisdom and Advice," you will find at least a couple of comments that will mean something to you.

13. In Chapter 12, I have some short stories of fun moments I've had in my car with my riders. I had to leave out dozens of other moments, but you'll enjoy these.

14. Some of the best quotes from my riders are spread throughout the book, but Chapter 13 will give you all the other ones. Remember, almost all of these are from people who are somewhat normal, sober people. An asterisk next to a quote anywhere means the quote was one of my best comments of the year.

15. Are you blinded by all the positivity and sunshine in this book? Just so you know that everything isn't sunshine and rainbows, I have some stories in Chapter 14 straight from *The Twilight Zone*.
16. What is my experience as a rider in an Uber? In Chapter 15, I walk you through my very first ride in Las Vegas and thank my driver again. Also, my ten thousandth ride was pretty special and I'm going to let you experience it with me.
17. The last two chapters, 16 and 17, is "And in the End." What have I experienced on this journey? More importantly, what have you learned on your journey with me? How can we use what we've learned and spread our sunshine? Your last destination is your seventeenth stop.

I hope you share this book, but I also hope you put this in a place that you can pick it up anytime and read a story or a couple quotes. Maybe it works for you to put it in on your coffee table, your nightstand, in your bathroom, or even at work when you need a break.

I wrote this book for you. I loved giving these rides. What made these rides even more fun was that I was able to share many of these stories and comments with so many of my other riders. Now, I'm turning the key, and we're heading to your first of seventeen destinations…

1

MY THREE FAVORITE RIDES

You might think that it would be difficult to pick three of my best rides out of more than ten thousand, but that's not the case. I've had many nice rides, dozens of good rides, fifty great rides—but these three rides were really the best of the best. These three rides represent the ten thousand rides well. Combined, they had it all: terrific, dedicated, funny, interesting, and inspirational people. One tourist was heading to the airport to go home, one was leaving a hospital to go to work, and the other was a tourist on a girl's weekend early on a Saturday night.

Join me on this adventure: you're only three inches tall on my dashboard, and you're about to meet some incredible people. We just reached our first destination.

#3. THE MAN WITH THE GREAT LIFE*

What made this a great ride? We all have struggles, challenges, and things in our life that we wish were better.

Through persistence and determination, this man overcame a seemingly insurmountable difficulty. His positive attitude and strength in character makes him an inspiration to everyone. This was an unforgettable ride and the only one for which I had to pull over after it was over and compose myself for a few minutes before I could take another ride. I wish every driver could take one ride with this man.

I accepted a ride to pick up a guy at a hospital. Immediately, I got a text from a veteran's organization that said he would have a walker and might have difficulty getting in my car. They said that he might not understand everything I say and that he was hard of hearing. I was told I didn't have to accept the ride and I would still be paid. I like a challenge, so I was not tempted to refuse it.

He came out of the hospital with no walker and got into my car easily. He had no problem communicating and I was mesmerized by his story. He had just left his wife in the hospital after she was diagnosed with a second form of cancer, and she was going to undergo radiation. He was in a very good mood and told me his life story.

He had been in the Army years ago and quit drinking, because he was told it was killing him. He was in a terrible motorcycle accident that almost killed him. He had brain surgery and had a plug or a cork put in his head. He still has not recovered some of his memory.

It took him thirty years to be able to physically work again. He works part-time in a local supermarket at night cleaning, and it's a job he loves. His wife sent him home to go to work because that's what he loves to do. He told me, "I've had a great life." He gave me a cash tip when I dropped him off. A few months later, my wife had the pleasure of driving him. His wife had passed away, but he was still happy and positive. It makes you wonder how wonderful the life we have is when you meet someone like him, who had such a "great life."

#2. THE MAGICAL EVENING RIDE

What made this a great ride? No ride has surprised me more, made me laugh more, taught me more, and has received more laughs from other riders than this 1.2-mile ride in Downtown Charleston at about 7 p.m. on a Saturday night. There are some drivers who don't like taking very short rides, but this ride taught me that any ride could be a great ride and that I needed to have more fun driving and in my life.

I picked up four young women about twenty to twenty-five years old from Pennsylvania on a girl's weekend. It was my last ride of the night, and I was meeting my wife at a nearby restaurant. It had been a long day, a very good day, and I was completely taken by surprise.

The four women crossed the dark street, and the one leading the group was raving about my driving rating. I had gotten out of the car to open the doors and started laughing, since almost no one ever mentions my rating. When she sat next to me in the car, she said, "I'm sorry, this is a short ride, is that OK?" I was still laughing because no one ever asks, "Is that OK?" I told her that since they were already in the car, "I'm stuck with you."

She was laughing, and said, "If you make us get out, I'm going to have to rate you a 'one.'" At this point, I was laughing more and told her that we rate our riders. Looking at my app for a name, I asked, "Who is Cathy?" She said it was one of her friends in the back, and I knew she was lying, which her friends confirmed.

I asked her a question I've only asked a couple other riders: "Have you ever done stand-up?" Her reply was quick and hilarious: "No, should I? We should do it together, maybe later tonight?"

At that point, I knew I had to shut her up or I wouldn't be able to complete the ride. She is the only rider I've ever had to stop talking. I told her that I blog about my favorite riders and that I'd have to write about her. I gave her the business card my wife and I use and told her that if she wanted to read the story, she could send me her email address.

I told her a rider's story, where a young black kid gave me the nickname, "Jeffro-No-Fro," and when I finished, she yelled out, "I have to show you something." I told her to wait a minute and tell me when I pulled over. At her destination, she showed me a second-grade picture of herself with very curly hair, which looked like a "fro," and she hated it. Since she no longer had curly hair, her message was clear: she was "No-Fro" too.

A day or two later, I got a text from her saying that she made some comments on the app she thought I would like. When I said, "I'll see if I can figure out which comments are yours," her reply was, "If you can't, our stand-up routine will be a flop." Her comments on the app are still the best ones I've ever received and some of the only funny ones. She wrote, "What can I say about Jeffrey. We had a magical evening ride that lasted only a mile. When he and his wife move to Charleston, we're going to have a nightly stand-up routine."

When I later told another rider about these comments, she replied, "That's really cute, like you rode up on a horse with a carriage." Telling this story to a middle-aged woman maybe a year later, the woman could not stop laughing, and I thought she was going to have a medical problem. Getting out of the car, she pointed her finger at me and said, "You have to do stand-up with that woman." Women especially love this story for some reason. This young woman and I had some kind of unusual connection and the idea of doing stand-up with her was so amusing to me, I actually wrote a comedy sketch about us doing that. There really was magic in this ride and the magic was her.

#1. THE MAYOR

What made this a great ride? It was one of the earliest in my first two hundred rides. He was a terrific guy, funny, down-to-earth, and inspirational. As a political science major who loves politics, I was talking to someone actively involved in it. After this ride, I told my wife I would love to have some of my riders over for dinner; she wasn't as enthused as I was about that idea.

My favorite rider was the mayor of a small town in Pennsylvania of 350 people. He had been vacationing in Myrtle Beach and I was driving him to the airport to head home. Right away I told him he looked like the actor/comedian Tim Allen, and he said, "No one has said that to me in twenty years." He was easy to talk to, very personable. He explained to me, "I'm not a beach person, but I just spent three days on the beach here, and when I'm on the beach, I always feel like a rotisserie chicken." I was laughing and replied, "I'm not a beach person either, but I love rotisserie chicken—I just never put the two together." We had a good laugh and I've gotten dozens of laughs from riders since then with his beach comment.

I asked him how he got to be mayor, and he told me, "When I came to the town, people would tell me that someone should do something about this and that and I just decided to be that person." One practical program he started was to improve the look of the yards in the neighborhood. By selecting a "Yard of the Month" and giving out a gift certificate, his town looked better almost immediately.

I would have voted for him at that point or donated to a future campaign of his. I asked him an important question. Explaining my interest in politics, I said, "I'm curious; are you a Democrat or a Republican?" His answer is probably the best line I've heard in my car. He said, "When people ask me that question, I tell them I'm an American." I don't need to know what party he's in, but I hope one day to drive him again and tell him why he's my favorite rider.

OCCUPATIONS—WHAT PEOPLE DO

I have asked this question thousands of times in different ways: What kind of work do you do? What do you do? What do you do where you live? I have had a few people say, "As little as I can," but almost all of them were willing to share what they did for a living. It's amazing to me to think back on all the different occupations, some I had never even heard of. I have listed 150 occupations below and a short comment on each one. There are additional comments listed by category following the below list.

1. SUPERTASTER: They have three more taste buds than most people.
2. AIR FORCE DRONE PILOT: Each cost $20 million. "I don't always tell people what I do."
3. PROFESSIONAL STALKER: Works for police gathering info on people of interest.

4. BORDER AGENT: She's twenty-four and regularly in 115-degree temperatures. "Number one priority is keeping us all hydrated."
5. ANESTHESIOLOGIST: He said, "I pass gas for a living."
6. BRITISH RACE CAR DRIVER: Me: "What's the best thing about being a retired race car driver?" Him: "I lived."
7. PROFESSIONAL SAILING TRAINERS: The couple trains 120 people a year at $6,000 each and takes a vacation for four months a year living on their boat.
8. ELEVATOR INSTALLER: His wife was upset the hotel elevator was slow. He said, "I know who installed it."
9. FLY-FISHING TEACHER: Taught country music star Thomas Rhett.
10. FAMOUS DJ: Got his big break in radio due to the attack on New York City on September 11, 2001. My favorite ride #44.
11. "THE HONEYBEE": Her nickname as vice-president of a honey company in the Midwest.
12. PODCASTER: Retired Air Force photographer asks the question: "If tomorrow was your last day on earth, what would your last letter be?" His podcast is "Last Letters."
13. KNIFE THROWER: I picked him up from the hospital after slicing off part of his finger.
14. PROFESSIONAL SINGER: She has sung in seventy countries. "It's a hard life."

15. AIRPLANE PAINTER: How do you learn to paint airplanes? My favorite ride #32.
16. "I'm in DEATH SALES; I sell plots, caskets and mausoleums." The hilarious young guy is an all-time favorite rider. My favorite ride #5.
17. FORMER FBI AGENT: He grilled me and asked, "What does Uber and Lyft do to keep you happy and driving?" I teased him about still being FBI.
18. AUCTIONEER: "I keep my voice fresh with whiskey."
19. FORMER UFC FIGHTER: "While trying out, I went up to the strongest guy and said, 'If I beat you, I'll make a name for myself,' and I did."
20. OYSTER FARM OWNER: In his first year of business; "I sell three thousand oysters a week."
21. SPINE SALES: Female: "I get the physicians what they need. I feel guilty liking my job this much."
22. SECRET AGENT MAN: Has visited one hundred countries helping our embassies get what they need done. "I can't tell you what I do."
23. CANCER DOCTOR for Steve Jobs: Has a very high success rate. My favorite ride #46.
24. DRUDGER: Excavates dirt to keep shipping lanes open around the country.
25. ESPN REPLAY GUY: "If I'm standing next to a famous guy on the sidelines, I don't care. I'm interested in the technical side."
26. AMUSEMENT RIDE BUILDER: From New York. "The only thing I don't like about New York is that there is always someone in front of you."

27. ANCHORWOMAN: Her puppy stole the show when it waved in her basket.
28. WHITE HAT HACKER: Recent high school grad working part-time to break into the computer system of a company and tell them how to better it.
29. OWNER OF A SURFBOARD COMPANY: Sales were up 300% during COVID; no foreign competition.
30. CRUISE SHIP ENGINEER: Took him to the new Star Wars movie and said goodbye. "May the force be with you."
31. CONCERT CONDUCTOR: He's an independent contractor just like me.
32. SAILOR: "I've wanted to sail around the world since I was ten, and now, I'm doing it."
33. CEO: Well-known company in the Midwest at the beginning of the pandemic; could not believe how crazy people were about it.
34. SANITARIAN: Health inspector who started his new career by seeing an ad in the paper.
35. ROBOTIC DRONE BUILDER: For pest control.
36. OWNER OF THIRTY-SIX AUTISM CENTERS: "I hated being an accountant."
37. PROFESSIONAL SOCCER PLAYER: "I once played in Iceland in below-freezing temperatures."
38. TWO THIRD MATES: Licensed to drive ships. "We're just regular people, not big deals."
39. PIPELINE WELDER: He said, "I lost $400,000 when Biden canceled the pipeline."
40. PRESIDENT OF A MEDICAL ASSOCIATION: This inspiring woman is my favorite ride #15.

41. OWNER OF A BEAUTY PAGEANT WEBSITE: An amazing success story, My favorite ride #37.
42. THE SURGICAL TECHNOLOGIST TRAVELER: She keeps everything sanitary in the operating room.
43. TRAVELING CRANE OPERATOR: He goes to different states emptying cargo from ships.
44. PUBLIC SPEAKER ON ENTREPRENEURSHIP: She said, "I was an awful employee; my mind is different."
45. LOADMASTER, AIR FORCE: She makes sure everything fits on the plane.
46. ENGLISH TEACHER IN KOREA: For ten years, she has taught military personnel.
47. INSTITUTIONALIZED FOREIGN SALES: She works for a Japanese company.
48. FEDERAL GOVERNMENT, HUMAN RESOURCES: His story with his famous mom is my favorite ride #24.
49. MOTORCYCLE CHAMPION: "I lived more life than most people by age thirty."
50. SOFTWARE DEVELOPER: He makes games for a cartoon, "Afro Man."
51. SHOT SALESPERSON AT STRIP CLUB: *I asked her, "Do you get good tips?" She said, "Oh yeah, I get tipped up the ass." (She really said that.)
52. DEPARTMENT OF AGRICULTURE INVESTIGATOR: In Charleston; "We're investigating an invasive beetle."

53. SNEAKER COLLECTOR: "I have two hundred expensive pairs and my dad has four hundred. They might be worth $500,000."
54. COMMERCIAL DIVER: He does underwater welding.
55. CYBERSECURITY AND EMERGENCY MANAGEMENT: The couple said, "We're dark humor people. If we weren't, we'd be alcoholics."
56. BUSINESS OWNER, COOK: In a suburb in Chicago, she cooks hot and cold healthy meals for about fifty of her neighbors and sells them out of her garage.
57. RETIRED OWNER OF A USED CAR BUSINESS: "I've cheated and lied about my earnings for many years."
58. OIL RIG WORKER: He once worked forty-two straight hours before he needed a break.
59. LAND SURVEYOR: "There's been a shortage for years." I suggested he open a school and he said he would if I ran it.
60. COMPLIANCE OFFICER: He worked for a movie studio doing COVID-19 testing.
61. SAILORS: The couple retired from retail management to raise their three small kids on their new sailboat.
62. MARINER: The woman is a freelancer who transports boats for owners.
63. EGYPTIAN PRIEST: Enthusiastic, passionate, and he taught me some Egyptian. My favorite ride #21.

64. MOLECULAR SCIENTIST: She worked on PCR training (nasal swabs) for COVID-19 around the globe.
65. ORGAN TRANSPLANT SURGEON AND PSYCHIATRIC SPECIALIST: "I worked in the Navy and Marines, helping our servicemen. If I told you any more, I'd have to kill you."
66. FRENCH MALE MODEL: From LA. "The modeling pays the bills, but acting is my real passion."
67. LAWYER: His wife said, "My husband doesn't enjoy law, but he loves bartending."
68. FAST FOOD WORKER: She: "My customer told me, "The coffee isn't hot enough," and then she threw it at me. I think I like doing customer service on the phone better."
69. CHIEF OPERATING OFFICER, UNITED NEGRO FUND (UNCF): He said, "We give out about $100 million in scholarships each year."
70. PART-TIME TRAVELER: She may be the most interesting rider I've driven. *The twenty-year-old woman said, "I take a three-to-five-day vacation every month." My favorite ride #16.
71. THE TRAVELING DENTIST: She is licensed in three states to fill in for other dentists.
72. SUPER SECRET SQUIRREL: Her husband said, "She's in logistics, but works for our government with top clearance to find and rescue things underwater."

73. SCIENTIST: She: "When I was young, I wanted to be a mad scientist. I was reading medical journals in junior high school."
74. SPECIALIZED TRAINER: He: "I'm training four astronauts in the Mojave Desert in a couple weeks on how to get in and out of 450-foot craters to take samples."
75. MARINE BIOLOGIST: Me: "How long have you been a marine biologist?" Her: "Forever." Me: "Since birth?" Her: "Yes, I came out swimming."
76. BUSINESS OWNER, LUXURY POOLS: "We finish expensive pools in Long Island. We send a group of twelve people out and pay them $1,500 for the day."
77. ONCOLOGIST: "Our cancer patients are more susceptible to COVID-19, but they've done very well with getting all the shots."
78. POLITICAL FUNDRAISER: She: "Sometimes I think it would have been a better choice doing fundraising for a college or charity."
79. BUG IDENTIFIER FOR AIRBNB: He calls himself this, although he's a software engineer.
80. ANESTHESIOLOGIST BITCH: She calls herself that. "I make sure they have all the drugs they need, I'm an aide."
81. INSPECTOR GENERAL IN THE AIR FORCE: "We're in charge of investigations, but not all investigations."
82. SINGER/SONGWRITER: From Florida. She charges $300 for an original song.

83. PROFESSIONAL BALLET DANCER: Right now, she works as a nanny.
84. POLE CLIMBER: He works for AT&T and climbs 300 feet up.
85. NEWS DIRECTOR, LOCAL TV STATION: She laughed when I told her I don't have a TV.
86. HOSPITAL BUILDER: Young guy who travels the country building hospitals.
87. INVENTOR: Has approval for a phone that prevents a driver from turning it on when the car is running.
88. PRO FOOTBALL PLAYER: The 6'6" offensive lineman played for the Cleveland Browns.
89. WORLD BANK EMPLOYEE: I asked her where she's from and she showed me the back of her phone with a picture of Putin.
90. BARBER: Working in my neighborhood. He told me that I had lost only 30 percent of my hair.
91. BARTENDER: "Bartending is like babysitting for adults."
92. CHIEF REVENUE OFFICER: At twenty-four, has six partners, selling $1 million worth of clothing apparel online.
93. MISSIONARIES: From North Dakota. Speak the Gospel to farmers with their three kids.
94. TECHNICAL ANALYST FOR INTELLIGENCE AGENCY: "We may wind up with 300,000 COVID-19 deaths." (Wish his estimate had been correct.)

95. MASSAGE THERAPIST: Making the case for her to get good tips, she actually said to me, "When I'm rubbing hard on your naked body." I got her point.
96. ENTREPRENEUR: He said, "CEO stands for Chief of Everything." (Wouldn't that be "COE"?)
97. POLICE OFFICER: Two female cops from Florida. "I hesitate to tell people what we do, since some love us and some hate us."
98. DISC GOLFER'S WIFE: Her husband is one of the top players in the country and she gave me a pin for my son, who enjoys playing.

99. BOWLER: "Bowlers hate each other, especially the good, young ones."
100. RETIRED AIRLINE MECHANIC: "There's a lot of confusion in this country about needs and wants."
101. HOMELAND SECURITY AGENT: Sixteen years; "A diversified position."
102. RECRUITER: She said, "Not a day goes by that I don't ask myself why I didn't go into the tech field."

103. STUDENT: She is completing her seventh degree. She has four bachelors, two associates, and one masters.
104. PROFESSIONAL SINGER: Country singer Lorrie Morgan: "I've been on the road for forty-five years."
105. LEAD INVESTIGATOR OF THE PARANORMAL: "Most spirits are grumpy, because they don't like where they are."
106. MCDONALD'S MANAGER : "Customers are blind; they are 98 percent wrong."
107. SUPERMARKET DELI WORKER: She said, "When our rotisserie chickens come out three times a day, one of us comes out and does a chicken dance with music and we turn around and shake our butt."
108. PHARMACISTS: When asked what they did for work, they said, "We're both drug dealers."
109. NANNY: She said, "I graduated college, but becoming a nanny was the best decision I ever made."
110. WEDDING FLORIST: She told me, "I've been doing this since I was fifteen years old."
111. SUPPLY CHAIN CONSULTANT: "The computer chip shortage was due to the fact that one of the two biggest manufacturers in China had a fire and their plant was destroyed, and they couldn't rebuild it during the pandemic."
112. CORRECTIONS OFFICER: She said, "It's not for me to decide someone's guilt."
113. PROGRAM MANAGER OF PROPAGANDA: He worked in Nigeria for us, "promoting the U.S. way of life."

114. PROFESSOR: She works for Stanford University "in countries around the world, teaching students how to improve their resources in their country."
115. CEO OF A NONPROFIT HEALTH ORGANIZATION: He's responsible for seven thousand employees.
116. VERY SUCCESSFUL ENTREPRENEUR: His inspiration for his invention came when his four-year-old son asked him a question. My favorite ride #17.
117. DEFENSE CONTRACTOR: "I'm looking for ISIS and al-Qaeda in Africa now."
118. ROBOTICS CONSULTANT: "The most important thing today is to be passionate about what you do and have people be able to see it."
119. ZOO SUPERVISOR: She has a master's in psychology. "I'm doing some work with *National Geographic*."
120. ALUMINUM EXTRUDER: "Sometimes, the temperature is one thousand degrees."
121. HOUSE MANAGER: She told me, "I manage a couple's estate which has three properties in three different states."
122. X-RAY PHYSICIST: He used to be this and has changed his occupation.
123. DOMESTIC ABUSE COUNSELOR: For eight years. She said, "I was working with the abusers, it wore me out."
124. NEW AUTHOR: "I just published my autobiography, my first book, *Fulfilling Your Destiny*, and it's available on Amazon."

125. CONCERT SECURITY GUARD: She: "I find out where all the stupid people are."
126. NEUROSURGEON: "I knew I wanted to be a neurosurgeon when I was in the fourth grade since my dad was one. My residency is seven years and I'm done with the first one."
127. COVID-19 TESTING NURSE: "I was raking it in; they paid me $44 an hour and paid for mileage too."
128. SCARE ACTOR: "I work in the Zombie House. I love scaring the crap out of people."
129. SINGER: He said, "I was on *The Voice* eight years ago and sang "Yesterday," and I got to go to California."
130. TV PRODUCER: Her husband bragged that his wife has won three Emmys and has produced "the Doctors," Dr. Phil, Montel Williams, and others.
131. RESIDENT DOCTOR: *"Are you due for a colonoscopy?"
132. TUGBOAT CAPTAIN: His former job and is now a harbor pilot helping ships dock.
133. SHIP SURVEYOR: Heading out to Buffalo after a blizzard, I asked if he could check on ships in this weather and he said, "I'm going to find out."
134. YOUTUBE VIDEO MAKER: She does it with six friends to promote their channel.
135. ESTHETICIAN: She used to answer phones in a spa. "I saw people walk out after five minutes with a smile on their face, and I said, 'I can do that.'"
136. CANCER COLON RESEARCHER: Going into the office on a Sunday, he said, "I have to feed the cells every day or they will die."

137. PRIVATE LUXURY CHEF: His business took off in New York during the pandemic because people wanted to have private dinner parties.
138. ROCK BAND MANAGER: The group, Widespread Panic, holds the record for the most consecutive sellouts—sixty-seven—at Red Rocks in Colorado.
139. SOFTWARE SALES: The middle-aged man worked remotely. "I sell software in my underwear."
140. BEER SALESMAN: He said he doesn't sell in his underwear. "I'm better drinking and talking, and I wear pants; it sucks."
141. WELDER: She said, "Welding is drawing with fire."
142. DEPARTMENT OF JUSTICE AGENT: He used to be undercover and specialized in "saving North American women from human trafficking."
143. STATE DEPARTMENT MUSICIAN: Performed for over ten years in thirty-five countries promoting America's music.
144. BUILDER OF MONSTER TRUCKS: In the family business for many years. He has appeared on TV and expects to do more.
145. PROFESSIONAL CORNHOLE PLAYERS: My four riders were four of only thirty-four professional women in the country.
146. HAIR STYLIST: He said, "I create an experience for my customers."
147. SHIPPING CLERK: Working in a lab. For the first time in his life, he's excited to go to work.
148. CPA: "Figures don't lie, but liars can figure."

149. CANCER DOCTOR: "I have two sons in LA; one is successful, and the other is an actor. He's still on my payroll."
150. CFO OF A NATIONAL COMPANY with many offices: He said, "It keeps me off the streets and out of trouble."

Salespeople

I may have had a couple hundred riders in sales, and six of them are in my top fifty rides. The rides are listed as 5, 7, 26, 28, 30, and 35. A few of them are naturally funny. Below are some of the interesting and/or funny comments I've received from salespeople.

- *Me: "What is the secret to being a top salesperson in your company in the USA?" Him: "I don't give a f---. I tell them you probably can't afford this anyway and I have other things to do. My girlfriend is hungry, and I have to feed her."
- *Female sales rep.: "I was speaking with three sisters from New York and a male colleague was teasing me. One sister leaned over and whispered, 'If you need him to be taken care of, I know someone.'"
- *Man in his early thirties in sales: "I speak to a lot of important people for work. We have a stupidity problem in this country. I told my wife that I have to make enough money to support the next seven generations in our family."
- *Him: "I can get you 15 percent off on a casket. Sometimes people ask if they can get the discount

- later on and I tell them that when it's time, it's too late for the discount."
- "We sell time together, not timeshares."
- "When I sold timeshares, I imagined that I was talking to my grandma, and I wouldn't want anything bad to happen to her."
- Young man selling timeshares in Myrtle Beach: "I'm selling my soul." I reminded him that "The devil went down to Georgia, not South Carolina." He said, "He had to make a pit stop."
- The young man said, "The fence business is booming. People were home for a whole year, and they hate their neighbors."
- Realtor: "I bought my first house when I was eighteen. I saved my money."
- Insurance agent: "I had a couple in my office and the husband said, 'How can you expect us to pick what kind of insurance to get, we can't even decide when to have sex.'"
- Insurance agent: "My client asked me, 'What kind of carpet should I get in my house?'"
- "Selling real estate is the hardest work I've ever done."
- She: "I'm the medical version of a Home Depot salesman. I sell plates and screws for knees."
- Male: "I sold magazines door-to-door in forty-eight states and did very well, but it was a pyramid scheme and I lost everything."
- She was the number one account representative last quarter in the country for her company. Me: "What's the secret of your success?" Her: "Whatever

challenge I have, I figure out how to get it done for my customers."
- GMC salesman: "I have several sold cars thirteen minutes from our dealership, but we can't get them because they're short truck drivers, and we have to wait to have them delivered."
- She sells timeshares: "I love selling timeshares. I look out the window at the beach and talk about vacations."
- He sells services to get people out of timeshares: "We've helped 550,000 people in the last seven years."
- Woman: "Selling cars was the worst job I ever had and the most money I ever made. The managers were mean and humiliating to everyone."
- Recruiter: "I sell people."
- Him: "I was a fitness trainer and bodyguard for a Kurdish prince when I met a guy at a bar who said he would train me to sell corporate jets. I quit my regular job and have done very well selling corporate jets."
- "I have the softest hands." Me: "I'll have to take your word for it." She: "I demonstrate the lotion by massaging people's hands. I like people. They have hands."
- Realtor: "I'm having too much fun making money to retire."
- Woman: "When I was eight, I sold my younger brother's action figures door-to-door. The neighbors thought it was cute; my parents and brothers did not."

- The young realtor from New York said, "It's against the law here for a buyer to give a letter to a seller. When I get a letter, I read it and throw it away. They are usually sob stories on why they should buy the house, like 'My dad's head exploded,' or some other thing."
- The nineteen-year-old guy said, "I recently got a job selling furniture, but they told me I was too young. I had no sales experience, knew nothing about furniture, and I didn't have a car to get to work. I told them I would Uber every day and be here an hour early. This job has literally changed my life."
- Timeshare sales: "When I was twenty-six, I made $250,000 in a year selling timeshares. It was great because I carried $500 in cash all the time and I could buy my girlfriend Coach purses and watches. My boss told me that if I went to Myrtle Beach, I would make twice that, and I did it."

Business Owners and Managers

I have some of my very best conversations with business owners and managers. Since I had a nontraditional business for ten years out of my house and I was a midlevel manager for many years, I could relate and communicate with these riders very easily, and I was fascinated by some of their stories. Thirteen of my top fifty riders were in this category, and those rides are numbers 7, 10, 12, 14, 17, 18, 19, 24, 27, 37, 42, and 49. Below are some other comments I've gotten over the years:

- *Female: "When I called my fast-food manager on the phone and told her that the doctor said I had a collapsed lung, she said, 'Are you going to be at work tomorrow?'"
- Me: "Did you go from selling commercial real estate to owning a store that sold and installed Jeep parts because you were making too much money?" Him: "Oh yeah, it's much better being in an industry that keeps me effin' poor all the time."
- She's a very successful marketing executive: "I grew up in a cult and I was the first one to escape when I was eighteen. The hotel chain that hired me moved me to Hawaii, far away from the cult. Later, I was able to convince my parents to leave the cult."
- Walgreens store manager: "My wife helps the world as a social worker, and I make money off it."
- Coffee shop owner: "I understand the manager mentality that you have to have workers coming in. It's like, if they call in and say they had their leg amputated, you ask, 'What time are you coming in? We'll set up a chair for you to work.'"
- "We own a towing business. We don't care how badly people drive as long as they are safe."
- Male restaurant owner: "You don't want to be in the restaurant business when you're older; it's a tough business."
- I asked her what she did for work, and she replied, "I put out fires with thimbles of water."
- "The chef training me said that I have to find my own style."

- Human resources manager: She said, "I once had someone who was upset, so he left his urine sample on my desk."
- Pastor: "I took over our congregation in January after our pastor was tragically killed by his son with a gun. We have a lot of healing to do."
- Female bakery owner: "Do you want to deliver bread for us? Our last driver drove our truck into the pond."
- Retired from forty-five years of owning an Italian restaurant: "I used to tell people in the business that we need to create something so customers can eat our food for breakfast."
- He: "My friend made about $500,000 last summer selling shitty food."
- Business owner: "My friend of mine had an idea when he was drunk at a bar to start a dumpster rental business. We started it and it was a great idea."
- Owner of a local public television station: He said, "I became the owner after I was asked, since I was running it."
- The store manager of a grocery store said, "Customers don't want to be happy."
- Manager: "The truck driver called me and said he was having trouble with his truck and he was working on it. On my way to work, I saw his truck in line at another construction company. I called him and told him he should lose my number because I was losing his."
- The owner of a Chinese restaurant: He said, "I'm a 'croggy' liberal so the goal for me is to make a good

life, but not to suck everything out of my business. I'm OK with paying my dishwasher fifteen dollars an hour."
- As the CEO of a large healthcare system, he said, "We had about two hundred out of seven thousand employees who left [because of] the vaccine mandate. I told everyone we can't have patients getting sick from us. About 90 percent of the two hundred were people who were always complaining about something."
- The assistant manager of a gas station told me, "The customer said there was a naked man in the bathroom building a bird's nest. I walked in and there he was with newspapers all around him on the floor. I walked out and said to myself, 'What do I do now?'"
- He: "My business [building surfboards] is up 300 percent over the last year since our country has stopped all shipping with Taiwan and China."
- I asked the Publix manager during the pandemic, "How is your staffing going?" He said, "Horrible, just horrible, but I'm getting a lot of overtime."
- Manager: "When it came down to cutting personnel, attitude and effort were most important."
- He loves to keep busy as I do, so I could really relate to this. He said he likes to fish, and I said, "How can you enjoy fishing?" He: "I have three or four poles in the water at the same time, or I would have to reorganize my tackle box three times."
- The twenty-year-old guy and his brother, a jeweler, are starting a business, turning ash into diamonds.

"We have an LLC and a patent to turn the deceased's ashes into diamonds. I got the idea when I told my brother that he liked diamonds so much that when he dies, I'll turn his ashes into a diamond. Two cups of ashes equal one karat."

- Woman living in Chicago with two boys, ages six and eight: "I don't do anything, but I started a business out of my garage providing healthy food for my neighbors. Each week I cook a large salad and a main dish over two days, and I have about fifty customers who pick up meals for themselves and their families. I make about $800 a week."

Medical and Law Professions

Talking to people in the medical field, especially ones that worked in a hospital, was a rewarding experience. I thanked many of them for what they do and there was no doubt that they had gone through some difficult challenges during the past few years. My favorite rider stories in this category are 15, 42, and 46.

- *Me: "What do you do for work?" She: "I do a lot of things; I'm a lawyer and a Danish knight. I've been an honorary counsel for the country of Denmark since 2014. I'm going to be officially knighted at a ceremony soon."
- Me: "How do you deal with the stress of being a trauma nurse?" She: "I get off from work and go into my car in the parking garage and take off my badge and then my bra, and it helps."

- "I went into the pharmacy field because I didn't want to touch anyone."
- Optometrist: "Not everyone needs glasses." I asked him, "How many people in their seventies and eighties don't need glasses?" He replied, "None of them."
- He: "My wife works in ICU, and she turns chicken nuggets into babies."
- I told a nurse and her friend the story about how the trauma nurse relieved stress from her job by finishing her shift, going into the parking garage, and in her car, taking off her badge and bra. Her friend said, "That's what I do when I get home from work." I laughed and said, "Thanks for sharing that," and she replied, "If you wore a jockstrap all day, you would take it off immediately too."
- She: "I went to the orientation at law school and knew that I didn't have the enthusiasm that others did there, so I quit to become a teacher. Everyone told me not to become a teacher."
- Woman: "When I started working in the hospital, cleaning rooms, I decided to lose weight. I drank a lot of water, and doing my job I lost sixty pounds in three months." Me: "That would make a great recruitment video; lose weight while you make money."
- Nurse's assistant: At nineteen, she has her own business helping elderly in the middle of the day, and she charges $50 an hour.
- Dentist: "I went to dental school in my late thirties." He's had a twenty-five-year career as a dentist and is an extraordinary painter of pictures.

- Lawyer: I asked him, "What kind of lawyer are you?" His reply was, "A good one."
- Lawyer: "When I found out I could help people, I decided to be a lawyer."
- She said, "I was a civil engineer, but I didn't love it. I went back to school to be a nurse when I was thirty after watching nurses take care of my dad after six brain surgeries."
- Respiratory therapist: From the Northeast; he said, "I almost got fired my first week living in the South for talking to a supervisor. You have to be cocky in Boston or no one trusts you."
- Lawyer's advice about law school if you're not passionate about being a lawyer: "Don't pay someone to make you miserable."
- My riders said, "We're both lawyers." I replied, "That's terrific." They said, "Some days it is."
- School nurse: She said, "The kids [have been] great during the past year, but some parents are stupid humans."
- Oklahoma man: "My passion is farming, but I have to practice law to afford to do it."
- Him: "I'm a lawyer, which really stands for 'a lot more work.'"
- Male: "I've been a real estate attorney for twenty years in Myrtle Beach. 2020 was the best year I ever had, and this year, for the first time ever, I had to turn down business."
- Female: "I don't math well, that's why I went to law school."

- Female attorney just won her first big case after an Amazon tractor trailer hit her client's car from behind. "We won $30 million for her. I have a cool life."
- Female nurse: "Three years ago, I had brain and neck surgery. I burst a ligament when I picked up a box of paper, not realizing it was full. My injury was like the one that Christopher Reeves had."

Government/Military Employees

I have spoken to many military personnel over the years and some people in government. In my favorite rides you can find some of them here: 1, 24, and 46.

- When the couple got in the car, I asked, "How are you tonight?" The retired cop from New York said, "Good, I haven't had the urge or desire to kill anyone today." Laughing, I said, "Is it urge or desire?" Him: "That's open to interpretation."
- He said, "I've seen a lot of unusual things. In Afghanistan I saw a man 'with' a goat." Me: "Was that when you were in the Army?" Him: "Well, I wasn't on vacation there."
- Young guy in the Army: "My choice in high school was to get a factory job, sell drugs, or go into the military. I wouldn't change a thing."
- The female physical trainer said, "After my husband was killed in the war in Afghanistan, I was in a funk. I decided to do something 'badass,' so I climbed Mt. Kilimanjaro in Tanzania. I've done it twice now."

- The three male postal workers from Boston were kidding when they said, "We came down here to buy guns; they don't give them out anymore up there. We'll go back and 'go postal.'"
- When the cadets got in the car, one of them said, "You're the guy who told me how McDonald's made their money." (Real Estate)
- The two cops from Maryland said, "We're in town for SWAT training." Me: "Where is the training?" Him: "Yes." Me: "I was going to ask if it was top secret." Him: "No, not top secret, but yes."
- Young woman: "I wanted to be a ballet dancer, but COVID changed that. I'm now going into the Marines."
- Looking at an entire field of dead cows after a severe hailstorm, his coworker said, "These are definitely hail-damaged cows."
- Member of the National Guard: "Anxiety does not have any control of my life anymore."
- The military guy said, "Some of the most well-rounded people are military leaders."
- The guy in the Air Force told me, "I jumped out of a plane and my chute didn't open, but I landed and rolled as I was taught. I was sore, but OK. Twelve years later, a doctor found that I had a healed vertebrae fracture, which had to have come from my fall."
- Mailman: "I've only been bitten twice in seventeen years. One of them came right through the screen door and bit my arm, and when I hit it, it bit me in the leg."

OCCUPATIONS—WHAT PEOPLE DO

- Fireman: "You don't become a fireman to make money."
- New York City transit supervisor: "Assaults are up because people are pissed."
- TSA agent: "There were forty-one agents from across the country that came to Myrtle Beach (summer 2021) due to the large amounts of passengers. It went smoothly, but in New Jersey, those people can be snippy with you."
- New York City actress: "I was in a military family and the theatre became life preserving for me, and today I'm in plays and do commercials."
- City employee for Kansas City: "I work for the city and if I told you what I do, I'd have to kill you."
- I asked him, "What kind of work do you do?" He replied, "I do all the things that no one else wants to do." Just out of the army, he works in a restaurant.
- She edits rulings for the Chicago supreme court: "My husband used to write some of the rulings that I edited, and I always tried to find something I could correct so I could tell him I did it."
- The young fireman said, "When I work a twenty-four-hour shift, I come home and work out for an hour and then go to my part-time job."
- Retired police officer: "If I didn't have a lot of hobbies now, I'd be in jail."
- Helicopter pilot: "When you see an orange sky in the morning, it means that a storm is coming."
- Young woman: "When we lived in Pennsylvania, there were some people who slashed our tires and

put alcohol in our pool because my dad was in the military."
- Male: "Working on a project, I had to go onto a military base, and when they wanted to scan my left index finger, he noticed I was missing half my finger. The guard said, 'You're the second guy this week.'" (Both carpenters)
- He was in the Army working for the Defense department trying to prevent another 9/11. He told me this story about 9/11: "When there was one plane left heading towards Washington, DC, two fighter pilots jumped in their plane without arming it. They had one goal: fly into the plane, and make sure it goes down before it gets to Washington. Shortly after getting in the air, the remaining plane crashed in Pennsylvania."
- In the Army for eighteen years, he loves to do dangerous things. He once jumped out of a plane 1,200 feet up when his parachute did not work. "I pulled the secondary chute, but it was so late, it just protected me some when I hit the ground. I got up and walked to my troop. They saw I was cut and bleeding on my face and got me to the hospital, where they told me I broke my spine.
- The retired IRS manager from Missouri told me, "The three toughest calls I had to take were people who threatened suicide if I couldn't help them stop the IRS from taking everything from them. We only do that after ten years if our efforts to get them to pay have failed. I don't sugarcoat it; I tell them like it is."

Hospitality/Customer Service

Each day I have driven, I have picked up someone in hospitality or customer service; Myrtle Beach and Charleston are very big tourist destinations. Below are some of their comments:

- Male housekeeper at a hotel told me, "A twenty-five-year-old woman at our front desk asked me for help. A sink had [overflowed], and she was going to clean it up with a mop. She was holding the mop and said, 'I don't know how to use this.'"
- Male cleaning hotel room: "I think I cleaned a room today that was a murder scene. There was a lot of blood. I mean it wasn't a lot, it was *a lot*, a lot."
- She works at a hotel at the front desk. "I still have a potty mouth. A customer said to me, 'Why is that effin' door always locked?' I said, 'Because the effin' door is supposed to be locked.'"
- Front desk worker at a hotel: She said, "I'm just not ready to deal with people today."
- Female front desk worker: "I can't wait for the season to end. People have been miserable and unhappy."
- Female bartender: "If I don't get a Mountain Dew today, I'm going to die."
- She works at the front desk of a hotel. She tells employers: "I'm the alpha female. [The person in charge.] Pay me what I'm worth."
- Hotel executive: I asked him how the hotel business was these days and he said, "Profitable."

- "When they gave away my car that I reserved, I asked the agent, 'What would you suggest?' She said, 'I don't know what to tell you.' I said, 'You're not very good at your job. I worked for Enterprise for seven years.'"
- Bartender: "We give people our energy."
- "The best thing about doing nails is seeing the before and after."
- Cook: "There are two kinds of people in the world: people who make food and people who eat it."
- Customer service representative: "I have twelve years of experience—I actually started when I was twelve in my grandfather's store and worked at McDonald's when I was fourteen."
- Bartender: Me: "How long have you been bartending?" Her: "A hundred years." Me: "Is that a lot of double shifts?" Her: "Definitely."
- Chef: "I became a chef when I saw how much food costs, and now, I get free food every day."
- Female bartender in the South talking to a customer from the North: "I said to her, "No ma'am, I did not say 'ma'am' to you because you were older."
- The chef was originally from Ohio, and he said, "When I was in jail, I did ten thousand pushups a day for several months, several hundred an hour. My doctor said that the workout actually changed some of the bone structure in my body."
- Passionate chef: "When I cook a meal at my restaurant, I cook as if I'm cooking for my family. Every table should be a VIP table."

- The recovering alcoholic is now a bartender: "I have a lot more fun sober now, and I remember it the next day."
- He told me that he has had a lot of different careers, but finally found that being a chef was the right one. I said, "That just means you're a man of many talents." Him: "I don't know about that." Me: "Let's debate it, I'll debate for you, and you debate against you."
- "I work as a bartender seven months a year, but it's twelve months of income."
- The female bartender said, "My hobby is cooking. It started as a joke, but I'm cooking one dish from fifty different countries."
- Getting a job in a restaurant when he was homeless, he said, "I wasn't going to take 'no' for an answer. I do the things that no one else does."
- He said, "One night serving in a fine dining restaurant, I was the only server and took care of thirteen tables at the same time. The bartender helped me make $400 that night."
- He said, "The pride and joy of our hotel at the front desk told our customer, 'F--- you,' and then walked out of the hotel."
- The bartender works in a strip club, and she said, "I had a sixty-seven-year-old man come in on his birthday looking to take one of the girls home with him. It didn't work out well for him. He gave me a lot of details on what he wanted to do with them."
- Female bartender: "One night as I was leaving, I warned the other bartenders about this guy who

needed to be shut off. The next day, I found he wound up in the parking lot harassing girls and then shot himself in the hand. I really dodged [a] bullet."
- "As a bartender along the beach here, I saved all my quarters a couple years ago and rolled them each night. When the summer ended, and three days before I went to Disney World, I brought all the rolls of quarters into the bank. The $1,000 paid for my trip."
- She: "I don't know how people dress in the morning. The other day, a man sat down on our bench in front of the restaurant, and he was butt naked. He may have come back from the beach. He wanted water, but we got him a cop. Some of the girls took pictures."
- He said, "I'm a server at Nacho Hippo. One guy had been drinking a lot and handed me the bill and said, 'I can't read it, put in the tip you want.' I put in $50 on a $300 bill and he said, 'That's not enough.' I said I'd take $100, and I did."

A Few More

- Nuclear power plant inspector: "When I tell people I inspect nuclear power plants, they frequently say I'm like Homer Simpson."
- Hair stylist: "Writing is a love language. When you have the gift of writing, you're touching people with words."
- He: "I'm a millwright, and sometimes I get fifty-four hours of overtime in a week."

- She: "I'm a stay-at-home mom without kids." Me: "When did the last kid leave?" Her: "Over a year ago."
- Former basketball player: "I played against the Harlem Globetrotters once and I played the bad guy." He's seven feet, eight inches tall, and he took a selfie with me.
- The research farmer who lives in Charleston said, "I own farms in South Carolina and Oregon. I've driven 2,800 miles to Oregon seven times by myself."
- Zamboni driver: After a couple drinks she said to me, "Don't f--- with me, I'm from Buffalo, New York."
- I asked the accountant, "Do you like numbers?" She replied very slowly, "Yes, as long as they are adding up in my account."
- The young engineer told me, "Going out in the field to help customers solve problems helps me become a better engineer."
- Male barber: "You earned your hair loss by living a long time."
- The hairstylist said, "I'm just a big ear."
- The farmer said, "I've worked on a farm most of my life. We had 25,000 chickens all together and it's easy for them to spread diseases. If we saw one with a bad leg, we would hit it in the head and kill it."
- She said, "When I win the lottery, I'm going to fund my cell phone invention and one day be on the cover of Forbes magazine."
- The security guard explained why he wore steel shoes: "I can't throw a punch, but no one wants to be kicked by a steel toe."

- The CPA said on Saturday at 9 a.m., "It's going to be a long day. I'm going to take a nap first."
- Electrician: "When I wake up at 3 a.m. and need to clear my head, I play classical piano."
- Retired accountant: "Being retired, I don't care what numbers add up to."
- Wedding florist: She told me, "I've been doing this since I was fifteen."
- Museum employee: She is "the Director of Public Engagement for a museum in Los Angeles."
- Boeing employee: The man in his fifties had a very thick Alabama accent. He told me, "My accent helped me get the job. There were five hundred applicants, then they cut it down to six and then two. The interviewer was from Seattle, but he loved my accent."
- Hairdresser: "About twenty years ago, I put the Nike swoosh on the back of someone's head. I thought at the time it was really weird."
- Female hair stylist: "The guy came in with blue hair and he wanted me to put horns on his head. It was difficult, but I did it."
- "As a second mate on a freighter, I work around forty straight days going to about a dozen ports and then do it all over again. I get four months [of] vacation."
- Wealth management: When he said, "wealth management," I thought he said, "wolf management." He said, "It's really the same thing."
- Dog watcher: The nurse in her mid-twenties: "My parents pay me $500 to watch their dogs over the weekend; it's a good gig."

- Finance: Me: "Do you like your job in finance?" She: "Yes, but I'm not doing it for fun."
- Photographer: "Photography was just a hobby until Vogue called me out of the blue after seeing some things on social media."
- I asked the woman who does accounting work, "Do you like numbers?" She said, "I like money."
- The female cement truck driver said, "I got tired of being inside four walls. I love to drive."
- The machine engineer with a very big smile told me, "I'm a joy in a field where not a lot of people smile."
- She: "I'm an airfield hands electrician. I handle all the lights on the airfield."
- The woman is a data scientist: "I help analyze numbers for my company."
- The pipe welder told me, "I was working in Wisconsin outside when it was twenty [degrees] below zero. My friend had icicles hanging from his nose."

3
WHAT'S IN A NAME?

I consider myself a collector of names, but not just any names. There are many people out there who have unique or unusual names. I have been able to discuss these names with hundreds of riders. Some people have funny explanations or stories on how they got their name and I greatly appreciate their willingness to share it with me. In my favorite rides, I have written one story about a unique name, "Night Train," which is listed as number 4.

Below are a few stories about people with unique names and some of their comments about their names. There are also a number of riders who have met or heard about other people with unique names, and some of them are priceless.

Part of my interest in people's names comes from naming our third child, Marisa. It was a good story, and I could not wait to one day pick up a Marisa and tell her my story. When the day came, I was excited about sharing the story, and then I was stunned when her story was better than mine. Although Marisa is not a very unique name, I have only driven about five Marisas, and two of them had very good stories.

Marisa

About ten years before my daughter was born, I worked at a business school. The school used to have high school students answering the phone, and one day, I came in and saw a girl I had not seen before, so I walked up to her and introduced myself. When I asked what her name was, she said, "I don't like my name." When she told me it was Marisa, I immediately said, "I like that name so much, I may name a child that one day." It was the first thing that came into my head, and I had never thought of it before.

When my first Uber rider named Marisa heard that story, she said, "I have a better story. My Dad named me after a Playboy pin-up he liked. In my baby book are pictures of the Playboy bunny." I would have loved to see the look on her grandmother's face when was looking at her baby book.

The second Marisa I picked up, I told both stories, and she said that she had a good story too. "When my grandfather heard I was going to be named Marisa, he hated it. He said it was the worst name he had ever heard and said, 'Why would anyone name their child that?'"

Forrest-Rain

This is my favorite name story, and I was so struck by it and my rider, I am not 100 percent sure I spelled his name correctly. I know it was hyphenated and I had to ask him how he got that name. He said, "My mom was Native American, and she lived way out in the woods as a child. She used to play outside her house under a very large tree which protected her from the rain, so she named me Forrest-Rain. If I had been a girl, she would have named me Reign-Forrest." Other riders have enjoyed this story, although one guy amusingly said, "It sounds made up, did you ask his mom?"

Trrrip

When I asked the young black kid how he got his name, he said, "I nicknamed myself Trrrip." I said, "Why did you nickname yourself Trrrip?" He replied, "Because, sometimes I'm a trip." He told me a number of stories about his life, and sometimes he *was* a trip. Approaching his house, he said, "You should have a nickname." I said, "OK, my name's Jeff." He said, "Jeffro-no-fro." Considering I have almost no hair and he had dreads, I thought it was hysterical. I was still laughing moments later when I picked up another young black kid nearby. I wanted to see if he thought this was funny, and when I mentioned Trrrip he said, "That's my best friend!" He called Trrrip up and said, "I just heard about Jeffro-no-fro."

Over the years, my new nickname has gotten hundreds of laughs, including one comment on the app, "Jeffro-no-fro, you're my hero." I badly wanted to drive Trrrip again to tell him how funny the nickname was, but it never happened. However, I picked up his best friend and I was able to talk to him on the phone and he said, "You really made my day." I replied, "You really made *my* day."

Santa

A young woman shared this story with me: "My name is Santa, which is *saint* in Spanish. My dad was buying my mom flowers at a shop from a woman named Santa. She told him that his wife was having a girl, although the doctors said it was a boy. She said that if you name her Santa, she will be very healthy and always happy. When I was born a girl, they named me Santa. A few days later, my dad went to tell the woman that they named me Santa, but he was told the woman had suddenly passed away a couple days ago."

Sean (Not a Unique Name)

"I got my name in a funny way. My mom was pregnant in New York City and was walking one day and literally bumped into a stranger, and she fell to the ground. The man helped her up and brushed her off, but was concerned when he saw she was pregnant. He offered to buy her lunch, and during lunch she found out that his name was Sean, and he was Jewish. She said, "I've never heard of someone Jewish named Sean, I'm going to name my son Sean." (He's not Jewish, but my son, Sean, is.)

Dynamite

I thought I might be picking up a black guy who had this nickname after the famous comedian Jimmy Walker, whose famous line was "Dynamite," but I was wrong. The white guy told me, "I was born four weeks early, and when my aunt looked at me, she said, 'He's a real firecracker.' My uncle corrected her and said, 'No; he's dynamite,' and that's how I got the nickname that I go by."

Stay At Home

It sounds made up, but my rider was not the joking kind of guy. He explained, "Names don't faze me anymore. When I worked as a prison guard, there was an inmate whose real name was "Stay at Home." I asked him if he ever talked to him, and he said, "He was not the kind of guy you talk to."

Hampton

It is a common name in the South, but I asked him how he got the name, and he said, "I was conceived in a Hampton Inn." He was joking, but the real explanation was pretty good. "It's a family name that goes back to General Robert E. Lee's time. My relative was General Wade Hampton who worked with General Lee."

Kmnop

A guy named Ashley was really into this subject. He told me, "The other day I was at the bank and the female teller asked me if Ashley was my real name. Her name tag said 'Sam.' I told her, 'Looking at your name tag, you shouldn't ask me that question.'"

But Ashley hit the jackpot with a name that really does sound made up. "A friend of mine knows a woman whose name is pronounced 'Noelle,' but it's spelled K-M-N-O-P, because there's no *L* in her name." I had one rider who said that this woman's parents shouldn't have been allowed to have kids, and you must admit that giving a child that name is pretty bad. Another rider said, "Her parents set her up to be bullied."

Candy Barr

He explained, "I know a girl named Candace who uses Candy as a nickname, and she married a guy named Barr. Her name is Candy Barr, and she's not a stripper."

Shondra Leer

Shondra isn't that unusual, but when you own a light company and your last name is Leer, do you really want your daughter to be Shondra Leer?

April May June

She told me, "I know of a girl named April and her middle name is May and her last name is June."

Unique

The woman from New Jersey said, "My mom said to my dad, 'We have to give her a unique name,' and my dad said, 'That's it—Unique.'" As unique a name as this is, her brother's name is Wulf.

River

It is his real name. "My mom named me after a soap opera actor she liked. My last name is Mann, so I'm River Mann. Maybe I'll name my kids Spider and Bat?"

Sharmilia

She: "It's a Hawaiian name. My great-great-great-great-great-grandmother and I are the only two people with this name, which means 'beautiful flower.' She lived to be 119 years old, the oldest Hawaiian to have ever lived."

Jantzen

She: "I was named after a swimsuit company. My mom needed a *J* name and she saw Jantzen on the wall of a store."

Unbelievable

My rider managed truck drivers and told me, "I had one driver who went by the name Unbelievable. His very first day of work, he left his driver's license at home and called me to see if I had a copy."

The Superhero

The young woman's first name started with the letter X (which sounded like "H") and a last name that had a Y and a Z in it. Me: "How did your parents come up with that name?" She: "They wanted to make my life miserable."

However, sometimes people would call me X and I felt like a superhero."

Booberell?

His name sounded something like this, but his explanation was hilarious. "My parents made a lot of mistakes, but it all started in a KFC bathroom."

Another Tripp

"My parents gave me the nickname of Tripp, which I got because I'm the third child, and I use it. I think they gave it to me so if the cops come to my door, I can show them my real ID and say [that] I don't know who Tripp is."

Ponyboy

The young woman told me, "My boyfriend's real name is Ponyboy after a character in an old movie that his parents loved. He doesn't go by that name."

Palace

He said, "I heard of a woman named Palace who had a last name of Steps, so she is Palace Steps."

Y'keshia

She said, "I was named after my dad's mistress."

Female

She told me, "My friend is a nurse, and she asked a woman who was expecting if she had decided on a name for her daughter. The woman said, 'I'm going to call her "Familia"' [or so it sounded]. I saw a woman with a bracelet that said, 'Female.'

Abcde

He said, "I know someone who spelled their first name A-B-C-D-E."

Vision

The young man from China told me, "I made the name up; probably from the Marvel character."

One

My mom named me One, because I was her first son. "I'm One Alexander. (His middle name) If I have a son one day, I want to call him King Alexander."

Chasing The Money

"My friends gave me the nickname."

River, Season, Rain

"I know a family that named their kids River, Season, and Rain."

Brooklyn

"My husband named our daughter Brooklyn, because he said it sounded southern."

Gary Jumping Eagle

He told me, "I knew a guy whose real name was Gary Jumping Eagle."

Sexyblack

She: "When I was a child, my uncle named me Sexyblack, and I still have some friends who call me that."

Sir James

"I have a friend who named his son Sir James. When his son was in school and a teacher called him James, he politely told them his name was Sir."

21

"In school I had a boy in my class whose name was 21."

Shark

"A friend told me that they knew someone with the first name 'Shark.' His last name rhymed with Shark and his parents were hippies."

Z

She explained, "My three sisters and one brother all have first names starting with a *Z*."

Jazieerd and Jazia

"My mom had a dream, and that's how she named me Jazieerd and my twin sister Jazia."

Zara

She said, "My name was supposed to be Patience, but they changed it. I don't know why. You'll have to ask them; they made me."

Mira

"My friend Mira was a miracle. When her mom gave birth, her baby was stillborn, but they didn't know that there was another baby behind that one. That's why she's named Mira."

Kennedi

She told me, "I was named Kennedi three weeks after I was born. I was originally Jordan, which is now my middle name. My mom was upset because there seemed to be too many people named Jordan."

Speedy Montana

From Louisiana. He said he was fast. I asked, "How did you get so fast?" He said, "Running from the police."

Noemi

In Italian, her name means "happiness."

Gotti

It is not a Greek name, but the GPS said to me, "Pick up the Greek letter symbol G." Gotti thought it was hilarious.

Blessing

"My mother was having a very difficult time when I was born, and they declared me dead with the cord around my neck. They were able to save me, so I'm her blessing."

Xavier

I asked the woman how she got her name and she said, "I don't know how my mom came up with the name, maybe she wanted a boy, or she was drunk."

Wyntre

"My mom was watching TV, and someone had a daughter named Wyntre."

Zhraemier

"My mom named me. The 'zhr' in Chinese sounds like a *D*, so my first name is pronounced 'Dreamier.'"

Unbreakable

He said it wasn't an interesting story; only the second person who did not want to discuss their unique name.

Kannon

He said he named his daughter Kannon. "I'm from Philly and we greet each other by saying, 'Hey, Cannon.'"

Haven

She told me, "I named my daughter Haven because she's a safe haven from my addiction."

Heaven

She said, "My mom gave me my middle name first, Molina, from her favorite video game, and then she found the name Heaven because it sounded well together. I'm Heaven Molina."

Wilhemema

"I once had a woman who insisted that I was spelling my name wrong."

Jenessa

"I really liked the names Jennifer and Vanessa, so I named my daughter Jenessa."

Sibikaia

"My sister's name means 'the seventh child.'"

Tata

She said, "My real name is Beatrice, but when I was one, I decided I would only answer to 'Tata,' and my family calls me that name today." (In her forties?)

Miluzka

Her name comes from Peru, and it means "the light of my eye."

Carlos Danger

His college friend gave him the nickname, and his girlfriend said, "When I heard his name, I was intrigued." His name wasn't Carlos, and he wasn't dangerous.

Cash

"When I set up the account on the Uber app, I was worried about losing my money, so I made up my name as 'Cash.'" (Only rider that day to tip me cash.)

Aerin

"My mom couldn't decide between an *A* or an *E* until she read a magazine article that said Estee Lauder's grandchild's name was spelled this way. (The *e* is silent.)

Christmas Carol

"I tell people to remember me as Christmas Carol, and some people call me that."

4

THE REST OF MY TOP FIFTY RIDES

Putting these rides in some kind of order was challenging. The numbers don't really matter much, and I'm sure if I put these in order as you read this, there would be a few changes. The important thing is that they were not ordinary rides, and they all mean a lot to me. I'll always remember them, and I've talked about some of these people for years because they are special.

#4. TWO GREAT NAMES AND ONE GREAT GUY

What made this ride great? Some people have very interesting or unusual names, but this rider wins the prize for literally having two Hall of Fame names. He has spent his whole life in and around baseball, and as a baseball fan, I could have talked to him all day.

You can't have a much better ride than I did taking this guy to the airport in Charleston. His dad named him Night Train after he met the former Hall of Fame football player

Dick "Night Train" Lane, who played his best years with the Detroit Lions. (Still has the fourth most interceptions ever.) He told me that his mom told his dad that he could name him "Night Train," but if he did, he would never have a say in anything [for] the rest of his life. He said, "My dad didn't realize how difficult it would be having this name and convincing people it was my real name."

Halfway through the ride, I was shocked to find out that his grandfather is the former owner of the Chicago White Sox, who is in the baseball Hall of Fame. His dad is a part owner of the Charleston, South Carolina, minor league baseball team. I have read a book on his grandfather, and I know that he and his son are famous for making promotions part of the game. Night Train told me, "My dad broke all the labor laws because I've been working since I was five and have done every job in a baseball stadium." He told me that he also had worked several years in Japan in cricket and that he was currently interviewing with baseball teams in this country. I wish my ride was longer with him and I hope I get lucky again and get to talk more baseball with him in the future.

#5. THE CLASS CLOWN CAPTURES HIS AUDIENCE

What made this ride great? He was incredible. The twenty-one-year-old is a very talented kid who can make anyone laugh and will have a great future.

I knew he was special immediately when the young couple from Pennsylvania got in my car. He was already talking, and sixty seconds later, I interrupted him and asked, "Are you in sales?" He said, "How did you know?" I told him it was how he was talking, and asked, "What kind of sales are you in?" His answer was hilarious: "I'm in death sales. I sell caskets, plots, and mausoleums. I can get you 15 percent off on a casket. Sometimes people ask if they can get a discount later and I tell them, 'When it's time, it's too late for a discount.'"

He did not stop, as if he had his material all set up for me. He used to sell insurance, but "I'd rather sell to people who are sixty with one foot in the grave." I told him I was six weeks from turning sixty, so I was still good. They had been dating awhile and I asked him when they were getting married, and I thought he said "Monday." He corrected me and said, "*Someday*; I need to sell a lot more caskets for that to happen."

His sense of humor runs in the family. His dad and grandfather were voted class clowns and he explained, "When my older brother was not, the pressure was really on me, but I did it without a problem." His girlfriend added, "His dad is worse than he is." I was able to entertain them with some stories, but his final comment was one of the best compliments I've ever had. He said, "I've never tipped an Uber driver before, but I have to tip you." I am certain he could have kept me laughing for hours.

#6. THE ATTITUDE ADJUSTER*

What made this ride great? He did; he is one of those special people that you meet that you will never, ever forget. I have written about fifty favorite riders and another twenty-two riders in the inspirational and motivational chapter. My wish is to be able to drive them again. I've been very fortunate to have driven this rider three times, and it's always a thrill.

He lives in the Charleston area, and he works at Trader Joe's. He caught my attention immediately when he said he was an "attitude adjuster." He explained, "I rap there. I greet them at the door and get them in a better mood to shop." Since I have read a lot of positive attitude books over the years and I've given some motivational talks in the past, I needed to know more about him. His story was inspirational for sure, but I could tell that who he is today was because of the challenges he went through in the past.

One time, I picked him up and I said, "How are you today?" He said, "Amazing; every day I wake up, I'm amazing." His attitude came from a near-fatal car crash he had in high school, close to twenty years ago. He had to have brain surgery, and the doctors told his parents that they would probably have to put him in assisted living. They gave him a lot of positive feedback that helped him recover. He worked for four years helping researchers assist people recovering from serious injuries and volunteered to help kids recover from injuries. He told me, "You have to talk about what you want; it creates the belief and what you desire."

That first morning I drove him, I dropped him off at a breakfast place that hadn't opened yet. As I pulled away, he made me laugh. He was standing in front of the door, and he had someone's attention. He was flapping his arms like a bird, making someone laugh and getting them ready for their day. I told him I was writing about him, and I can't wait to give him a copy of this book. I know he's going to enjoy it.

#7. THE MOTIVATOR*

What made this ride great? He might be the most successful person I've ever driven, and his story was incredibly inspiring. He was very easy to talk to and he was very willing to share his story with me. I have repeated his story many times.

He is an executive for one of the major hotel chains, and he told me it is the largest hotel chain in the world. The fifteen-minute ride turned out to be a forty-five-minute trip due to construction, and I was very lucky it happened. He's in charge of training sales representatives and other employees and has spent most of his life in the Las Vegas area; he was moving to South Carolina soon. He told me he had given five speeches outside of work to groups and charged $10,000 for a forty-five-minute speech. I could tell he knew what he was talking about. I said to him, "I'm feeling a little guilty I haven't paid anything for your seminar today." I've read many success-oriented books over the years, and I think he was amused that I was able to finish some of his sentences. He had an amazing story:

"When I was twenty-three and about to graduate college, I was selling cars, and I sold a $14,000 car to a twenty-year-old kid. He told me he was going to pay cash, but my boss didn't believe him and told me to go to the bank with him. I asked him how he could afford to pay cash and he told me that he sold timeshares [in the 1980s] and he made $23,000 in the past two months. He was not a very outgoing kid either. I decided right then that when I graduated, I would drive four hours away to California and get a job with that company. I did, and I've been with them for thirty-five years."

Since he came from a working-class background, his dad cried when he saw his son first make $100,000 in one year when he was in his twenties. He talked about how important passion and commitment are, and that "you become what you think about." He told me, "We sell time together, not timeshares." As the ride was ending, I asked him if he ever thought how different his life would have been if he hadn't asked that twenty-year-old what he did or if he hadn't sold him his car. He said, "I believe that somehow I would have found the right track, because it was my destiny." He gave me a twenty-dollar tip for my extra time, and I went to pick up my next rider. Her name was Destiny, the only one I picked up in my first ten thousand rides. I had some story to tell her.

#8. THE DISNEY PRINCESS

What made this ride great? What happens when two big Disney fans have thirty minutes together talking Disney? The only thing missing was Walt Disney himself, but his spirit was with us for every mile.

She was in her mid-twenties, and she worked at Disney World while she was in college. Just before everything closed due to the pandemic, she got married in an incredible wedding at Disney World. She had seventy people there to help her celebrate, including her grandfather. He had always said that he had taken her mom and aunt to Disney World and Disneyland many times, but when he got there, he said, "I've never been here." She enjoyed putting him on the ride Soarin'. They gave her group a few hours in Epcot in the evening, and she was up for twenty-four hours straight experiencing what she said was "a magical wedding."

We talked about our favorite Disney movies, did Disney trivia, and could have talked for hours. She shared an amazing story that she learned from a Disney employee when she worked in costume design. "The day before Disneyland opened in 1956, the Governor of California, Ronald Reagan, brought his two kids to Disneyland. The kids wanted to ride the monorail, but the monorail had not been working and the conductor did not know how to stop it. Walt Disney said OK, and they got on the monorail, and somehow it worked, and they stopped it. The Secret Service was angry when they heard about the problems it had before and wanted to sue Walt Disney for kidnapping."

When I dropped her off at the airport, I noticed her Disney suitcase, her Disney mask, and her shirt that said, "Dreams Do Come True." As I pulled away, I was grinning from ear to ear. Before I left the airport, her very generous tip popped up on the app and I knew that she enjoyed the "Disney ride" as much as I did.

#9. A DEVOTED MOM AND LONELY WIDOW

What made this ride great? She didn't stop talking, completely dominating the fifteen-minute ride. She was interesting, entertaining, hilarious, and outrageous. I have no idea what kind of work she's done in the past, but she should have been an actress for this incredible performance.

Her son in Boston, Massachusetts, ordered the ride for her while he was plowing snow. I found her in front of a pharmacy in a town thirty miles west of Charleston. His name was on the app, and I didn't see him. I got out of the car and called him, putting him on speaker. It's no surprise she recognized his voice; she was missing him. She told me her life story with virtually no questions or prodding.

Her best lines were these: "My son could have any girl, he's so handsome. In high school, he was dating two girls, and one of them jumped out of his bedroom window so I wouldn't see her. I don't like his girlfriend now; she came over for Thanksgiving and didn't bring anything or say thank you." Her very best line may have been this one: "My son was born on the fourth of July—he came in with a bang and out with a bang."

The widow said, "I'm not desperate, but I'm lonely. If I don't find anyone down here soon, I'm going to have to go back to Massachusetts and bring someone back before I lose my juiciness." I couldn't believe what she had just said; however, she made it a point of repeating it two more times before she got out of the car. My wife later explained to me that she was flirting with me. I had absolutely no clue. I was laughing too much. What a show!

#10. THE SUPER BOWL RING

What made this ride great? It was stunning, shocking, and amazing. The ride was over, and suddenly, there were two more minutes left, and it's those two minutes that thousands of my riders have been able to enjoy. It doesn't get much better than this.

Early morning rides are almost always good and sometimes great, but nothing could have prepared me for this ride. The woman I picked up has worked in management for the Kansas City Chiefs for twenty years. She was wide awake, articulate, and friendly. We had a very good conversation about her job and football. Her office gets many requests from the public and fans and they do their best to help people out when they can. She told me one story of a family who had their house burned down and they had lost all their Chiefs' merchandise; her office was able to replace everything for them. There was no doubt in my mind as I spoke with her that I was talking to someone who is very good at what they do and is passionate about it too.

About 6:30 a.m., I pulled up in front of the airport to drop her off. It was still dark out and I had just told her that I was giving her my list of my favorite rider comments from last year. Her next comment was one of the very best lines of any year. She said, "If you promise not to mug me, I can show you something." As my head slowly turned and I suspiciously said "yeah," there in front of me was her Super Bowl ring from a couple years earlier. She had been on vacation with her girlfriends and was showing it off to them since they had never seen it. I asked her if I could take a picture of it on my finger and I did. I thanked her and said goodbye and kept looking at the picture in disbelief.

It was a generous, thoughtful, and kind thing for her to do. She knew that it would give me a thrill, but what she didn't know was that thousands of my riders would enjoy seeing a blown-up picture of the ring hanging in my car. Below are some of my favorite comments about her ring:

Woman: "Why are you selling your Super Bowl ring?"

She said, "So it's yours now?"

He looked at the picture of the ring and said, "Where did you get that ring? I have the same one. My family built Arrowhead Stadium and Kauffman Stadium." (The baseball stadium.)

Woman: "I'm sorry I don't have a Super Bowl ring to show you."

She took a picture of the ring. "My cousin used to play for them; he'd love to see this."

Seeing the picture of the Super Bowl ring hanging in my car next to the $500 bill from South Sudan from another rider, she said, "Here's a paint stick from Home Depot, you can show that off too."

He said, "You should have mugged her."

The Kansas City Chiefs fan couldn't wait to get to work after seeing the Super Bowl ring. "My boss is a San Francisco 49'er fan, I can't wait to see him." (The Chiefs beat them in the Super Bowl.)

Talking to the young Jamaican guy about the picture of the Super Bowl ring in my car, he said, "What does the *KC* stand for? "Me: "Kansas City." Him: "It doesn't stand for witchcraft?" (Another rider told me that the initials have to do with voodoo.)

#11. THE DISNEY COUPLE

What made this ride great? Two weeks after the "Disney Princess" ride, I was somehow fortunate enough to get another Disney ride that was almost as much fun as the first one, and I was able to drive two big Disney fans.

The young couple, about twenty-one years old, was from California, and the forty-minute ride to the airport was so they could rent a car to drive eight hours to Disney World. When I told them that my trip to Disney was just canceled due to the pandemic last month, they said, "Why don't you come with us?" I would have loved to, but it would have been difficult to explain to my wife.

They met three years ago on a dating site. Their first date was planned to be at Disneyland. Since they hadn't met before, they decided to talk on the phone the day before their date. They talked for twelve hours (really)! She graduated high school the day after their date. One of their goals is to visit all the Disney parks in the world and they told me about their trip to Paris Disneyland where they ate amazing French food throughout the park.

I told them about the "Disney Princess" ride I had two weeks earlier and I gave them a bunch of suggestions for their trip. I suggested they might get married at Disney and it wouldn't surprise me if that happened. I know they had as much fun as I did because they gave me a very generous twenty-dollar tip. They were a joy to drive and I'm certain they will have much success in the health careers that they are going into and in their future together.

#12. WONDER WOMAN*

What made this ride great? She was the most inspiring female rider I have ever had. I told her that she should find some way to speak with young women, because her story was so important for them to hear. She is a terrific role model.

I was impressed with her before I met her. I was picking her up at the tennis stadium and some of the roads were blocked off. She texted me several sentences that were very specific so I could find her, I really would have lost out if I had missed her. She had been working at the stadium representing a hair company as an independent contractor. It had been a long day doing the tennis player's hair and she told me that she was tired. She told me she was thirty-three years old, and she had to drop out of high school during her senior year due to family problems. She was eleventh in her class at the time. She put herself through cosmetology school, became a hair stylist, went to a four-year college and opened her own salon. She still does hair today, teaches hair styling, and owns two houses.

As the ride was ending, she said, "I was a little grumpy getting out of work, but after this ride, you really changed my mood." I told her that I got more out of the ride than she did, and I've told her story many times over the past three years. She felt good that I was so impressed with her accomplishments and her generous tip showed that she really was a special woman. She didn't have superpowers like Wonder Woman, but she had persistence, determination, and one incredible success story.

#13. THIS GUY HAD IT ALL

What made this ride great? He may be the most unique person I've ever driven. He had personality, enthusiasm, humor, an incredible work ethic, and he somehow came across as a regular guy that you wish was your friend.

I knew almost immediately I was going to write a story about him. The thirty-two-year-old guy from California used to sell $70,000 cars for three years, until he decided, "I didn't like what I had become." I'm sure he was very good at it too. He told me he's afraid of the ocean, but when he arrived in South Carolina, he was on a golf course and saw an alligator. Sneaking up behind the gator, he picked it up and it started to hiss. I said, "What did you do then?" He replied, "I dropped it and ran."

He's a jack and bore specialist, which deals with sewer construction. He loves it and calls himself "a certified laborer." He works eighty hours a week, and after working twenty-one straight days, he gets two days off. He is not dating now, and he said, "The women down here are thirsty; that's not what I'm looking for." He enjoyed the ride as much as I did, because at the end he said, "I don't have a lot of friends here, but my buddy from work and I get together sometimes to play cards, smoke cigars, and pretend to be old men; do you want to join us sometime?" Me: "I don't smoke cigars, but I got the old man thing down." I would have loved to hang out with him. I think he could do anything he wants to do and I'm sure he will.

#14. THE SURPRISING YOUNG MAN*

What made this ride great? He was six feet, three inches tall and maybe 250–275 pounds, with a full beard and an inspiring success story that really impressed me.

He was sitting next to me and talking about his job as a ramp supervisor for American Airlines. He told me that when the planes come in, he has a group of people who quickly get the plane ready for it to fly out again. He was dedicated, knowledgeable, and enthusiastic, and then he told me he was twenty-one years old. He had been working for the airline for less than a year and he had already been promoted.

I was shocked; I thought he was around thirty. His stepfather suggested he apply, and then he said, "They were impressed with my moving business." Now I was confused, and asked, "How do you have a moving business?" He replied, "In high school, I was helping people move and a woman from my church suggested I should start my own business, and she gave me $25,000 to start it."

Obviously, it wasn't just American Airlines and me who were impressed with this guy. He oversees the moving business and has someone else running it. I suggested to him that he should go back to his high school and encourage young people, because they need to hear from people like him. I thanked him for the ride, and I know he enjoyed it also. As I pulled away, it came up on the app that he gave me a twenty-dollar tip. I should have tipped *him* for the ride, and over the past three years, I've told his story many times.

#15. THE MEDICAL ASSOCIATION PRESIDENT*

What made this ride so great? She was impressive, inspirational, delightful, and unforgettable. It was a *wow* ride, and if I had a recording of it, I would have watched it many times.

I would have given this ride for free; it was that good. She was halfway through her one-year term as president of the top medical association that has been around for 175 years. Their purpose is to "Promote the art and science of medicine and the betterment of public health." She is the first black woman to be elected to the position. She had to campaign for it by interviewing and debating her opponent. She also had to answer questions from a panel of professionals.

She told me her background: "I became a doctor (psychiatrist) because of the television show, *Marcus Welby, M.D.* I was inspired with how he cared for his patients and his commitment to his community." People discouraged her from studying medicine due to her race, but Dr. Welby made the difference. She went to nursing school but knew immediately it wasn't for her.

We talked about medicine and the opioid crisis. She said, "We're making progress." This ride was right before the pandemic hit; we had no idea how much medicine was about to change. It was an amazing experience spending thirty-plus minutes talking with her, and I'll never forget it.

#16. THE PART-TIME TRAVELER*

What made this ride great? A rider once asked me, "What was your most interesting ride?" The answer has to be this young woman, whose ambition and ability to set goals for her life is impressive for anyone of any age.

It did not make a lot of sense. As she spoke to me, I was trying to add things up. Being a numbers guy, I did not understand what I was hearing. I was taking her to work, which I was soon to find out was at a Waffle House. However, when I asked her what kind of work she did, she told me, "I'm a part-time traveler." She was wearing a mask during the pandemic, and I was certain I misheard what she said, so I had her repeat it two more times. She explained, "Every month I take a three-to-five-day vacation and I go to places I haven't been to. I want to fill up my passport." She has several places already picked out for the next couple months.

She was twenty years old the first time I drove her; she's a server at Waffle House and she's also in culinary school. "My real goal is to be a chef who travels the world." As I was driving, I was still trying to figure out how she was doing this, until she told me that her mom recently retired as a flight attendant. That explains her ability to travel, and she wants to follow in her mom's footsteps and be a flight attendant. She told me that she had already made the decision not to have children, because she doesn't like to take care of people. Her solution is that since she wasn't going to use her eggs, she would sell them so someone else can have a child.

To top it off, she is publishing a cookbook this year and the title is going to be *One Hundred Ways to Make Your Mouth Climax*. She was extraordinary and fascinating, and she has a great future ahead of her. She's decided that the sky is the limit and she's reaching for it. I've driven her twice, and I'm looking forward to the next time to hear about what she's doing in her life.

#17. BEACH WEEK: OHIO-STYLE*

What made this ride great? Two very nice people had two incredible stories for me, which is the only time this has ever happened. I'm not sure which story is better, but together they made this ride very unique and very special.

The outgoing couple from Ohio had been married thirty-nine years, and you could tell they had a great relationship. The first week in August is a special week for their family because they always visit North Myrtle Beach. The family tradition began seventy-three years ago—yes, seventy-three years ago. There were three brothers who were in World War II, and they made a pact that if they survived the war, they would vacation in North Myrtle Beach for the rest of their life. Their father bought ten small plots of land to build on that cost maybe $175 each. The three brothers were all golfers, because growing up, their dad had built a golf course around their house. The dad knew that North Myrtle Beach would be a big tourist area and it was a great place for his family to vacation.

The second story, I almost missed, because I was so fascinated with the first story. The husband is retired from an invention he patented in 1986. The idea came from his four-year-old son. They were feeding the dog together and when the father poured water into the bowl of dog food, his son asked, "Why does the water turn red?" He had no idea since dogs can't see color.

He said, "I drove one hundred miles to a dog food manufacturer and asked the manager if I could watch their manufacturing process, and the guy thought it was the craziest idea he ever heard." He developed a process to make colored mulch and fifteen years later, sold it to a large company that sold millions of dollars of it. The moral of this story is to listen carefully to your children's questions—you never know where they might lead.

#18. "WILL YOU MARRY ME?"

What made this ride great? I wish I hadn't been driving, but instead, sitting next to the driver while I spoke with this woman. Funny, unique, and outspoken, she had an uncanny ability to attract men.

The car had hardly moved when I heard her struggle in the back with the seatbelt. When she said that she was pregnant, I asked, "Your first child?" Her answer was, "No, my last." She told me right away that she wasn't a big fan of marriage or of having kids, which was a remarkable comment to a stranger. She had been married for six years and had one child, and she's in her early thirties and runs a maintenance business. I laughed when she told me, "I was funnier before I was married." She's had a very interesting life, having lived her first two weeks in Siberia, Russia, and then several other European countries. She told me, "I waited until I was twenty-one to come into the United States so I could drink legally."

"I was engaged five times before I was twenty-five, because when someone asked me, I said 'sure.'" She worked on a cruise ship and had met her husband when he walked on board. She told a coworker, "He's so hot; I'm going to marry him." They pretended to be engaged so he could cruise with her while she worked. Her real engagement happened like this: "We were watching the movie *He's Not That Into You* and he thought I reminded him of the character who really wanted to get married. I told him, 'I am not desperate to get married,' and he said, 'Would you marry me?'"

She said "yes" again, and I think she was happy with her decision, just a little uncomfortable with another baby on the way. One day, someone may write a book about her life; unfortunately, I only heard a small part of it.

#19. "I'M IN SO MUCH TROUBLE"*

What made this ride great? This could easily have fit under inspirational stories since I inspired this woman; however, her circumstances were so unusual and I worked harder on this ride than any other ride.

I saw the couple walking toward my car in front of a hotel in downtown Charleston. I thought they were both getting in the car, but he gave her a kiss, which I really didn't see, and put her in my back seat. As I started to drive, she said, "I'm in so much trouble." She probably said this five times during our ride. I offered to help her and asked her what kind of trouble she was in. She said, "My mom tracks me on her phone, and I didn't go home last night, but nothing happened." She told me her mom just called her and she needed to call her back when I took her home. I was thinking that she was in her early twenties and living at home, but she was really thirty years old. She was an engineer and a supervisor for a big company, and she had been living on her own for ten years.

Being a dad with three kids in their twenties, I told her that she needed a game plan. I explained that the best defense is a strong offense. I told her that she should show her appreciation to her mom for being worried and loving her but let her know that she's fine and that she knew exactly what she was doing. She told me, "I just didn't feel like going home." Her parents were on vacation and the guy, a pilot, offered to get her a ticket to go where her parents were. I told her when she calls her mom that she should stand up, because you're more confident standing than sitting, and she agreed that it was true.

By the time she got out of my car, she realized that she wasn't in any trouble, and she could handle this situation because of who she is and what she has accomplished. Who knows, maybe she's dating or married to the pilot today?

#20. SHE'S A WHAT?

What made this ride great? I have met only a handful of naturally funny people in my car, and this woman is one who could make anyone laugh. I had a short ride with her, but she was throwing out line after line as if she was preparing for her next show.

Sometimes you know immediately that you're going to have a special ride, and this woman wasted no time letting me know. As she got in, I said hello to this woman in her fifties and asked her what she did for a living. Her reply was quick: "I'm a whore and massage therapist." She did a lot of things, but I'm pretty sure "whore" was not one of them. When the GPS said to turn left when it was clearly right, she said, "That bitch makes my life miserable every single day." (Her townhouse is difficult to find.) I had no idea what she was going to say next, and I don't think she did either.

She had no problem telling me this: "What's wrong with men? They are always listening to their little head instead of their big head." I'm certain that was not an original line, but she had an unlimited supply. She told me, "People think I'm crazy because I speak my mind." She started talking about family problems and I added, "Sometimes families can be a challenge." She answered by saying, "Yes, yes, yes. They are all apples from the same tree." She told me that twenty years ago, a friend told her that she could do a talk show, and I promise you that nothing has changed. I would love to drive her again, but if I do, I will expect the unexpected—she was terrific. What is she? She is a very funny woman.

#21. THE EGYPTIAN CHRISTIAN PRIEST

What made this ride great? I'm Jewish, and I think this is the only time I have had a conversation with a priest. It was a fascinating ride, and when I wrote my Uber song, which is at the very end of this book, I had to mention him in the song.

I drove up to the church and I did not expect a priest to get in my car wearing robes. I drove him to the airport to get a flight back to his home in Indiana. I liked him immediately, since he had an extremely outgoing personality. He told me that he'd just performed a wedding for a couple who live in Indiana. He may have laughed at everything I said, and of course I liked that. He taught me two Egyptian words which I have taught other riders. *Coptic* means "Egyptian" and when we say *shalom* in Hebrew for hello/goodbye, in Egyptian you say *salem*. A future rider told me that salem means "hello" or "welcoming," and that's why it's the last part of *Jerusalem*.

He told me that in Egypt there are "more than ten million Christians, and they are a large majority." He said that the biggest problem in Egypt is terrorism from the radical Muslims. He was full of life, and not what I would expect a priest to be. But, then again, I don't know any other priests. When I have a passenger from Indiana, I always mention my favorite priest.

#22. JUST LIKE AN OLD FRIEND

What made this ride great? I have been fortunate in over ten thousand rides to have a lot of very good conversations, but only a handful of conversations were so easy that I felt like we were old friends catching up. This ride is one of those, and it's the only time I have had two great rides on the same day. The two rides were less than thirty minutes apart, and both women had the same first name.

I was in a great mood. I had just had an incredibly inspiring ride and never expected a second great ride. Some rides are filled with laughter, or me telling entertaining stories, or the rider having a great success story. This ride was special because our conversation was so natural. I picked her up at her house and she was dressed for a Saturday night. She was in her mid-to-late twenties. I said, "How are you today?" Her response was, "I'm not in a 'bachelorette-y' mood." I told her I would help her out and get her into the right mood. It was her second night in a row of bachelorette parties, and she didn't want to go out again, leaving her young son. For the next twenty-five minutes, we talked about a wide range of subjects—her job, country music, a few of my riders like the one I'd just had, and the kind of work her husband did.

She was very well-spoken, and I told her that she should be in sales. She started laughing and told me, "My husband tells me the same thing." I added, "That's because he's right, and you tell him that I said so." She was not a nurse, but she was in the nursing profession, and she enjoyed it. When the ride ended, she got out and said, "Thanks Jeff, I feel more 'bachelorette-y' now." I laughed and said, "Thank you. I really enjoyed the ride." I have thanked riders at the end of the ride or for a story they shared, but this time it was different. I think I felt more in a "bachelorette-y" mood too.

#23. A HILARIOUS MOM

What made this ride great? One of the funniest women I've driven was worthy of winning an award by the time she got out of my car.

A mom from Pennsylvania, she was taking her two daughters, eight and ten, to Medieval Times. I asked her, "What brings you to Myrtle Beach?" She answered, "My girls are here dancing for the Future Strippers of America." Her delivery was so perfect I had to ask her a second time, and then she admitted they were here for a dance competition. As a mom, she said, "I am not a maid, my kids have to do chores—I have things to do." She has a special game she plays with her kids: "I tape three dollar bills to the wall, and I line my three kids up in front of the wall. [The youngest is four.] They have to put their nose to the bill, and the last one to move gets to keep the three dollars. One game lasted forty minutes."

She saved her best comments for last as she kept looking around my car. I asked what she was looking for, and she said, "The camera." Egging her on, I asked, "What camera?" She replied, "The one where you watch what your passengers are doing." Me: "Why would I want to do that? I'm driving." She said, "What if two girls pass out in the back of your car and accuse you of something you didn't do?" I answered her, "I don't worry about that." I think any subject we talked about; she would have made me laugh—she was truly unforgettable.

#24. NOT JUST A GOVERNMENT EMPLOYEE

What made this ride great? A thirty-minute ride turned into a two-hour ride, and my rider not only loved history like I do, but he had a connection to history unlike almost anyone else.

I was taking him to the airport in Myrtle Beach so he could rent a car to drive back to the Charleston area. It was raining, and we were having a very good conversation—I suggested that I could drive him all the way home. He agreed, but if he didn't, I would have missed out on his great story.

He worked in human resources for the federal government, and since I've hired/contracted many people over the years, we talked shop, which might have put other people to sleep. He told me that there are special programs to get young people involved in public service. He was responsible for hiring people around the country, and he said, "Millennials these days are more interested in how much time they have off, job flexibility, and when they can work at home and less about the actual job." (This was before the pandemic.) It was easy to see how dedicated he was to his work, and he was very cost-conscious for taxpayers.

We started talking about history, and it was fascinating. His mom worked as a secretary in the federal government, and she was the first woman in South Carolina to volunteer to enlist after Pearl Harbor. She was told by supervisors three times not to ask to enlist in the war effort, and she ignored them. She later worked for the Navy's military intelligence, interviewing captured Germans from submarines. Her drive and ability were recognized quickly, and she became known as Eleanor Roosevelt's "right-hand woman." He took out his phone and showed me a couple pictures of his mom and Eleanor Roosevelt. There is no doubt in my mind that he was his mom's son, and I'm pretty sure she would have been proud of his career. What a ride this was!

#25. DESTINY OR FATE?

What made this ride great? She was inspirational, funny, and an absolute joy to be around. There was no doubt that we were meant to be in the same car together.

Picking up a man and a woman from a hotel to go to the airport is very routine, but there was nothing ordinary about this ride—it was extraordinary. When I heard that they were from Indiana, I told them, "I have some great rider stories from Indiana." I started to tell one of my favorites about the Egyptian priest who had performed a wedding in Myrtle Beach. She started laughing before I said anything funny and said, "Do you want to hear something funny?" She told me, "I'm a wedding officiant and my friend here is Egyptian."

She continued by telling me, "I have my own chapel, because I believe that every woman deserves to be able to afford a beautiful wedding." She started her own business as a legacy to her late husband, who died suddenly in her arms. (She started to tear up when she mentioned her husband.) She charges only $400 for the chapel and her services. She said she was just a regular girl, and I corrected her and said, "When they gave out personality, you got three big scoops."

Her friend did not say a word the whole trip; he had the best seat in town. Her two children were the same age as my oldest children, and I asked her, "Is your birthday this month?" When she told me it was August 18th, I pulled out my driver's license and gave it to her so she could see I was born August 19th. We had an immediate connection between us, and we both had an incredible ride. Arriving at the airport, she said, "I really needed you today, you're a blessing." She never knew that I needed her that day, too, after having a rare, difficult ride that morning. I still remember the difficult ride, but it happened on the day I met the wedding officiant from Indiana.

#26. WHO KNEW THAT PHYSICS WAS FUNNY?

What made this ride great? How often do you get to meet someone who is obviously brilliant and incredibly funny? We didn't talk much about physics, but his performance was hilarious, and I was fortunate to be his only audience.

It was another great ride to the airport. My rider said he was in physics, and he spent twenty years fixing nuclear cameras. What he does now is different, but since I didn't do well in Physics class forty years ago, I didn't really understand. I only have a few words to explain it: atomic particles and radioactive isotopes. I don't know his job title, but I'm going to say he is a comedic physicist. (He may be the only one, and I'm sure he'll love his new title.)

It was clear immediately that he was not just some intelligent scientist with no personality. His performance should have been filmed. He did tell me he's never performed in front of people, but explained, "When I ride in an Uber, I figure if I make them laugh, they won't hit me." His education was different because his dad had wanted two kids and he had five. "There was no money for me for college, so I borrowed $5,000 from a bank." He had his uncle cosign for it. He went to an electronics school for two years and said, "You can get a good education without going to college." Whatever his job is, he does make a six-figure salary.

At the age of sixty-two, he has two adult children around forty years old. He said, "My wife kissed a lot of toads before she found her prince. I married the first girl I kissed; I didn't think it would happen again. On our honeymoon, my wife's antibiotics messed up our family planning." And to top it off, he's been married forty-two years.

Here's a few more of his greatest bits: "My dad taught me all about physics in how he disciplined. His hands were as big as dinner plates and his fingers were like sausages.

"I thought it was odd that my grandparents in Kentucky were first cousins also, until I realized that in Kentucky, the only options you have are cows, corn, coal, and cousins.

"My dad never told me about the four rings of marriage: the telephone ring, the engagement ring, the wedding ring, and the suffering."

I didn't want to end the ride and I'm sure he enjoyed me laughing at everything. He said, "The ride is on a company account, so if you want to take a few left turns you can." I think he could talk about anything and make it funny, even physics.

#27. THE UNLIKELY COMEDIAN

What made this ride great? He looked like a New Yorker—successful, tough, and mean. Somehow, he made me laugh so much, I was wiping tears from my eyes when the ride ended.

Before the pandemic, when a single rider approached my car, I would open the front passenger door and offer to let them sit in front if they'd like to. As he approached me, he didn't answer my question; he pushed the door shut, almost getting my hand. He then quickly grabbed the back door handle before I could unlock the door. He did not look friendly, and since it was early in the morning, I figured it would be a quiet ride. He had worked on Wall Street in securities and had recently moved to the Charleston area. I asked, "Did you move down here to slow down and retire?" His answer stunned me and cracked me up. He said, "Slow down? No, I'm going to speed up. Look at the demographics here. You have to be a effin' moron not to be able to make money down here."

When I asked him if he had ever done stand-up comedy, his reply said it all: "No, but I've had people ask me that before." I wish I could have taken notes, but I wrote everything down that I could when he left the car. He went on a rant against the government, that they take too much money from us, and hit on several other subjects. I loved this ride partly because it was so unusual and I've always remembered him as a great example of the fact that any ride could be a great ride. I know he enjoyed himself too; maybe he was just as surprised as I was?

#28. WINNING THE COIN TOSS*

What made this ride great? I've had so many fun rides talking sports with people from the Boston area, I thought he was another one. However, I realized that his career success was much more interesting and entertaining.

I wish I hadn't talked about sports with him for the first fifteen minutes. He was dressed immaculately, probably in his thirties, and he could have been a model. He had a good story about Tom Brady, the New England Patriots quarterback, who many consider to be the greatest quarterback of all time. "One of my friends is a physical therapist for the Patriots, and one day Brady needed someone to catch some balls. Brady told him to put his hands out and not move them and he would hit them. He had gloves on, but the force of the ball was so strong it hit his hands and then his chest and knocked the wind out of him. And then, Brady said he was going to throw some hard ones!"

Many years ago, he owned an arena football team, and that led him to be the owner of the largest beauty pageant website in the world. Here's how it happened: with the opening game in Georgia, he wanted a pretty girl to do the opening coin toss. He contacted Miss Georgia; she agreed to do it, and they started dating. She told him all about the world of beauty pageants and he saw an opportunity.

He said, "There's one to two million women involved in pageants across the world. Any woman can go online and find out when the pageants are and what they need to do." When he visits other countries for work, he would get tours from beauty pageant winners. I joked, "That must be a difficult job." He admitted, "There are more difficult jobs." Before I dropped him off, he said, "I'm married to Miss Massachusetts." He definitely won the coin toss.

#29. SOUTHERN CHARM

What made this ride great? He was charming, funny, and enthusiastic, with a long career of success. My two rides with him were definitely like riding with a friend.

The sixty-three-year-old man had the energy and enthusiasm of a twenty-three-year-old man. He sells timeshares in Myrtle Beach and was number one in his office for ten of the last seventeen years. He also had business success with his wife, who he lost a few years ago. He said, "My wife and I owned several photo shops, and we made ugly women beautiful. She would just get you laughing, and you'd hand over your credit card." I couldn't imagine how funny his wife was, because he was hilarious. I asked him, "What is the secret of your sales success?" He said, "Ask for the friggin' money. When someone says no, I take it as a challenge."

He has a new wife, and he said, "When my wife doesn't like how something sounds the way I say it with my southern accent, I tell her this: I can say anything I want. I make more money than you do." There was no way I could keep up with all his amusing comments, but he added one about his mom. "My mama told me that if you don't have something nice to say about someone, shut your mouth up." He is still succeeding in sales, and I bet he'll be doing well and entertaining people into his eighties.

#30. THE MOST GENEROUS TIPPERS

What made this ride great? It was a good ride, until the final minute I was sitting in their driveway. Generous, thoughtful, thankful, they made that moment unforgettable.

It was my first ride of the day around 5:30 a.m. I picked the couple up at a bar that had been closed for some time. They were thrilled to see me, since two drivers had passed on picking them up. They were afraid they wouldn't get home, and they told me they would give me a good tip for the ten-minute ride. They were celebrating his thirty-second birthday and they obviously had enjoyed a few drinks.

At times they were a little loud, both talking at the same time, but it was a pretty good ride. They told me an amusing story about a vacation with their kids in a Cadillac Escalade.

The wife said she had met Chipper Jones, the Hall of Fame baseball player and then said, "I would have had his babies." When I started telling my Super Bowl ring story, the husband asked if he could record me telling the story, and that was a first for me.

When we pulled up in their driveway, the wife got out and immediately tipped me twenty dollars on the app, which was very nice. The husband was having too much fun talking to me and slowly got out of my car and took out his wallet. He handed me a hundred-dollar bill, and I was so shocked, I said, "I can't take that." He insisted and said, "You're the best Uber driver I've ever had. We were just hoping someone would pick us up." I thanked him, and several times during the day, I pulled that bill out just to make sure it really happened. I've been fortunate to have thousands of riders tip me, and some of them were very generous. However, this couple, who live only ten minutes away from me, were my biggest tippers, and I will always remember that moment on their driveway.

#31. THE CHARACTER

What made this ride great? I have met some people while driving who have such an interesting and unusual life that I am certain I could write a book about them. This guy would be near the top of that list.

If you invited him to a party, he would be the life of the party, and he would constantly have a group of people around him. I'm sure he has been called a lot of things in his life, but "a character" fits him best. At twenty-nine, he's a successful commodities broker who is sincerely interested in helping people. He told me that his parents were poor and used to eat "rice and tomatoes three times a week." His dad started a construction company, which built a significant part of an exclusive section of homes in the Charleston area.

Today, he spends a lot of money "spoiling his friends." He already has plans for a Las Vegas bash celebrating his thirtieth birthday next year. He explained, "When a woman hears I'm a broker, they ask if I have a lot of money. I tell them, 'I'm not hurting, but that money isn't going to be spent on you sweetie.'" Apparently, his old girlfriends are all mad at him, because he's "run through all of their friends." He had a Jekyll and Hyde personality, but what a personality!

#32. THE YOUNG AND POWERFUL VOICE*

What made this ride great? She is dedicated to helping others, and the short ride with her made a lasting impression on me after I read some of the things she had written about her career.

Her name was Angeline, and she was headed home to Ohio. She told me, "I'm in charge of marketing for a cancer foundation." When she said she had been doing it for fifteen years, I joked with her, asking if she had started in junior high school since she had a very young-sounding voice. She said, "I've only been full-time a couple years; I've been volunteering since I was ten when I lost my mom to breast cancer." The Karen Wellington Foundation sends families on vacation while they are battling cancer to give them a break from the disease and make some great memories for them. We spoke briefly about what she did, and she gave me her card to contact her if I knew someone that she could help. She inspired me to check out their website and I read the "KWF Living" blog that she writes. She writes stories about the people they've been able to help. She's a terrific writer, and I really regret not being able to talk with her about her writing.

One of her articles was about her mom who celebrated strangers. The article, "Celebrating Strangers," was outstanding, and it meant a lot to me. It is not a coincidence that both those words are on the front cover of this book, because this is what I do in my car and in this book. She wrote this about her foundation: "Although our mission is rooted in *fun*, our goal is to give back to thousands of deserving strangers *living* with cancer." She summarized this blog with words I believe in 100 percent: "Never underestimate the significance of the time you give to others. Don't forget to slow down just enough to be aware of those strangers who need a bit of extra love along the way. You never know the impact you might have."

I have this blog post hanging in my office and I have read it many times. Her mom lived a very full life, and her daughter is making each day count too. She is an inspiration, and I'm sure her mom would be very proud.

#33. HE PAINTS AIRPLANES

What made this ride great? It's never too late to change jobs, and sometimes a small investment can give you incredible rewards.

When do you ever get a chance to talk with someone who paints airplanes? The work he does today is as interesting as how he got there. He worked in retail in Florida for eight years and was ready for a change. He found an ad in the newspaper for a technical school that had a two-month course for $2,000. They taught people how to paint airplanes and he signed up. (I worked eight years at a business and technical school, so I was really interested in his story.)

He graduated with only seven people and put resumes out and contacted companies online. Only one company responded, but it was Boeing. They offered him $38,000 to start, but he said, "I wasn't convinced it was enough until they said I could work overtime." His first year, he made $80,000. He told me that every ten years, planes come in for a paint job, and it usually takes seven to ten days for a staff of over fifty people to finish the job. He said that just buying the special paint for one plane costs $1 million. He said that completing the whole job usually costs a few million dollars. He loves what he does and believes he was lucky to fall into his job just at the right time.

#34. THE ACCOUNTANT WHO CHANGED HER LIFE*

What made this ride great? Out of all the top fifty rides and the twenty-two inspirational and motivational rides

I've written about, this woman is one of only four people I have had the pleasure of driving a second time. However, *her* second ride was the best of those second rides, because she overcame significant personal and professional problems in a short period of time. I was absolutely thrilled to hear how much better her life had become.

I had picked her up in March, and she had had an incredible amount of stress. She was an accountant in tax season with billing hours she had to do. What complicated things was that she had hit her head and was suffering from concussive symptoms that affected her work and sleep. She was trying to work through it, but her doctor told her to take time off or she risked permanent injury.

Eight months later, she was relaxed, smiling, and almost completely healthy. When her boss gave her a review, they said they could not give her a raise due to her performance. She gave her two weeks' notice and found a job doing the same work. It paid $20,000 a year more and paid overtime, which she hadn't been getting.

She told me that her accident was also a good thing because that night, she met her current boyfriend. She did not remember meeting him at all before she hit her head. At that second meeting he said to her, "Don't you remember? We talked all night and fell in love." When I told her that she has a gift in her ability to work with numbers, she said, "It's not a gift unless you use it to help people."

I hit the jackpot toward the end of the ride when I started to give her my trivia question about what the Ravenel Bridge in Charleston was built to look like. She didn't know the answer, but then said, "I was the first person to officially cross over the bridge." In 2005, she was in third grade and entered an art contest. She submitted a picture of the bridge and won first place. She was able to cross over the bridge in a limo with two other winners, which had to be fun. Her artwork of the bridge and her picture is below. She is also in the chapter "Driving in Charleston, South Carolina." As great as the year has been for her, I have no doubt she has a great future ahead of her.

1st place
Heather Jervey, third grade,
Belle Hall Elementary

#35. THE MARATHON RUNNER RAN AWAY FROM TWENTY-ONE WINES?

What made this ride great? Two friends from North Carolina met in North Myrtle Beach to run a half marathon, and they gave me a priceless story about drinking and running.

I was driving them at 7 a.m. on a Sunday morning. They told me that they don't get out much, and they were very happy to see each other since they live in different parts of the state. They arrived at 4 p.m. Saturday, went out to eat, and went to a winery to drink. One woman was an accounting and finance professor who said, "I have a messed-up sleep schedule." She grades papers at 2 or 3 a.m., with tequila. She explained, "If I look at some numbers and it doesn't look right, I take some tequila and check it again. If it looks the same, I know I'm good."

The other woman said, "I'm going to have to go home today and pretend I'm not tired, so my husband doesn't think I was up all-night drinking." I asked, "Isn't that what you just did?" I told her she has to have a strong offense in order to defend herself. I wrote her a note for her husband that said, "She only tasted twenty-one wines and did not drive. The Uber Driver." We all had a good laugh about it, but I've had many laughs about it since.

My very next riders were two more women running the marathon, and I told them about this story. One woman said, "The note should have said, 'She was doing more than drinking wine last night,'" and the other one added, "Her husband would probably think she was having an affair."

#36. THE VIBE GUY

What made this ride great? The young man was genuinely funny and gave me possibly the best laugh I've ever had with a rider, and it was after the ride ended.

The first time I saw him was just after 6 a.m. on a Sunday morning. I was driving my first rider of the day and he was walking along Ocean Boulevard. He looked out of place since he was dressed very well. He became my second rider, and he made my day. Sitting next to me, he immediately was fixing his hair and checking his breath, because he was going to a "hook-up." I think that meant he was meeting someone for the first time, and they weren't going to watch television. He sold timeshares for a major hotel, and I could tell that he did well by the way he talked. He said, "I'm sixth in my office, "and I replied, "You're not going to tell me that there are only ten salespeople in your office?" He replied, "You're killing my vibe," and that made me laugh.

He said he had walked into something last night that he wasn't prepared for, but I didn't ask for details. He hadn't slept at all either, but he was making sure that he looked good. The thirty-minute ride was entertaining, but he saved the best for last. We said goodbye and he took a few steps away from my car, then suddenly turned around and came back toward my car and said to me, "Make good choices." As he walked away, I burst out laughing. If he had looked back, he would have found me slumped over the steering wheel laughing. *I* should make good choices?

#37. EDUCATING THE BRITISH YOUTH ABOUT THE BEATLES

What made this ride great? Like many people, The Beatles are my favorite musical group. The movie *Yesterday* (about The Beatles) was about to come out and I had been promoting it. I never imagined that I would wind up promoting The Beatles to young people from England.

The three eighteen-year-olds from England were going to Walmart. They were in the British Army and will eventually be called on for emergency situations. They were visiting

Charleston and doing something with our military. Most of the conversation on the ride involved me talking to them. I immediately asked if any of them were from Liverpool. One of them said, "How did you know that?" I replied, "You know why I asked about Liverpool, don't you?" No, they really didn't have any idea. I explained, "I'm a big Beatles fan," and one of them said, "So you really like The Beatles?" I sarcastically told them there were a few of us here.

I asked the guy from Liverpool if he had been to The Cavern, but he didn't recognize the name. After, I explained to them that that's where The Beatles were discovered and how their manager heard about them. Finally, the guy from Liverpool said, "Is The Cavern where bands play?" I told them it was and gave them more information about the most famous band in the world. They seemed to be surprised that The Beatles were so popular, which is just bizarre. They did ask if I liked other British groups and I named several that I liked. I realize it's a different generation, but this was not just a local group that had some success; it's The Beatles. When they got out of the car, I was looking around to see if someone had set me up, and it is still one of the most amazing rides I've ever had.

#38. THE IBM COMEDIAN

What made this ride great? I have entertained many riders with stories and comments from other riders. Occasionally, the tables are turned, and the entertainer is my rider, and I am his only audience. He was a very successful guy, and he was very amusing.

His wife was in the car, but only said a couple words. She was obviously used to his stories and his comedic talent;

she was probably entertained at how much I was laughing. Her husband had been with IBM for fifteen years and was in management. Years ago, he was given what he said was the best financial advice from a multimillionaire. The guy told him simply, "One house, one spouse, no boat."

The night before, they were at a wedding where they didn't know a lot of people. He explained, "I had people ask me if I was on the bride's side or the groom's side. I just made stories up. I told some people that I was glad the groom had gotten the sex therapy he needed." At that point, the wife said, "You didn't!" He said he did. I asked him if he had ever done stand-up comedy and he told me he had not. I said, "When you do your first comedy special, I want a copy of it." His immediate response was simple and hilarious: "It's going to be inexpensive to make, because I'll need only one copy." I told him that if that IBM thing doesn't work out, he should try comedy. He really had a gift, and I told his wife she's lucky to be able to enjoy his humor, but I'm not sure she enjoyed it as much as I did.

#39. WHO KILLED MARTIN LUTHER KING JR.?

What made this ride great? I've always enjoyed history, but how often do you get to go back and look at history from a different perspective? My rider was able to turn back time and make me really think by asking some questions that few people get to ask.

The long ride to the airport was fascinating. The couple I was driving from Tennessee had been married for fifty-five years, and they were entertaining. I asked them what the secret was to a successful marriage, and he immediately answered, "Yes, dear." She laughed a little and said, "It's important to do things together."

He told me he was a corrections officer for thirty years in a men's prison, a women's prison, and skid row. His most famous prisoner was James Earl Ray, who had confessed to killing Martin Luther King Jr. in 1968. Three days later, he recanted his confession and said he was set up. My rider said, "No one in the prison thought he was guilty. The other inmates could have killed him anytime, but they only cut him up so he could go to the hospital." It's important to note that James Earl Ray was white and, of course, Martin Luther King Jr. was black. This was in the 1960s, a very difficult time for race relations. The rider told me that he spoke with Ray's son frequently and that Ray had a suitcase with $40,000 when he was finally captured. Ray wrote a book and signed it for my rider, who was offered $500 for it but kept it.

After looking up the story, I found that Ray convinced Martin Luther King Jr.'s family that he was innocent, and they tried to get him a trial. Since he confessed immediately, he was never tried for the crime and died in prison. I'm not a believer in conspiracy theories but getting this kind of information made me think that maybe he was innocent. It was a fascinating ride.

#40. THE OUTGOING LIBRARIAN

What made this ride great? She was my best ride of the day and one of a kind. We had chemistry immediately and she was an absolute delight to drive.

She was visiting Charleston from Chicago and she surprised me when she told me, "I'm the kind of librarian that my kids say to me, '*shh*.'" She told me "There's a lot of outgoing librarians," but I can't imagine there are any who are more outgoing than her. She's been a librarian for over twenty years. Her funny lines were coming out quickly and I told her, "We should do a podcast together and call it 'Ebony and Ivory.'" (I am white, and she is not.) It was not difficult to get her laughing again and I told her I wished I had a tape recorder to tape her laugh. (I never thought of my phone.)

Some of her interesting and amusing comments included: "Growing up in LA, you know mobility is a big issue there, so when you turn five, they give you a car." I suggested she would be a terrific Uber driver, but she said, "I hate driving, but if there was a job looking out the window at things, I love doing that." She said, "I could teach diversity at companies, just pay me all the money spent on it and I would go in and play 'Walk This Way' by RUN DMC and Aerosmith." (A black and white group singing together.) She looked at the signs in my car and told me, "You would make a good librarian, we love to make signs." She then added, "You should get a Pulitzer Prize," before I told her I had a blog or was writing a book. She did admit that she could do a talk show, and I would listen to that every day; wouldn't you?

#41. THE FIRST-TIME GRANDPARENT

What made this ride so great? I don't have any grandchildren, and I got to share this woman's excitement and get her to the airport so she could get to her daughter.

I've given a lot of early-morning rides, but this ride had more pure excitement than any other one. It was 6:30 a.m. on a Sunday morning and she came running out of her house to greet me. She was extremely excited. She was talking in a loud voice, and she told me that her pregnant daughter in Maryland was two days early and she was already at the hospital. She needed to get her big dog to the "dog place" and then get to the airport. We loaded everything into my van—the dog, the dog's bed, the dog's food, and her big suitcase. She was getting texts from her daughter on how far apart the contractions were. I was driving, trying to stay calm, but she was giving some of the play-by-play from the hospital.

As we pulled up to the airport, her daughter had passed the phone over to her husband. He started texting for her because she was starting to push. I know my heart was beating faster, and although I missed the conclusion, I'm sure everything turned out well. My rider was even more excited when I dropped her off. I can't imagine sitting next to her on that plane.

#42. THE SUNSHINE COUPLE MEETS THE SUNSHINE MAN

What made this ride so great? I was absolutely destined to pick up this couple, and the wife knew it too. You never know how much a little sunshine can make a difference in someone's life, and this was a great example.

I picked them up in Conway, about twenty minutes west of Myrtle Beach. The truck driver and his wife were going to the beach. Fortunately, it was hot and sunny on the beach, unlike the cloudy skies in Conway. She hadn't been to the beach in a long time, and they were going for an hour after his last delivery. Yesterday had been her birthday, and she said, "I was forty-one yesterday and seventeen the day before." I told her, "You had a very long day," and we had a good laugh.

I recently had put a sign up in my car that said, "If you can't find the sunshine, be the sunshine." She told me that she calls her husband "Sunshine." When she was going through a difficult marriage, she would see him around the apartment complex and that his friendly greetings were the only kind words she heard all day. She loved my sign and said, "That's the reason you picked us up." When I told her that my business name was "The Sunshine Man," she was amazed at the coincidences.

As we approached the beach, she started to cry, she was so happy. She was a photographer and she asked if she could take a picture of the three of us. I would have gotten a copy, but we were wearing masks and we looked like we were about to rob a bank. I said goodbye, and thirty minutes later, the clouds of Conway had reached the beach and it started to rain. However, I know she got the sunshine she needed, and it made her day and mine too.

#43. HELPING THOUSANDS*

What made this ride so great? I've been fortunate to hear a number of good success stories, but how do you really make a difference after your career is over? This man took his dad's death and made a big difference for a lot of people.

I knew when he got in my car that he was successful; he had that look and he carried himself in a different way. Originally from New York, he was probably in his sixties.

He started as an engineer and then worked in the healthcare field with Dupont before owning his own healthcare business. We talked about the differences between living in the North and the South, and he had some fascinating conclusions. He had lived in both parts of three different countries, and he concluded, "People in the South are always friendlier. They are outside more since the weather is nicer. However, people in the North are more loyal and have closer relationships with people, since they are inside more."

He got into the healthcare business watching closely how his dad was treated in the hospital. He said, "They made three serious mistakes treating him and I watched him pass away at ninety-two years old." With his knowledge and experience in the medical field, he told me, "There are 97,000 fatal mistakes in hospitals every day. Ninety-five percent of hospital workers are great and professional, but the hospital system is what fails." His business helps people get quality care at home. Since I had lost my dad a year ago, I told him that I thought it was a tremendous tribute to his dad that he's been able to help so many sick people. We shook hands before we said goodbye; it was a terrific ride.

#44. A BRILLIANT AND UNIQUE COLLEGE STUDENT

What made this ride great? The twenty-one-year-old was more mature than his age, and he was an intellectual who was very comfortable with who he is. He was sincere, curious, and inquisitive, and I'm positive that he has an interesting and successful career ahead of him.

He told me right from the start that he had overcome some health challenges and was definitely an individual. I explained some of my experiences being different and he appreciated my openness. He said, "Embracing being an individual helps make me feel better about it." He used to ask people a simple question: "What makes you happy?" My answer was easy. "My wife."

I asked him my usual question for guys from the College of Charleston. "How are you managing with the seventy-thirty ratio of girls to guys?" His reply surprised me: "I haven't had sex in a year and a half and I'm fine with it. I found that it wasn't important to have sex with random girls several times a week." I told him that sex was one of the few topics I haven't discussed with riders, and he wanted to make sure I wasn't uncomfortable discussing it. I told him I wasn't, and we continued. He observed that a lot of women come here and try to fit in by dressing and being like the people from the South instead of being who they are.

He's very interested in psychology and the sciences, which did not surprise me. He is working while going to school as a chef, which he enjoys. He explained, "I'm the kind of guy who craves chaos." I asked him about his experiences with other Uber drivers and he said, "They all have different personalities. Sometimes a driver says almost nothing, but he's a good driver and gets me where I'm going and that's a good ride. Other times, I have someone that we talk so much that we hug at the end of the ride." We didn't hug when I dropped him off, but I'm certain we both really enjoyed the conversation and hopefully we can do it again sometime.

#45. A FAMOUS DJ

What made this ride great? He was obviously very successful, and on the weekend of 9/11/2001, he shared an incredible story of that morning that changed his life dramatically.

I've driven DJs before, but I knew he was different immediately. He was exhausted from working the night before and he started talking about working as a DJ in Europe. The ride may have lasted fifteen minutes, but he generously talked with me about his life and career. He was heading to New York City that morning of September 12th, for a 9/11 benefit at Madison Square Garden with several comedians like Dave Chappelle.

I asked him if COVID-19 had affected his work and he said, "I just worked in red states where governors didn't care about their people." If it wasn't early morning and he wasn't exhausted and the ride was longer, I might have asked him a follow-up question to that statement. He told me that he has worked with all the big rappers and also radio personalities like Howard Stern and Opie and Anthony.

I had a framed picture of the Twin Towers that I had put in the car for riders to see that weekend, remembering the anniversary of 9/11. He saw it and told me one of the best stories I've heard from a rider. He began, "I was there that morning. My studio was next to the World Trade Center, but I left there at 8:30 a.m., shortly before the first plane hit." He told me that a famous DJ had lost his pug that morning and could not work until he found it. He was asked to substitute on the radio for him for three shows, and then the dog was found (unharmed). He was offered a job because he was funny. He added, "I owe my radio career to that pug. I call him 'devil dog.'"

He's been on the air since then and can be heard on Sirius XM. My wife really would have loved this ride, since she enjoys rap. When I got home that night, we looked up his first name on the internet and we found him. He is the real deal, and I greatly appreciated his willingness to share some of his life with me.

#46. THE SUNSHINE FARMER

What made this ride great? There was no doubt that I was meant to pick him and his son up, and I knew before they got in the car that this was going to be a special ride. I was not disappointed.

It was my very first full day driving my new orange van. As I approached my riders, I looked to the left and saw the Charleston Harbor and the cruise ship that said on the side of it in big letters, "*Sunshine*." My rider was standing with his five-year-old son and a very large suitcase, which was bright orange. My business name for more than ten years has been "The Sunshine Man." I told him he had the perfect suitcase for my car. The five-year-old almost stole the show with his comments about his dad. "He's getting old and fat and my sister and I beat him up all the time." His dad was in his mid-thirties and didn't have an ounce of fat on him.

They were from northern Maine, right near the Canadian border. He farms just about everything. He said, "When the weather is good, we work twenty-hour days. If you want to survive in northern Maine, you must work eight days a week." He got his work ethic from his dad. His dad worked many jobs and he helped with his snow plowing. As young as nine years old, he was shoveling snow for him, and he told me, "I still hate it." He never got paid, and I told him he should tell his dad he owes him back pay. In high school, he wound up with nine W-2s. He got a great deal on the cruise and got to spend some quality time with his son. I'm glad they got to spend some time with me; it was a lot of fun.

#47. A CANCER SURGEON

What made this ride great? He was obviously very successful and dedicated to his field, but he was also a very down-to-earth guy who was willing to share part of his life with me.

He turned down a job at Harvard and accepted one in Charleston, South Carolina. He is best known as one of the doctors who treated Steve Jobs, the founder of Apple. He told me that his success rate with cancer patients was 70 percent compared to 7 percent for other doctors.

A few years back, a supervisor told him that his "methods were not acceptable." Four years later, the same supervisor offered him his present position in front of an auditorium crowd, and he pretended not to hear him. He joked, "The supervisor owed me some drinks, because he was the motivation for my success and persistence." He offers his students this advice: "When you are convinced you are doing something right, you should always be persistent in your efforts." It was obvious to me that he wasn't pretending to be successful; he really was.

#48. 131 MINUTES OF LAUGHTER

What made this ride great? My stomach hurt from laughing when I dropped them off. We connected immediately, which led to some hilarious conversations.

The young couple had been dating for only four months and they needed a ride from Myrtle Beach to Charleston Airport. There is no doubt that I was meant to get this ride. He was from Long Island, New York, and since I was from New Jersey, it was our first connection. They both live in Colorado, where two of my children are living, and we were planning on visiting that summer.

His family was meeting her for the first time, and it was no surprise that it went well. The night before, they ate at The Claw House, one of my wife's and my favorite restaurants.

He works answering 9-1-1 calls, and in the past, worked as a chef and baker in a bed-and-breakfast. She was in marketing for USA Volleyball, a nonprofit organization which was founded in 1928 in New York. I told them with their background they should open a bed-and-breakfast. He was just about to tell me they had discussed that idea. I suggested that they should have volleyball-themed rooms or suites with an actual net in the room, maybe over the bed. His girlfriend said, "There would be no spiking." We talked about a big mural inside the place with all the different USA volleyball teams across the country and they suggested the perfect painter. I had told them about a dentist who I drove who was an incredible painter and we figured he could have an office and do check-ups in the bed and breakfast.

I told them about the guy from Minnesota who wasn't big on mini-golf, but said he'd thought his whole life about "stripper-mini-golf." He suggested that the stripper would drive around from hole to hole, but she said, "There should be a stripper for each hole." There is no doubt that this couple has a great future ahead of them and I told them that my wife and I would stay at their bed-and-breakfast when they made their dream a reality.

After sending him the original story I wrote about them, he emailed me this kind message: "You truly were an unforgettable person and we both appreciated your positive outlook on life. Please never change yourself, because you've reminded me that there are still people that look at the bright side and look for the good in people." They have a lot of good in them.

#49. THE BARTENDER WHO WANTS TO BE REMEMBERED

What made this ride great? I have driven many bartenders, but this bartender is the most unique one. He doesn't like to talk but wants to be remembered—maybe this story will help.

It was early in the morning, maybe 6–7 a.m., and it was just getting light out. He told me he usually doesn't talk to Uber drivers, but for some reason, I lucked out. He doesn't like talking to his customers either, which is very unusual for a bartender. He said, "I'm different. I don't talk much with my customers. I just bring them what they want, and they love me." He was smart and explained, "I'm situationally witty. I like it when someone says, 'Can I ask you a question?' I say, 'You just did,' and I walk away."

He seemed to be more of a private person, but he made it clear that he really wants to be remembered. He said, "There are seven billion people on the planet. I'd like one billion to remember me." If he made a conscious decision to talk to people, how could they not remember him? When I pick up a bartender, I usually talk about him. I wonder how many people he's done this to.

#50. A VOICE FROM IOWA

What made this ride great? This was one of the earliest rides I had in my very first month of driving. I was able to talk a little about politics with someone who enjoyed it as much as I did.

My favorite movie is *Field of Dreams*, where a voice tells Kevin Costner to build a baseball field on his farm in Iowa. The voice I heard came from Iowa, and she was involved in politics, one of my favorite subjects. She told me, "I've been working on the Iowa caucus for many years." She'd gotten to hear many speeches by candidates, including Hillary Clinton, who ran for President in 2016.

Our ride was almost forty-five minutes long, and she told me at the end of the ride that her professional mentor was the Republican Governor of Iowa, although she is a Democrat. She said, "It's too bad we can't talk more," and I agreed and offered to drive her around another half hour. We both laughed and enjoyed our conversation. This was one of the rides that made me realize there was a lot more to driving rideshare than I had previously thought. She was easy to talk to and very willing to share her political experiences with me, and I'll always be grateful to her for making this ride so memorable.

5

DESTINATIONS FROM EVERYWHERE

One of the best things about being an Uber driver is getting to meet so many people from so many places. It is true that people are different, but one of the reasons that's true is the places they are from are so different. These are a few stories about places and some of the best comments made about them. Southern hospitality and driving in Charleston, South Carolina, are in separate chapters.

From Russia:
She worked for the World Bank and had a degree in engineering and economics. She was very excited about vacationing in Myrtle Beach. She was told the Hilton was giving her a big room, but "I asked for a smaller one and they charged me $50 more." When I asked her where she was from, she took out her phone and showed me the back, pictured below.

She said, "It's very common for Russians to have a picture of Putin on their phone."

From New Hampshire:
Two riders who live there told me on different rides about "River Dave." He is a famous squatter in New Hampshire who lived in a shed for twenty-seven years on someone else's property. The owner of the land died, and the two sons had him arrested for contempt when he wouldn't leave the shack. While in jail, the shack burned to the ground. A GoFundMe site was started for the eighty-year-old man and raised $200,000. A year later, River Dave went back to live on the same property and was arrested again. In the end, he moved to Maine to live with family.

Los Angeles, California:
He said, "When I lived in LA, my friend bought tickets for a charity event at the Playboy Mansion. He invited me and my brother. I was kind of disappointed, other than the beautiful women serving sushi, who were only wearing body paint. The mansion and the grotto were smaller than I thought. My brother was drunk, and he got kicked out

because supposedly he was trying to take pictures of Khloe Kardashian's feet."

Hawaiian Vacation:
"My wife and I were stuck with a layover at Honolulu Airport, and we heard that there were 27 seats on a plane going over to Maui. I asked the woman at the desk if we could get on that flight and she said, 'Did you pay for it? You got what you paid for, now go sit down.' If they tell you to sit down twice, they send you to jail."

Egyptian Vacation:
With restrictions to many countries due to COVID-19, my rider went to Egypt for ten days. He said, "What amazed me were the highways. There are lanes on the highway, but no one pays attention to them. It's a mess and they are always honking at each other. People here complain about following rules and laws, but [in Egypt] there are none; it's awful."

Atlanta, Georgia:
"When I lived in Atlanta, I worked twelve miles away in the city and it took over two hours to commute each way. I don't miss it." Today, he works from home in South Carolina. "I've driven only eight thousand miles in the last six years. My dealership keeps asking when I'm coming in for an oil change."

An Uber Movie?:
I told the woman that I once gave a ride from Myrtle Beach to Atlanta, and it was about six hours long. She said, "I think

it would make for a great family comedy movie—an Uber cross-country trip where you see how the relationship changes. At the end, the Uber driver says, 'I can't charge you, you're my best friend.'"

Foreign Countries

Europe:
"On our European vacation, the four of us drank sixty-seven bottles of wine in ten days; we counted them."

Secret Agent for the United States:
"When you visit a city in Europe, don't spend too much time on the big attractions. What you really want to do is walk down a local street and have a family invite you in for dinner."

"You can't talk English with a New Jersey accent in Europe and expect to be understood."

In the Army for eighteen years and living in many places, he told me, "Our two favorite places to live were Italy and Germany. The culture and the ability to travel were great."

Morocco:
She: "I was on a cruise in Morocco not long ago and the people there didn't want us to be there. They were throwing rocks at us, and the police had to escort us."

New Zealand:
"There are sixteen sheep for every person and the mountains have rings around them from the sheep climbing up the mountains in circles."

Greenland:
Him: "I loved visiting Greenland. It's like a whole different world."

Jordan:
"We have everything you could want for a country—mountains, ocean, snow. We're small, we just have less of it."

Dubai:
She: "I lived in Dubai. When I first got there, it was 120 degrees. I thought I was in hell."

Japan:
The young man said, "My dream is to live in Japan; I'm fascinated by their culture."
"Did you know in Japan they have Kit Kats that are seaweed-flavored and salt-flavored?"

She: "My dad was in the military, and we lived in Japan for a few years. The day we arrived, I was completely out of it after the plane ride and the jet lag. He was showing us around and I said, 'Where are we?' It was complete culture shock. I tried to learn Japanese, but I couldn't do it."

France:
Two sailors in the French Navy spoke almost no English and were docked in Charleston. I gave them a brochure to go to Patriot's Point and to go on an aircraft carrier, although they had just gotten off a ship they had been on for five months!

She: "We didn't see many French restaurants in Paris; we had to look it up. There were a lot of restaurants for Americans. We found a French restaurant down an alley and in a basement and it was packed, and the food was amazing."

Greek Island:
"The people are very laid back there, like they are in the South."

China:
She lives there and said, "I find it interesting that people here move from the city to the country, because we move from the country to the city for better education and access to resources."

He explained, "People here really don't want to be bothered with you. They are focused on their life and what they are doing."

He told me, "When I go to my office in Shanghai, during the thirty minute [commute], I see 300,000 to 400,000 people."

Russia:
She said, "We don't send cards or wrap presents."

I told another woman from Russia about the woman who had Putin's picture on the back of her phone; she said, "It's the idol of stupidity. It's funny that someone likes him."
After telling her about the woman with Putin on her phone, she said, "One of my friends has a whole box of them and he sells them."

"In Russia, there are forever gloomy days."

Italy:
Me: "What's it like being in the Army and living in Italy?"
Him: "The beer was better, and the girls were too."

England:
From London, she told me: "I hate tourists. They walk too slow and speak too loudly."

The English woman said, "If you ever go to Britain, you have to go to Liverpool. It is the best place in the country. The people are wonderful."

The British guy said, "When I got my visa, I put down that I was from the U.K., but they thought it said 'O.K.' I told them I was from Oklahoma, and I still go with that."

Jamaica:
I told him that I had never been to Jamaica, and the Jamaican said, "You should take a small vacation to Jamaica for two to three weeks." (They think differently about vacations.)

The DJ said, "All the stations play every kind of music, so you get used to listening to great music."

The Jamaican man said, "I can't get enough of rain; I'm the little boy who used to run outside in the rain."

Malaysia:
I asked the three guys from Malaysia, "How do you guys stay looking so young?" He said, "We eat a lot of rice and drink a lot of water."

Africa:
"My friend flies to Africa to get her hair braided because it costs only $5 there. It's a few hundred dollars here, but her flight costs $1,600."

Mauritius:
Woman: "I live on an island off the east coast of Africa." (It has one million residents.)

South America:
From Columbia, she said, "I love living there because people are very kind and happy."

Bosnia:
The military guy said, "Bosnia has been one of the best places I've visited."

Thailand:
"I loved living in Thailand because of its culture and friendly people."

Greece:
"In Greece, most people wake up at 9 a.m. and have dinner at 10 p.m., and the bars get busy at 1 a.m. and close at 5 a.m."

The Philippines:
"The best part of living here is that it's a calm lifestyle."

The Caribbean:
Two young people told me, "We stay young by drinking coconut water and working out."

Nova Scotia:
"It has great food prices, fresh food, and beautiful scenery."

South Korea:
"When I lived in South Korea, I took up biking and biked the four hundred miles along the border of the country in five days."

The American businessman lived there sixteen years. "We loved it, it was like living in the US in the fifties."

The United States of America

*The young woman in her late twenties from a military family: "I've lived in sixty-three cities in my life."

The young Cuban rider told me on the morning of July 4th, "You can't tell Americans what to do; that's what I love most about this country."

The woman from Italy on what she likes in the US: "You can go outside in your pajamas, and no one cares."

He told me, "I worked as a pilot in Hong Kong for five years. I was really happy to go into a supermarket yesterday and see thirty different barbecue sauces I could buy."

She: "I want my son to visit all fifty states, and we've done fifteen now, including Alaska. Ten-year-old: "My mom has been to all except Rhode Island."

She: "I was born where the Gila monsters live. They were cute." (Southwestern US, and the lizards can be twenty feet long.)

The West Coast

Alaska:
He told me: "I just came back from Alaska where I was helping a friend remodel his kitchen for the past two months. It was ten below zero there, but we had a great time fishing, hunting, drinking, and doing Alaskan shit."

Female physical therapist living in Fairbanks, Alaska said, "I love it there, the outdoor activities and scenery."

"I grew up in Anchorage. Alaska is a beautiful place to visit, but not to live."

Washington:

From Seattle, she said, "We tell tourists that it rains all the time, but most of the time it's very light and you don't need a raincoat."

Him: "The Seattle Freeze is when you're not acknowledged at all."

Woman: "Washington is beautiful because of all the rain."

"In Washington State, summer always begins exactly on July 5th."

"If you don't like downhill skiing or walking in the rain, Seattle is not for you."

Oregon:

The woman explained: "The food in Oregon is amazing. You can get anything you want and its high quality. It's like New York."

When I told the guy from Washington State that I've had people from Oregon tell me that Oregon is known for its food, the guy said, "I just think of biscuits and gravy."

Man from Portland: "The government is very weak. They wouldn't let the local police do their job."

"Oregon has the best drivers in the country; they are always driving the speed limit."

She said, "The news media exaggerated everything. The rioting in Portland was only in a four-block radius."

Hawaii:
"It's a great place to visit, but not to live. It's crowded and expensive."

"Hawaii has the most perfect weather on the planet."

Me: "How did you decide to move to Hawaii?" Him: "One day I just got up and said, 'Why don't we move to Hawaii and buy a coffee shop?'"

He said, "When I was in Hawaii, I saw a petrified forest that had multicolored trees."

She told me: "I chose the University of Hawaii because they have one of the top cheerleading programs in the country."

"I once bought a gallon of milk in Hawaii for $12."

Nebraska:
"Omaha is a big city with a small vibe."

Wyoming:
"The best thing about living in Wyoming is that it's the least-populated state."

Woman from Wyoming in the first weekend of April: "We're expecting a foot and a half of snow today. We've had 700 percent of the snow we normally get in the winter."

"The weather in Wyoming is horrible. It snowed the other day." (May 1)

The woman from Wyoming told me, "Your car isn't orange enough; my jeep is a fiery orange."

Arizona:
"The people in Tucson were rude. I was there five years, and it was four years too many."

The couple from Las Vegas explained, "We loved the thunder and heavy rain here. We only get two to three inches of rain each year."

She is from Las Vegas: "When I went to Vegas, I played slots for three days and lost $500." Me: "Did you at any time think to yourself, 'This really isn't working out'?" She: "Yes, on the third day."

"We go to Hawaii when we go on vacation."

New Mexico:
She explained that it's called The Land of Entrapment. "It's too beautiful there to move, but there's absolutely nothing to do there."

Montana:
Me: "I heard there were only eight people living in Montana." Her: "Yes, it's true. We actually only hit one million people a few months ago."

Couple: "We lived in Hawaii for 6–7 years and just moved to Montana." Me: "Why did you move to Montana?" She: "We're not very smart."

"It's as cold as shikees there." ("shit")

"The people in Montana are friendlier than South Carolina, and it's cheaper to live there too."

"It was a beautiful place when I lived there."

Woman: "My husband won't leave Montana, so I brought my mom with me on vacation."

Him: "I drove across Montana and drove up to 140 mph in a Trans Am. The steering got a little shaky and I decided not to pass anyone."

"I was sick and tired of the snow and cold in Montana, so I moved to South Carolina."

Utah:
"It's a beautiful state, but it's becoming overcrowded. We're going to move to Idaho; no one knows it's beautiful." Me: "I won't tell anyone." (Oops.)

California:
Him: "I pay $22,000 a year in property taxes in San Francisco."

He said, "I used to live in the capital of Mexico: Los Angeles. I decided to get back to the US, so I moved out of LA. One of the things I miss most from living there is real Mexican food."

She: "We moved out of California when I was almost kidnapped at two years old. A woman grabbed me from my crib through an open window and was at the street when my mom started yelling at her."

A male finance mortgage guy from San Clemente told me, "The Richard Nixon estate is for sale for $60 million, we can go fifty-fifty on it." Me: "I'll check with my accountant, just get us a good rate."

Male: "I find it relaxing driving in LA. When I'm in traffic, it's 'me time.' I get a lot of things done in my car."

Me: "What's the best thing about growing up in California?" Turning to her friend, she said, "The first time I got high was with her and her sister. My mom, dad, and grandmother all grew weed."

The young man told me, "I like living in LA, because you can walk down the street, and no one gives a f---."
The twenty-year resident said, "LA is like a socialist environment, trying to solve all the world's problems."

The trucker said, "I paid $900 a month in gas, and I really didn't go anywhere."

He said, "My colleague in San Francisco pays $3,400 a month for a tiny apartment. It's a hellhole in a dirty city."

"San Diego has the best weather in the country."

Male: "I moved to San Diego to chase women when I was young and stupid. I found her and married her."

The first rider I had from San Diego told me, "It was so weird this week. I kept checking the weather for my trip here. We don't look at the weather in San Diego."

"I had to move out of San Diego, because the weather was always the same."

Young man from San Diego: "The beaches there are contaminated due to chemicals from Mexico."

He: "I moved from New York to Los Angeles last year and I can't believe the amount of homelessness in LA."

Woman who lives in Tennessee: "A lot of people from California are moving to Tennessee where we live. Many of us say, 'You're welcome to enjoy our beautiful state, but leave your politics at home.' We have a saying: 'Don't California our Tennessee.'"

He explained, "Once you get out of the cities in California, it's mostly a conservative state."

He: "I could talk to you for twenty hours about how California is a shithole."

"California just has some stupid laws."

"People in California are in their own bubble."

"I moved near Los Angeles and the weather is pretty much the same every day, but I can't break the habit of looking at the weather."

The Midwest

Missouri:
Woman who works for the city: "If there is an apocalypse, there is a plan for dignitaries to go into the caves of Missouri, and they'll have everything there, strip clubs and everything."

He: "Kansas City is a great place to grow up and also to move away from."

Guy from St. Louis: "Some people have actually asked me if I've gone into the ark." (It's an arch.)

Minnesota:
The woman with her nine-year-old daughter told me about the "Minnesota Goodbye." She: "We start saying goodbye an hour before we're leaving somewhere." The daughter interrupted, "They never stop talking." She explained that the "Minnesota Goodbye" is when you first say goodbye, you're just telling people that you're going to leave, but you're not leaving yet.

*He told me, "In Minnesota you're nice to your neighbors, because if you're not, they'll freeze and die, and you might be the next one to go."

Male: "In Minnesota, we're not friendly waving at each other, we help change people's tires in the snow."

*Explaining my idea for an educational mini-golf course, the young man from Minnesota who owned a distillery said this: "I've always been disappointed with mini-golf, but I've thought my whole life about 'stripper mini-golf.'"

Me: "You're from Minnesota, the friendliest state in the country?" He wasn't friendly, and he replied, "It is now after I left."

Him: "The difference between Minnesota and South Carolina is it takes twelve minutes to get a cup of coffee here."

The guy in his late twenties explained: "In my city of Minneapolis, the damage to the city is going to cost taxpayers 250 million dollars. Half of the restaurants won't open again. I'm thinking of moving." (Referring to the riots.)

Me: "Where are you from?" Her: "Up north." Me: "New Jersey?" Her: "Further north." Me: "Connecticut?" Her: "North, Minnesota." Me: "You know you're on the east coast?"

Teenager from Minnesota: "We're friendly to outsiders in Minnesota, but not so much to each other. We don't like each other."

I apologized to the couple from Minnesota about the bad weather on Valentine's Day and they said, "This is like spring break, we just left minus-seventeen degrees."

Indiana:
"When I lived in Indiana six years ago, we had a whole week of forty degrees below zero. People here were throwing hot water outside and it would freeze before it hit the ground."

"We had a New Year's Eve in Indiana that was sixty degrees below zero."

The woman from Indianapolis said, "Is there a hood in Myrtle Beach?" I replied, "Yes, but I don't go there often."

South Dakota:
She: "South Dakota is like heaven on earth, it's the most beautiful place in the country."

"The best thing about living there is you can go eighty mph on the highway, and everyone knows you."

"The only traffic we have in South Dakota is cows and tractors."

North Dakota:
"We have three cows for every person in North Dakota."

"In North Dakota, it's freezing all the time."

She: "There were only fourteen kids in my grade in North Dakota."

Ohio:

I asked the couple from Ohio why they were in town, and he said, "We're thinking of moving here." His wife said, "Thinking? We're going to meet our builder." Laughing, I said, "Does your builder know that you're just thinking about it?"

Me: "I don't know of any good Ohio stories; I've only been told that that they're bad drivers." Her: "So in addition to us being bad drivers we're also boring?"

She: "I like the wind here [in Charleston]. We don't really have wind in Ohio."

"We used to come down to Myrtle Beach every year. One year, I pulled up to a light here and my next-door neighbor in Ohio was next to us. We had no idea we were both coming here."

"Ohio has the largest fresh water preserve in the country."

"We're a little meaner in Ohio than here in the South."

Me: "Where do you live in Ohio?" She: "In the middle of nowhere. We don't have a stop light, but we have two restaurants."

"Ohio drivers are bad, but not like a New Yorker."

"In Ohio, if someone was as nice as the people down here, they would think they were being set up for something."

Just arriving from Ohio, he asked, "Do you have a funny bone here?" (Asking about comedy places.)

"If you take drivers from South Carolina and put them in the snow in Ohio, I'm pretty sure they would be bad drivers too."

Woman living in the South: "There are a lot of people here from Ohio; is there a program where we can send some of our people to Ohio?"

Michigan:
She and her husband moved from Buffalo, New York, to Detroit, Michigan. "Our first winter day in Detroit was minus-forty-three degrees. We found out that the cold in Detroit causes the snow in Buffalo. You have to have serious long underwear in Detroit."

"Most of the year we get no sun in Michigan."

He told me that the roads are bad in Michigan. I said, "Is it the highways or the local roads?" He replied, "Both. You have no idea."

Iowa:
"I grew up in the cornfields of Iowa. The cornfields in the movie *Field of Dreams* are not corn you can eat. It's just for cows."

Illinois:
"Anyone who says they enjoy the Chicago winters, they are lying."

"Chicago is seven months of cold."

Me: "How is Chicago?" Him: "It's cold and dangerous."

She: "I moved from one Chicago suburb to another two years ago, but it's not feeding my soul."

Kansas:
She: "We live in Manhattan, Kansas. We call it the Little Apple."

Colorado:
Living there, he explained, "We get teased for being 'the mile high state,' but no person has passed away due to pot. There is a problem with pets and small children getting it in the house."

He lived there for thirteen years and is a chef and guitar player. "I've seen five hundred shows at Red Rocks. There's nothing like it in the world. If you have a chance to see a concert there, just do it. Talking about it is bringing me to tears."

She: "I'm a CPA in Colorado, and two of my clients are Robert Wagner and Jill St. John."

Many, many riders have raved about Denver and described it as "great" or "awesome."

"San Diego has the best weather in the country, but Denver has the best weather if you want four seasons."
"I love living in Denver because of all the seasons."

"The best thing about Denver is the weather diversity."

She: "I'm a foodie; I love walking around Denver."

"My sister is moving to Denver for the weed."

She: "I love living in Denver because of all the seasons, and you can go to different parts of the area for different weather."

She: "The people of Denver are horrible, there are a lot of drugs there. They are not friendly."

The Northeast

Man from the South about people in the North: "I'd be unhappy too, if half of my wages were being taken away from me."

He said, "I was born in Poland and lived in Canada, California, and Denver, but my favorite place, because of the people, is the Northeast, where I lived for a semester of college."

Pennsylvania:
His dad was in the Navy, so as a child, from four to seven years old, he lived on an island off Italy. "I came home to

Philadelphia when I was seven and it was 1976, the bicentennial. They were having parades and celebrations and I thought America was like that all the time."

"The people in Pennsylvania are naturally pissed off."

She: "Philadelphia is my favorite city because it celebrates black culture, and it has great food and music."

New York:
She: "New York is like an old boyfriend—I miss it not being there, but when I'm there I realize why I broke up with it."

*She: "I lived in New York for ten years and didn't drive. I'm a terrible driver, but very good at parallel parking. My dad says I should stay parallel parked."

She: "I love New York, but they have a rodent problem. Last time I was there, I saw an entire parking lot filled with rats."

Pro softball player: "Every time I go back home to New York, they have a snowstorm."

When I told the two New Yorkers that people in the South almost consider honking your horn to be cursing at other drivers, he said, "That's the first thing we learn in driver's ed."

"I plowed snow in upstate New York where we had 140 inches of snow in the winter. One time there was fifty-four inches that came down in twenty-four hours. We had to clear the roof to open the door."

The New Yorker cursed twice in the same sentence, and I said, "You know, down here they don't talk like that much." He laughed and said, "I get your effin' point."

He: "In New York, people always look angry."

She: "New Yorkers are friendly, we just don't have the time to talk a lot."

Growing up in the South, her dad always complained about "the Yankee" doing something. She said, "I didn't know until he died that he was born in New York."

I told the retired woman from Queens, "People here think there's a lot of traffic." She said, "Traffic! My sidewalk is busy in Queens! There are kids and bicycles and animals and everything going on."

She: "People are not as nice up there."

Me: "It sounds like you miss living in New York. Her: "You bet your ass I do."

"New Yorkers are narcissistic."

Him: "I moved down to the South to get away from all the terrible people who live in New York."

Asking her how they got through the rough winters, she replied, "Since the world is ending soon, we'll be OK in Buffalo."

Due to global warming, he said, "We think Buffalo is going to be the new Florida in the future."

Student from China visiting New York, "It was crowded, noisy, dirty, and there [were] drugs everywhere." I don't think she was impressed.

Williamsburg section in Brooklyn, New York: "That's where the hipsters live."

Williamsburg section in Brooklyn, New York: "The young people dress like they're homeless, but what they wear is expensive."

"All of New York is New Jersey's hat."

"I never met a nice New Yorker."

She: "I was working in New York City on 9/11. I walked six hours to get out, but fortunately a store was giving away sneakers and I took a pair."

The guy in commercial real estate said, "I've lived in New York City for ten years, but I don't know how much longer my wallet can take it."

Young woman from New York: "I miss home; other than the weather, just about everything—my family, friends, and boyfriend." Me: "I'm sure your boyfriend would like to have heard where he ranked."

New Jersey:
The rider told me that in New Jersey it is said, "The only problem with the Jersey Shore is the beaches are filled with people from New Jersey." (I've never heard it before and I'm from New Jersey.)

"They weren't super jacked about winter."

Talking about all the "yes sirs" and "ma'ams" in the South, the guy from New Jersey said, "The only time we hear 'sir' in Jersey is when the cop says, 'License and registration, sir.'"

Woman: "When I worked up in New Jersey, they were giving me lip for saying 'ma'am' and 'sir.' They're not that nice up there."

"There's more to do in New Jersey than the Charleston area." (New Jersey is a lot bigger.)

"All the nice people in the South are from New Jersey."

"I like the food in New Jersey and that's it."

"No one stays in New Jersey." Me: "My parents did, they had the same house for fifty years." Him: "So they're the one."

She: "My boyfriend was puzzled when we moved to Salem, New Jersey, because he didn't see anything witchy." (Salem, Massachusetts)

Him: "One of my fondest memories of New Jersey is buying a big sub in Long Branch."

When I told the guy from New Jersey that a guy had driven a woman three hours home after her car broke down, he said, "If that happened in New Jersey, he would have shot her and taken her car."

"I may be the only one to say it, but Newark Airport is great; it's empty these days." (During the pandemic.)

She: "You're the coolest person I ever met from New Jersey." (I may have been the only one.)

A New Yorker told me, "You're very friendly for someone from New Jersey."

New Jersey man: "People in New Jersey are born with a silver spoon in their mouth." Me: "Next time I pick you up I'll have a spoon in my mouth." Him: "Will it be silver?"

Me: "I'm from New Jersey." Her: "You're so lucky."

Connecticut:
She told me, "The only thing to do in Darien is go to the CVS."

Massachusetts:
The Canadian told me that his family vacationed in Cape Cod for many summers. Before I could ask him if he knew Old Silver Beach (where I vacationed almost fifty years ago), he said, "We always go to Old Silver Beach."

Him: "We live in Fenway Park. We can see the stadium from our living room."

Me: "What do you do in Massachusetts?" Him: "I do as little as possible and I'm planning on doing more of it."

Me: "Where do you live?" Him: "Massachusetts, unfortunately."

Young woman from Massachusetts: "We call people from Massachusetts 'assachusetters.'"

Maine:
After telling the guy from Maine that another Maine rider worked twenty hours as a farmer when the weather was good, he said, "And there was still time to mow the lawn."

New Hampshire:
*Me: "I don't get too many riders from New Hampshire." Pilot: "It's a small state, it's really just the four of us. We have to get back before someone declares squatter rights."

She told me, "People say they are from Boston when it's really New Hampshire, because people don't know where New Hampshire is."

"We have the largest arcade in the country in New Hampshire."

Rhode Island:
Male: "In Rhode Island we don't even like each other."

Washington, DC:
Him: "I'm sure that when you walk down the street in Washington, DC, there are some people who are thinking, 'Please don't talk to me.'"

"The people in Washington are awful. They are stuck in their own bubble and can't even discuss things they don't agree on."

The South

Most southerners hate cold weather, but this guy said, "When it gets cold, I'm in love."

Australian woman from LA: "When I get out here, it is so calm and relaxing."

I asked the young woman who grew up in the South, "I noticed you don't have an accent and you grew up here." She: "I took care of that. It's not very attractive to sound like a country bumpkin."

The woman from New Hampshire who lives in the South told me, "I'm a Yankee Southern Belle. I'm a Yankee in the butt."

The woman who moved from London to Summerville, South Carolina, said, "I learned it's OK to take your time."

"You can't shovel sunshine; my friends up north don't like me saying that.

Woman from New Jersey said about living in the South, "I love it when people say, 'Have a blessed day.'"

Woman raised and living in the South: "It should be cold in the winter; I wish it was 40 below zero."

He said, "When you come down here you have to be 'Southified.' If you expect someone to come over to do work, it could be this week, next week, or the following one."

"Moving here was a culture shock. Even fast food is not fast."

I told the couple that a southerner once told me that when you come down here from the North, you have to be "Southified." The man said, "That sounds like becoming institutionalized up North."

The young woman from Boston in Charleston for a bachelorette party was surprised when another young woman in a restaurant actually yelled at them, "You have to be nice here, because you're in the South."

Arkansas:
The mom said to me, "Arkansas is a terrible state." When I said that President Clinton had a library in Little Rock where they lived, the fourteen-year-old boy said, "We don't condone him."

"It's a dreadful state." (Four-year resident.)

Louisiana:
Working away from home in the Charleston area: "I can only go without a woman so long."

Georgia:
She explained, "I like Savannah more than Charleston because Charleston was more rundown. Savannah had more flavor."

Me: "How did you like Savannah?" Couple: "It was fine, OK. After a few days we were looking to do more everyday things. Our desires did not fit with the expensive restaurants and things downtown."

Mississippi:
She: "There's too much humidity there."

"The people in Mississippi are hardworking, patriotic people."

Alabama:
Him: "When I was driving once in Birmingham, I ran over a wrench. The roads are so bad there, if you're not clenching your teeth there, they will fall out."

Kentucky:
"Louisville is the un-Kentucky like Nashville is the un-Tennessee."

West Virginia:
"It is one of only two states that have lost population in the last twenty years."

Tennessee:
"Where else but Nashville can you go into a McDonald's and see a country music singer performing live?"

"Nashville isn't just about country music; alternative and pop music are very big there too. The airport hires singers to sing in the airport so even people who have a layover in Nashville get to enjoy the Nashville experience."

From Memphis, I asked him how long he lived there, and he said, "Too long." Me: "What's the best thing about living there?" Him: "Leaving."

Virginia:
Him: "My friend was stuck on Route 95 in the snow. It took him twelve hours to go eleven miles."

Florida:
"In Florida, we're our own special kind of humans."

"When I was younger, we would ride our bikes past Trump's Mar-a-Lago before it was his. The security was so old that on top of the gates there was broken glass bottles to keep people out."

He told me, "South Beach in Miami is dangerous today. If you melted me like butter and dripped me on South Beach, I wouldn't go."

"People in Florida don't think they live in the South, because there are so many people from other places."

Texas:
"Texas is the best country in the world."

"Texas is so hot that you can look outside and start sweating."

South Carolina:
She: "When we moved from New York to South Carolina, it was an adjustment. My son went to Publix for the first time and told me it was like Disneyland."

"I moved to South Carolina for the quality of life."

Young woman: "I hate all the food in the South. I mainly eat sushi and salad."

Myrtle Beach, South Carolina:
The woman told me, "If you don't like the weather here, just wait five minutes."

"A bad day in Myrtle Beach is better than a good day at work."

She: "I was told Myrtle Beach is warm, but the people are warmer."

"Myrtle Beach is like Las Vegas on water."

From New Jersey; she explained, "Myrtle Beach is like Wildwood [New Jersey] on steroids."

"The weather here is bipolar."

Woman: "I truly believe that God brought me here to save my life." (Great healthcare.)

She said, "Living here is like being on vacation every day."

She got in the car and said, "It's as hot as Hades out there."

Man from North Dakota in Myrtle Beach: "The food is good here. If I lived here, I would weigh five hundred pounds."

The Romanian student said, "Myrtle Beach is like a different planet than Romania."

Getting in my car early in the morning was a guy from Las Vegas who had two bloody knees and a cut arm. I said to him, "What happens in Myrtle Beach, stays in Myrtle Beach."

Tourist: "I heard there are sharks on the beach." I assured her they were only in the water.

Woman: "We came from Chicago just for the safari."

"Everything's better down here compared to the North."

"Myrtle Beach had the most perfect pizza and sushi," said the visiting student.

She: "Until I get richer, Myrtle Beach is where I'm going to come for vacation."

"Myrtle Beach is cleaner than Miami and Atlanta."

Me: "What's the best thing about Myrtle Beach?" He replied, "The education; I have eight kids."

"In Phoenix, it's 115 degrees, but we had to adjust to the humidity here."

Woman from California: "I love it here, but it's too hot in the summer and too cold in the winter."

She asked me, "How come there are no high signs in Myrtle Beach?"

After a morning of rain, the weather was great in the afternoon. I asked the local woman, "How about this great weather this afternoon?' She said, "It sucks. [Referring to the humidity.] I wish it would have stayed cloudy."

Conway:
I asked her what the advantage is of staying in Conway, and she said, "The beaches are nice." (There are none in Conway.)

North Myrtle Beach:
"Being stuck in North Myrtle Beach for a month while we wait for our visas is not a bad place to get stuck."

6

SPORTS-TALK UBER

Living for fifty-seven years in New Jersey, I have spent hundreds, if not thousands, of hours listening to sports talk radio, mostly WFAN out of New York. I have had many great memories of listening to Steve Somers overnight while I delivered newspapers and magazines and also the legendary Mike and the Mad Dog show with Mike Francesa and Chris Russo during the day. As much as I enjoyed listening to them, I never had any interest in calling into the station and talking sports with them.

However, one of the most amazing things about being an Uber/Lyft driver has been how much fun I have had talking sports in my car. I have talked about every possible sport, from boxing and wrestling to golf and hockey and everything else in between, like adult kickball and disc golf.

The two most-talked-about sports have been baseball and football, which have separate sections. Each one has a few stories and then rider comments below. There are two great stories, one Yankee/Red Sox story and one Pittsburgh Steelers story, that you can't miss reading.

Baseball

I have loved talking to people from the Boston area since they are frequently Red Sox or Patriots fans, or both. There is nothing in sports like the Yankees/Red Sox rivalry and the number of stories I have collected, and the comments really say it all. These stories have entertained many baseball fans and have helped me give Red Sox fans more fun than they could imagine having in an Uber, even being driven by a Yankees fan.

The Red Sox Fan's Revenge:
I was telling him one of my Yankees/Red Sox stories when he interrupted me and said, "I only have five minutes left in the ride, I have to tell you this story because you're going to love it. From Connecticut, half his family are Red Sox fans and half are Yankees fans, but his grandfather was a die-hard Yankees fan. All his nieces and nephews were Yankees fans except him. His grandfather would needle him about being a Yankees fan, but in a loving way. In 2004, the Red Sox won the World Series for the first time in eighty-six years.

He said, "One month later, my grandfather passed away, and everyone came to the funeral. All the Yankees nieces and nephews brought Yankees trinkets to put in the casket surrounding our grandfather—baseballs, caps, pictures of them with him at Yankee Stadium." He didn't tell me this, but I have to figure that his grandfather was wearing a pinstripe suit. (The Yankees are known for their pinstripe uniforms.) He continued, "I took a newspaper that said, 'Red Sox are World Champs' and stuck it under his arm in the coffin."

Red Sox fans have all agreed that his grandfather would have enjoyed this, but my rider was not done. Three years later, the Red Sox won again, and my rider, who was a good guy, went to the cemetery with his best friend and brought his grandfather's favorite alcoholic beverage. He told me, "We toasted the Red Sox, and on the gravestone, I left another newspaper that said, 'Red Sox are World Champs.'" If you ever talk to anyone who doesn't understand why sports are so important, tell them this story. It is unforgettable, and when the Red Sox fan in my car finished his story, I dropped him off. I should have tipped him for sharing it with me.

"I Would Have Paid to Be at That Funeral.":
The Red Sox fan's response to my great Red Sox story about the grandfather's funeral.

The Marriage Arrangement:
The Red Sox fan: "When my uncle and aunt married, they made a compromise. He was a die-hard Red Sox fan and a Christian, and she was a big Yankee fan and Jewish. It was so important to my uncle to raise his kids as Red Sox fans, he converted to Judaism, and they live in New York with two kids who are Red Sox fans." Can you imagine those kids being hassled their whole childhood: "How can you be a Red Sox fan, you're in New York?" Maybe they said, "Our dad converted to Judaism just so we could do this!"

Halloween and the Red Sox:
My rider was a big Red Sox fan, and he told me that in 2013 on Halloween night, he and his brother were celebrating another Red Sox championship. It was the third time they had

seen them win, but their dad passed away and never saw them win. His drunk brother said, "Can we dig dad up?" He said, "No, but we can go to the cemetery. I grabbed a pumpkin and the three of us went to his gravestone and toasted the Red Sox together."

The Red Sox Server:
The huge Boston Red Sox fan told me that his daughter was a server and one day she gave a guy wearing a Yankee hat a really hard time. "She took his order last only after he checked his New York hat, and then gave him his food last and treated everyone better. The guy enjoyed it and personally gave her a $50 tip when he left."

"You Should Be a Sportswriter":
The two good friends from Connecticut were around twenty-six years old and had just played golf. They were discussing how the Yankee/Red Sox rivalry wasn't the same as it used to be. I said, "It really hit its peak with the 1978 playoff chase." I looked in the rearview mirror and realized how young they were. I said, "You know the Bucky Dent game?" and the Yankee fan said, "I think I saw that once." I gave them a five-minute summary of the entire season. Although the Red Sox led the Yankees by fourteen-and-a-half games in July, they each finished the season with ninety-nine wins.

I took them right up to the bottom of the ninth where future Red Sox Hall of Famer, Carl Yastrzemski, faced future Yankee Hall of Famer, Goose Gossage, with the tying run on third base. Yastrzemski popped the ball up to Graig Nettles in foul territory to give the Yankees a 5-4 win. One of the friends said, "You had us on the edge of our seats. You should be a sportswriter." I gave them homework to look up the 1978 race and I told them it was even better than I'd said.

Babe Ruth's Home Run Ball:
He told me this amazing story: "My grandfather worked for the Pittsburgh Pirates as an usher for sixty-four years. His friend worked there until he was ninety-eight. He was working in 1935 at Forbes Field when Babe Ruth hit the last three home runs of his career. The last one landed in the parking lot [estimated six hundred feet] and my grandfather said that he and another guy saw it roll under a car. They didn't realize what it was until later." (Ruth retired eight days later.)

"It All Started in New Delhi.":
The older man said it several times before telling me his Yankee story. As a child, he lived a few years in New Delhi, India. His parents were good friends with a neighbor, George Weiss, who was the general manager of the Yankees, and his wife. George Weiss was elected to the Baseball Hall of Fame, and he introduced him to all the Yankee stars in the 1950s, like Berra, Mantle, Rizzuto, and DiMaggio. He ran out of time, but his story started in New Delhi.

Meeting Derek Jeter:
He told me this great Yankee story: "A few years back, I went to see the Tigers play the Yankees in Detroit. I was one of the first ones in the stadium, but there was an older woman in my row who I was talking to and then she started yelling, 'Derek Jeter!' He came over and talked with her. Every time he came to Detroit, he left tickets for her since she was one of his grade-school teachers. She introduced me as her friend,

and when I shook hands with him, it was the first time in my life I was speechless."

Meeting Actor Bill Murray:
"My wife and I were at a Charleston baseball game and saw Bill Murray, who is a part owner of the team. I asked him for his autograph and handed him a pink bat I'd just bought my wife and a pen. He looked at the pen and said, 'I can't sign this with a pen. Hold my beer, I'll be right back.' He came back with a Sharpie and signed our bat and then said, 'Give me my beer back.'"

Meeting Jerry Remy:
Woman: "I went to Fenway Park for the first time and we went into Jerry Remy's [former Red Sox player] hot dog place to eat some hot dogs. As we were eating, suddenly, my husband jumped up and ran over to this guy and got his autograph. I couldn't understand it and asked him, 'Why did you get the autograph of a guy selling hot dogs?' It was Jerry Remy."

Autographed Baseball:
"I was at a baseball game about twenty-five rows up with my son. Luke Voit of the Yankees had thrown a ball in the previous inning to a fan, and I watched him coming off the field the next inning and he threw one to me. My dad is a neighbor of his and he talked to him, and he autographed the baseball for my son."

A World Series Ring:
The Phillies fan said, "When I was ten, I was a bat boy for the Philadelphia Phillies when we won the World Series in

1980. They gave me a World Series ring. Mike Schmidt gave me his bat and Peter Rose was good friends with my grandfather and they used to have dinner all the time."

Celebrating the Atlanta Braves:
He said, "In the early 1990s when I was in grade school, we had 'Brave Day' in Atlanta to celebrate the Braves being in the World Series. Kids brought in headdresses and fake tomahawks, and it was a lot of fun. We couldn't do that today."

"The Giants Win the Pennant" and "The Band Is on the Field":
The thirty-year-old woman was a cook in a restaurant in Myrtle Beach and she was a very big sports fan. She had never heard two of the greatest sports calls of all time and she played them on her phone. She loved it and said, "I can't wait to tell my dad about what I heard."

"That play that Derek Jeter made diving into the stands is the most overrated play in baseball history.":
I told the Red Sox fan that it will always be considered one of the best ever. Even better, it was against the Red Sox and the Yankees did win the game.

A Mixed Marriage:
The die-hard Red Sox fan told me, "Our son married a big Yankee fan and recently sent us a picture of the two of them after getting their COVID shots. She was wearing a Yankee hat, but he sent a revised picture with the hat changed to a Red Sox hat."

Satisfied Rider:
After telling the Red Sox fan a number of Red Sox stories, he got out of the car and pointed to me and said, "This is the best Uber ride I've ever had." I said, "Of course it was, we talked about the Red Sox the whole trip."

Criticizing the Future Hall of Famer:
The Red Sox fan said, "Years ago, my friend and I were at a bar and overheard two new Red Sox players talking about writer Peter Gammons, who was also there. One player said, 'I'd like to go over there and knock him out; he said I can't play defense.' The player was future Hall of Famer, Wade Boggs."

"My favorite Red Sox player was Jason Varitek, because he was good-looking.":
The wife told me that, and her husband added, "She thought he had a great ass."

"I can already see my two-year-old in pinstripes [playing for the Yankees] and paying for my private island.":
I told several guys who had young kids that the greatest accomplishment they would ever have is seeing when their kids are in their twenties and this was his funny response.

Woman: "I met Chipper Jones [Hall of Fame baseball player for Atlanta Braves] and I would have his babies.":
She obviously thought he was good-looking.

"I like the Yankees too, because of their hats.":
The guy from Massachusetts who is a Red Sox fan said this and probably doesn't admit it too often.

"I've never been more ready in my life.":
I asked the two young couples if they were ready to hear the best baseball story ever, and the girl, who was not a baseball fan, gave me this answer that made me laugh.

The Red Sox Trophy:
Yankee fan: "I was working in upstate New York in a guy's house, [whose owner] was not there. I came across a World Series trophy in an enclosed case. I think it was the Red Sox trophy for 2007 since the homeowner was a part owner of the team."

Foul Ball:
Red Sox fan: "I was at a World Series game at Fenway when a foul ball was hit right to my good friend, and he missed it. The very next pitch was a foul ball in exactly the same spot, and I pushed him out of the way and caught it."

Brotherly Love:
Yankee fan: "My brother got married last night. He's a big Red Sox fan, so everyone at the reception had to sign a Red Sox jersey. I signed it, 'GO YANKEES.'"

Young Woman: "I met Matthew Stafford [football player] and Clayton Kershaw [baseball player].":
"Kershaw gave me my first beer when I was fourteen."

Fenway Park Prank:
Red Sox fan: "Every time my friends and I went to Fenway Park, we would go into the bathroom and hide and yell, "F--- the Red Sox, go Yankees!"

Yankee fan: "We're not going to have anything in common with a Red Sox fan."

"We have the championships, and you have Fenway.":
The Yankee fan said this about Red Sox fans.

"My parents didn't have sex until 1990!"
It was a very funny response when I started talking about the 1978 Yankee/Red Sox playoff season.

"My favorite player was Pete Rose because of his passion, he'll beat you any way.":
Said by a baseball fan.

The Green Giant:
The woman from Boston is a Red Sox fan, and she told me, "My aunt is the biggest fan, she used to work at the Green Giant." I first thought she was talking about a supermarket or the vegetable company, and then I said, "Do you mean the Green Monster?" (The famous wall in left field.) Her: "Yes, oh, she would be mortified if I told her what I said."

Meeting Derek Jeter?:
I explained to the Michigan couple that Derek Jeter mostly grew up in Kalamazoo, Michigan. The woman said, "I met Derek Jeter. He has long hair and plays for Boston, right?" (No.)

Really Meeting Derek Jeter:
The man was from Kalamazoo, Michigan, where Derek Jeter grew up, and he has met him several times. "I also played

football in high school with Greg Jennings." (He played with the Green Bay Packers.)

Birthday Present:
The Yankee fan said, "I had a choice for my birthday to go to Yankee Stadium or San Diego for the first time and I chose San Diego." Me: "What kind of Yankee fan are you?"

Amazing Red Sox Fan:
"I've caught about one hundred baseballs at Fenway Park in my life."

Remembering His Grandfather:
Red Sox fan: "My grandfather was a big fan, but he died six months before the Red Sox won in 2004 [after eighty-six years]. I believe he was still rooting for them up there."

Unforgettable Yankee Moment:
"My friend got tickets for the World Series game from Yankee Wade Boggs that Jim Leyritz hit the big home run in 1996 in Atlanta. We went back to the hotel and partied with the Yankees."

The Pessimist:
The Mets fan said, "I'm waiting for something to go wrong." (It did.)

Not a Baseball Fan?
I asked the two women from Massachusetts, "Are you Red Sox fans?" They said, "We're more football fans. We're not retired yet and baseball is more of an investment of time."

A Yankee Ring:
He: "I was at a meet-and-greet with my son to hear Brian Cashman, the general manager of the Yankees, talk. Afterwards, I met him, and he handed me his World Series ring and let me try it on."

High School Job:
He: "I worked three years as a ball boy and in the clubhouse for the Pirates when I was in high school. Sometimes I worked sixteen hours in a day as an attendant for the opposing teams. It was really good money and I got good tips. When I was sixteen, I once drove Joe Torre around downtown when I'd just started driving."

Courteous Red Sox Fan:
"I missed my flight in the airport and I was upset, but I saw David Ortiz there. I went into the bathroom, and he was standing at the urinal. I didn't say anything then; I waited until he was leaving."

Big Chicago Cubs Fan:
He's from Chicago: "My sister and brother-in-law won a raffle the year the Cubs won the World Series and got four tickets to the World Series. They paid $1,400 for four tickets. I offered $1,000 for one ticket and they turned me down. They sold them for $1,400 each."

Red Sox Memory:
"I have a large, framed newspaper from when they won in 2004 and it says, 'FINALLY.'"

Red Sox Fan Giving It Back to Me:
"My son doesn't even know that the Yankees used to be a good team." Getting out of the car, he wasn't done ribbing me: "At least you still have the Giants and Jets."

Married to a Professional Baseball Player:
"I hate all sports, but I'll watch the luge. I would never try it because I'd be afraid of getting my fingers cut off." Me: "So gym wasn't your favorite subject in school?" She: "NOO!"

His Dad Cried:
The security guard said, "When the Red Sox won in 2004, it's the only time I've seen my dad cry."

Football

As a New York Giants fan, I have their cap on my dashboard. You would think that the Giants would dominate the stories and comments I've had in my car, but a few other teams have dominated my football conversations. My tenth favorite ride that I wrote about earlier was when I got to put a Kansas City Chiefs Super Bowl ring on my finger. You should read that story and some of the comments I've received about it in my earlier chapter. Pittsburgh Steeler fans are dedicated and devoted and they gave me a number of good stories and comments, including the best football story you've never heard below.

The Immaculate Reception:
The catch made by the Pittsburgh Steelers running back Franco Harris in 1974, is recognized as the greatest play in

NFL history. It won a playoff game in a miraculous and spectacular way in front of a euphoric home crowd. It was the first playoff victory for the Steelers, who became the team of the 1970s. If you have never watched this play, "Google 'immaculate reception'" If you like football, you need to see this play.

My rider grew up in Pittsburgh and he told me this incredible story. "One of my closest friends growing up was a kid whose dad was the photographer for the Steelers and the Pittsburgh Pirates. His dad was also good friends with Roberto Clemente, one of the greatest baseball players of all time. Clemente called him and said he was going on a humanitarian mission and asked the photographer to go with him and document what they were doing. He agreed, but when Franco Harris caught that pass, he had to call Clemente and apologize, because he had to work the following week.

"Clemente was fine with it, but five days after the 'Immaculate Reception,' Clemente's plane crashed, killing everyone on board. The photographer told Franco Harris that he saved his life with that catch." For this family, the Immaculate Reception really was something very different than it was to the rest of the country—it was an immaculate reception that saved the father's life.

The Football Wedding:
The couple was from Pittsburgh; they were big Pittsburgh Steeler fans and told me about their son's wedding. She said, "We're proud Pittsburgh Steeler fans. When my son got married, they had terrible towels on each table at the reception." (Used to cheer on the team.) They were in black and yellow, the Steelers colors, and had the wedding couple's name on it.

You Learn Something New Every Day:
The thirty-six-year-old male Pittsburgh Steeler fan, who lives in Pittsburgh, had never heard of the Immaculate Reception, which is considered the greatest play in NFL history. After explaining it to him, he watched the play on his phone and said, "I'm kind of mad my dad didn't tell me about this."

Seeing Double:
Him: "I used to work in a movie theater here in Charleston, and several times, football great Dan Marino would come in with his kids during the day in the middle of the week. He kept to himself and wanted his privacy. One day they came to see the movie *Bad Boyz 2*, which he had a cameo in. During the movie, one of his kids yelled out, 'Hey Dad, there's you.' After the movie, a guy came up to me and said he just had something really weird happen. He was watching the movie and he heard the kids yell out and when Dan Marino was on the screen, he turned around and there was Dan Marino."

The Cute Patriots Fan:
She was sitting in the middle with her boyfriend on one side and a male friend on the other. She was a big football fan and told me, "When my dad was in college, he put his name on a list to get Patriots tickets. Almost thirty years later, they called him and asked if he wanted to buy tickets and he said yes. They turned out to be near the fifty-yard line." A very big smile appeared on her face, and she was definitely twirling her hair when she said, "I was the most popular girl in high school; everyone wanted to date me." I wish I had a picture of her face at that moment.

The New Jerseyan Green Bay Packers Ticket-Holder:
He explained, "My family was buying tickets from a woman in Wisconsin for years and made a deal with her to transfer the tickets into my name [as her fake nephew]. I go to three to four games each year. We pay for four seats at seven games that cost $150 a ticket." He does have to travel from New Jersey to Wisconsin also.

Friendly Tradition:
Heading to meet his friends, he told me, "The four of us get together every year and go to a college football game somewhere. Two come from England, one from Florida, and I'm from New Jersey. Due to the virus, we weren't going to a game this year, but the two of us decided to get together so our wives couldn't say next year that we didn't go this year. We didn't want any chinks in the armor."

The Washington Commandos Fan:
The football fan from Washington, DC, told me, "I'm a fan of the Commandos, but they can't afford to wear underwear because their owner took all the money."

"I'm the Kurt Warner of grocery stores.":
He compared his career to Kurt Warner, who after college, stocked shelves in a supermarket and then went on to win the Super Bowl. "I worked in the grocery business for twenty-two years. I started out making four dollars an hour bagging groceries and I finished making $65,000 a year."

The Head Coach:
When he said he lived in Dallas, I asked, "Are you a Cowboys fan?" His reply was, "I don't root for them, but if they played ISIS, I would." He knows Jerry Jones, the owner of the Cowboys, and he's not a fan.

Cowboys Fan Has a Plan:
"All the Cowboys, Giants, and Redskins teams need to put together one team to beat the Eagles this year."

The Pawn/Porn Shop:
Talking about the picture of my Super Bowl ring hanging in my car, he said, "Athletes don't know how to manage their money. Some of those rings probably wind up in a porn shop." His wife corrected him, "He meant pawn shop." He added, "For some athletes it could be the same."

The Former Pro Football Player:
He was 6'9", and for a year and a half, he was an offensive lineman with the Cleveland Browns. He's currently a computer science teacher at a middle school and an actor doing some commercials, and it was very enjoyable giving him a ride.

The Eagles Super Bowl Ring:
He said, "Ron Jaworski, the former Eagle quarterback, owns a bunch of golf courses. He was talking to my dad and had a Super Bowl ring and let me put it on."

"Can I puke in your New York Giants hat and pretend I don't know what happened?":
The Green Bay Packer fan, who was not drinking, sat in the front seat right in front of my New York hats and couldn't handle it.

"Do I really have to sit in front of a New York Giants hat? I live those Super Bowl losses every day."
The New England Patriots fan was disturbed and obviously still traumatized by Eli Manning and the Giants beating his team twice. I said, "Yes!"

"Do we have to talk about that game?"
When the big New England Patriots fan asked that question, I answered with a big smile, "Yes!"

"I want Brady to mess up so he can come back to the Patriots.":
Said by an angry Patriots fan.

Eagles Fan:
"My brother was dropped on his head when he was little; that's why he's a Giants fan. The whole family are Eagles fans."

"When I was considering the Navy and playing football, my dad said I had to consider this not as a four-year commitment, but as a forty-year commitment."

"She's seen me cry only twice, and once was when Brady left.":
Heartbroken Patriots fan.

"You're going to a fantasy meeting with a bunch of women?"
My female rider's previous Uber driver said this, not realizing it was a women's Fantasy Football draft.

"When the Eagles won the Super Bowl, I knew he was the man I had to have.":
She was a pretty serious football fan, but what if they lost?

"This looks like a trashy place. They must have the Eagles game on."
Just a few big Eagles fans wanting to feel like they were home.

"We're used to winning."
The Red Sox and Patriots fan told me this.

"Anytime I fly into the Philadelphia airport, I always put on all my Dallas Cowboys attire,":
Said by a devoted Cowboys fan.

"I was a New England Patriots fan until they started kneeling during the national anthem. I haven't watched a game since.":
A former NFL fan who is still angry.

The Cowboys Fan:
She said, "My husband said he would not date a Dallas Cowboys fan, but we've been married for ten years." Me: "How did you overcome that?" Her: "I'm irresistible; we went straight to the altar."

Female Cowboys Fan:
Me: "Do women in Texas really wear cowboy hats?" Her: "Yes, I wear one with boots and with Dallas Cowboys outfits."

"I decided to be a Buffalo Bills fan instead of a New York Giants fan because it was cheaper to go to Buffalo for a game than New York."

"When I was a kid, I would help shovel out the Buffalo Bills stadium and they would give all the workers a free ticket to the game."

Father Puts His Foot Down:
"My dad said, 'If you're going to live in my house, you're going to have to be a Yankee and Giant fan.'"

Nightmarish:
My rider said, "I'm from Massachusetts." Me: "Would you be more comfortable if I put on my Yankee hat or my Giant hat?" He answered, "Neither, they both give me nightmares."

A Confident Woman?:
"We don't have a Super Bowl ring to show you, but my lack of knowledge is probably enough."

Educating a Bears Fan:
When the young Chicago Bears fan said he had never watched Gale Sayers highlights (the Hall of Fame running back) and he had never seen "Brian's Song" (one of the best sports movies of all time), he said, "I must be the most disappointing rider of the day."

"Philadelphia Eagles fans are not smart.":
Said by another dedicated Dallas Cowboys fan.

"Packers fans are sick and tired of Aaron Rodgers.":
He told me that, "You can't get a lot of help when you have that big of a salary."

A Giants Fan and A Cowboys Fan?
The Dallas Cowboys fan living in Texas said, "I like the Giants too, because their uniforms are blue."

Advice from a Coach:
When I asked the seventy-five-year-old man, "How long did it take you to get used to retirement twenty years ago?" He quoted the old football coach, Bum Phillips, when he said, "I'm not planning on doing nothing and I'm not starting until noon."

A Disappointed Cowboys Fan:
Me: "So you're a Cowboys fan?" Guy from Dallas, Texas: "Unfortunately."

A Bills Fan:
"There's only one football team in New York and it's the Buffalo Bills."

A Football Spiderman:
Him: "I use the name Spiderman. When I was in high school, I weighed ninety pounds playing football. My coach called me Spider because I was always knocking passes down."

"My friend's husband is a jeweler and he's worked on Tom Brady's rings."

"A friend of mine lost $7,000 when the Giants beat the undefeated Patriots in the Super Bowl."

Reaching a Goal:
"As an offensive lineman for the Navy, I weighed 290 pounds at the beginning of the year. I had to lose weight for their nuclear program, and with a group of friends, I lost eighty-five pounds in four months, and I've kept it off."

Woman: "I'm friends with Daniel Jones [the Giants quarterback]. Actually, we dated for two years in middle school.
"He's a great guy. He liked me when I had braces."

"My boyfriend rooms with Dwight Clark's [retired football player] son and I've been able to try on his Super Bowl rings."

"Sometimes it just seems like something white people want to complain about.":
The Washington Redskins fan (now the Commanders) had no problem with them changing their name.

"Tony Romo is a much better quarterback than Eli Manning.":
Said by a Dallas Cowboys fan.

"My dad watched Johnny Unitas in his [lifetime] but believes that Tom Brady is the best quarterback of all time.":
(Not a Patriots fan.)

"When I saw Dan Marino of course he didn't have a Super Bowl ring on.":
(Never won one.)

Proud Cowboys Fan:
Me: "Are you a Cowboys fan?" Him: "Isn't everyone?" (No.)

Colorful Football Fan:
Male: "I have a love-hate relationship with the color orange. I hate Clemson on Saturday but love the Cleveland Browns on Sunday."

Dedicated Steelers Fan:
Young guy: "I collect Pittsburgh Steelers Super Bowl rings. They are only worth $100 each, but they look real."

Washington Football Fan:
"When I was in high school, I worked in the Washington Redskins football stadium selling programs and making ten dollars an hour. Eventually, I was in charge of all of it." Me: "What do you think of the recent name change?" Him: "I'll always be a Washington Redskins fan."

"He got up and just ran down the sideline.":
He was coaching quarterback Steve McNair and missed one of the all-time greatest plays in NFL history because his back was to the field. In 2000, the Tennessee Titans won a playoff

game on a last second play, which is called "The Music City Miracle."

All Other Sports

*"I've thought my whole life about stripper mini golf.":
The guy in his twenties from Minnesota who owned a distillery said, "I've always been disappointed with mini golf." When I mentioned I had thought about a mini golf course where each hole was an important moment in history, he brought up beer mini golf. He said there would be different beer you could buy at each hole, and that a hole-in-one would get you a free cup of beer. The two couples and I laughed a lot, but when the idea of stripper mini golf came up, things got out of hand.

Special Lacrosse Moment:
The story meant a lot to him: "I was very close to my grandfather, and a few years ago he passed away. The service was at the same time as my big lacrosse game. I went to the game and scored the winner with nine seconds left, and I'm convinced that he was there at that moment helping me."

Different Golfing:
Arriving without clubs at the golf course, the New Yorker said, "We're just going to throw the balls around today."

Dressing Up for Golf:
The woman was wearing a $310 New York Gucci hat to go golfing. She said, "I'm really an LA fan, but I like the hat."

"We're here for the kickball tournament.":
The male and female told me they were in Myrtle Beach for the adult kickball tournament. They were from Wisconsin and said, "We're here on business. We're here to make money," since the winning team at the end of the year splits $125,000. Twenty teams were playing to win a $3,000 prize. They play on a baseball field with baseball rules.

Top Golf: "It sounds like a foreign language.":
Her boyfriend was explaining how Top Golf worked and she wasn't impressed. When she was told that the large net protects car windshields from being hit, she said, "The car windshields being hit sounds more interesting than golf; it would be very entertaining to see."

Basketball Idol:
"When I was seven, I went to Madison Square Garden with a large group of kids and was waiting to say hello to the Knicks, but they ran right by us. Magic Johnson ran across the court to talk with us and that's when he became my favorite player."

"I've been on 548 golf courses in my life.":
The eighty-four-year-old man was boasting, but his son added, "that he remembers." He also told me that when he was twenty years old, he got tickets to a College Bowl game in Miami. "I lived in Denver, Colorado, so I hitchhiked to the game and back."

Golfing in Myrtle Beach:
"My Uber driver said that when he came here, his goal was to play all one hundred golf courses, and he did."

"My boss said, 'If you hit under one hundred your first year, I'll give you a $5,000 bonus.'":
His boss was concerned about his health since he was playing softball five days a week, so he suggested he take up golf. In seven months, without lessons, he collected his bonus.

Woman On Hockey:
"I met my husband when he interviewed me for a summer job. I'm not sure if I got the job because he was interested in me, but it might have been the season tickets for the Boston Bruins that I had."

She: "My husband and I used to live in Augusta on the second hole of the Masters golf course. One year we were offered $20,000 for someone to rent our house for the nine days of the tournament. My husband said we didn't need the money."

"Our goal was to play all the mini-golf courses in the area.":
She and her husband loved playing and mapped out 123 courses, and over two years they played fifty-seven of them.

"Golf and I had no relationship.":
The very competitive guy taught himself how to play golf years ago by reading a book and was very good. He stopped

playing because he didn't have any relationship with golf, and years later, he started again and is playing well again.

"I'm Americanized as shit. When I feel stupid, I watch soccer."
Living here twenty years from Latvia, I picked him up from a bar where he was watching soccer.

"Some parents bought their three-year-old a real golf club.":
The golf pro in Ohio works in an exclusive club. Management set him up with a special class of twenty-two three-year-olds to give lessons to. He hired two other people to help, and they were using plastic golf clubs with the kids.

"I want to go to Top Golf so I can drink and look cute,"
Tthe young woman told me why she wanted to go to Top Golf.

*"I work hard every day of the week; I don't want to chase a little golf ball on the weekend."**

"Bowlers hate each other, especially the good, young guys."

Golf For One:
I was taking a guy to a golf course, and he said, "I was coming here with twelve guys, but eleven did not come. The one guy who I came with got bit by a copperhead and he's on crutches, so I'm playing by myself."

"We really roughed it here playing one hundred holes in three days; my back hurts."

"I played shuffleboard once with a sixty-year-old woman and I beat her and retired,"
he said.

"Those golfers really know how to party; my wife doesn't want me hanging out with them anymore."

"Sorry to see you're a Knicks and Giants fan."

Pickleball:
The tennis coach said, "Pickleball is not a fad. I knew a guy in college who was an average player, and he went pro as a pickleball player."

"At the NASCAR race, the cars were so fast that if you blinked you would have missed them. They were so loud you had to wear earplugs."

"A year after 9/11, I won a golf tournament in Idaho and the trophy was a large picture of the Statue of Liberty, the American flag, and the World Trade Center."

"Stay away, it's an awful game.":
The golfer gave me that advice and added, "One day you feel like you've learned something and the next day it looks like you bought your clubs on the way to the course."

"I went to my first NASCAR race. I'm for Louisiana, but I was surprised how everyone was dressed, it was a different kind of country than I'm used to."

"Cats by Ninety,"
They told me that it is a common phrase in Kentucky college sports. It means that when the team wins even by one point, fans like to think it was ninety.

Basketball Rings:
She told me, "My friend is a DJ for the Miami Heat and has three championship rings."

Kick Boxing:
Young man: "I just won my first kick boxing tournament here in Myrtle Beach last night."

Sports Program at a Military School:
She said, "I'm going to the Citadel for golf." (She was a student athlete.) "We have a women's team, but no men's team; since they have a men's tennis team, but no women's tennis team, it evens out."

"It's a lot better talking sports in an Uber than listening to Indian music the whole trip."

"Were you a sportswriter?":
After talking sports with him the whole trip, he just had to ask.

Hunting:
He told me, "My ten-year-old daughter loves to shoot deer. She's eight-for-eight, and we eat the meat."

New York Sports Hats:
Looking at my New York sports hats, he said, "My dad roots for all those teams." I said, "Tell him he has good taste." Him: "If I do, he's going to laugh."

Putt-Putt Can Be Dangerous:
She was in Myrtle Beach and her family went to play golf. The first ball she hit was hard and right at her dad. In moving away from the ball, he fell and shattered his ankle. She said, "I've never placed since."

7
RELATIONSHIPS ARE THE BEST

I have been very fortunate over the years to have had so many riders who were willing to share friendship and family stories with me. During the rides, there were some funny and unusual relationship moments, and some of those moments were in my fifty favorite rides. I picked out a few stories that are relationship-related stories, and I'm listing them here so you can read about them earlier in the book if you haven't already:

#9. A Devoted Mom
#11 The Disney Couple
#18 Will You Marry Me?
#19. I'm In So Much Trouble
#23. The Hilarious Mom
#35. Marathon Runner/Twenty-One Wines
#41 First-Time Grandparent
#46. The Sunshine Farmer

You will also find some relationship stories in the chapter on sports and the inspirational/motivational chapter. Below, there are some short friendship/family stories and then a section on comments about friendship, children, dating, and marriage.

Short Stories

o   The woman told me this incredible story about her amazing husband: "I was out of town and my husband was watching our two small girls. Our two-year-old got cut badly near her private parts while taking a bath. My husband, a surgeon, was afraid to take her to the emergency room because they would ask questions. There was blood everywhere, but he sewed her up himself and kept her calm by giving her M&Ms and turning on Mickey Mouse. He didn't tell me what happened until I got home."

o   *The twelve-year-old girl grew up in Hawaii. "My friends and I were convinced that snow was made up by mainlanders to make us look bad in Hawaii. When I was nine, I was in New York and it started snowing, and I ran out of the house yelling, 'It's real, it's real!' I sent messages to my friends in Hawaii; they thought I was lying."

o   Married for ten years with three children in a beautiful house, the woman told me, "I first saw my husband when his picture was in the company newsletter. I brought it home and told my parents and friends that

I was going to marry him. When we [had been] dating two months I said to him, 'I don't know what you're doing the rest of your life, but I'm going to marry you.' He said, 'I'm going to marry you.'"

- With his wife sitting next to him, the Dallas, Texas, truck driver said, "I tell people that my marriage has lasted twelve years for three reasons: 1) I married my best friend, 2) I know that she's really trying to kill me slowly and I'm not going to make it easy for her, and 3) she knows that she can leave anytime she wants, but I'm going to go with her." He added, "Early in our marriage we had an argument, and she went into the bedroom, opened a suitcase, and started packing it. I followed her in and did the same thing. She said, 'What are you doing?' I told her if she was leaving, I was too, and that was the end of the argument."

- "Being in the Air Force, I had a friend fly my girlfriend and I over the beach at Hilton Head. Earlier, with another friend we spelled out, 'WILL YOU MARRY ME' in the sand. When we flew over it, I said to my girlfriend, "What does that say?" and I got on my knee and gave her the ring. I told the pilot to shake the wings, which meant she said yes, but she thought we were going down and she got sick."

- The woman told me, "My dad has a refurbishing business, and he had a chance to do work for Paula Dean. He was invited to her house, and after waiting a while, he was told that she wanted to see him up in her bathroom. When he walked in, she was working on a painting of a pig in her bathroom. He made a formal presentation, but didn't get the job."

o   My rider was upset about his day. He had worked with several people to throw a surprise party of a hundred people for a friend. He said, "Everything went perfectly until I left to go home, and I changed my shirt. My girlfriend was thrown out of the restaurant/bar for yelling at the owner. I was going to take her home, but somehow, she wound up with my keys and locked the door. She wouldn't pull over and a cop followed her home and arrested her for DWI. She was spending the night in jail, and I missed most of the party."

o   Just married yesterday, he said, "I knew I was going to marry her when I was thirteen [now twenty-seven]." She is four years older, and he was shy, and he tried to date her younger sister so he could be around her. Him: "Our first dates, I had to travel out of state to see her." Her: "Our second date, he drove six hours one way." He was persistent, and after fourteen years, he got the girl.

o   The nine-year-old boy was with his older sister, and he said that he "loved history." I told him I did too, and I said that we should each give the other one a history question. He asked me the date of the Pearl Harbor attack and I gave him the right answer. I asked him, "Who was President of the United States when Pearl Harbor was attacked?" He said, "Roosevelt and not

Theodore." I said, "Eleanor?" but he didn't fall for that. I did have to tell him it was FDR, but he had as much fun as I did.

- Woman: "We heard there was three feet of snow in the mountains of North Carolina, so we rented a cabin there. It was literally up a mountain, and the roads were really bad. We were driving a Cadillac Escalade and my husband had the kids and I walk up the road because it was so dangerous. All the neighbors were watching him, and they wanted to hook our car in case it fell, but he made it."

- She told me about her ex-husband who was in the Marine Corps seventeen years ago. "He was supposed to be home for Christmas, but the plans changed, and they had him overseas in the Middle East and they weren't allowing him home until the end of January. We were disappointed and worried about him. I was with his parents Christmas Day and his dad went out and picked him up, and he just walked through the door to surprise us. It was a special moment, and his mom was crying, because she didn't know he was coming home either."

- "I told my daughter growing up that the South was winning the Civil War, but when they went up North in the winter they wanted no part of the cold weather, so they gave up the war. I got a call from her middle school teacher about it. That's my story and I'm sticking with it."

- She told me this hilarious story: "I was with a girlfriend in Conway, and we were drunk. My friend said, 'Do you want to go to the graveyard?' I said, 'Sure.' We walked for about an hour and forty-five minutes, and I said to her, 'Do you know where the graveyard is?' She replied, 'What graveyard?'"

- She: "I worked for a guy who put an ad in the paper that said only 'I need a wife' and his phone number. That's how he met his wife and they've been married a long time. The wife told me that she 'wanted to see who had the guts to do that.' I never understood what she saw in him."

- I asked a manager in the Marine Corps, "What made you decide to go into the military?" He replied, "I was pissed off about 9/11. When I was in third grade, I was in class, and someone said that planes had gone down from Los Angeles to Boston. A girl in our class said her dad was flying from LA to Boston. The teacher turned pale and said, 'We have to get you home.' Her dad was on the plane that crashed. I just wanted to give something back."

- The male barber from Ohio said, "I was in Brooklyn, New York, with my girlfriend at a concert and I saw a woman with green hair. The next day, I saw the woman in line at the airport to go back to Ohio on my flight. A short time later, I was looking at paintings online and the painting I wanted to buy was painted by the woman with green hair whose picture online was taken at the concert

I was at. A few months after I bought the painting, we went on our first date, and several people thought we were married. We've been together for two years."

- Her inspiration for becoming a lawyer and working on child trafficking came from an unusual place. She told me, "When I was six to nine years old, we had two male family friends who were cops. They would sit with me and tell me about all the horrors of the world. My sister said that I was thirty years old out of the womb."

- I picked up a young couple dressed immaculately for a wedding. I spoke with the guy about many things and suddenly he said, "I took her to her first strip club last night. They almost kicked us out; they don't like it when you dance with each other." Since he was visiting, I asked him how he found out about the strip club, and he said, "I picked up a flier in a convenience store." I said, "Is that the story you're going with?"

- Husband: "We met on a blind date. My friend insisted I go, and I said I would only go if it was 'one and done.'" Wife: "I had a coworker who told me one day that she had met my next husband." Him: "I was one and done, but not the way I thought."

- "My dad is a urologist. He got in an Uber and the woman was upset that her husband [had gotten] a vasectomy and she just got pregnant. My dad realized that the vasectomy was done in his office, which he didn't tell her. He looked it up later and found out that his colleague did the procedure, but the husband never came back for a follow-up appointment to make sure everything was OK. It was his fault."

- The young couple told me how they met. She: "We met in high school. He was a bad boy then [three years ago], not like he is now. The first time I saw him, he walked into the classroom where we had been split up into partners and he said, 'So no one wants to be my partner, because I'm ugly,' and then he flipped over a desk."

- She: "When I was about ten years old, my friend came over three days after Christmas. She was wearing a beautiful pin on her shirt, and I loved it. I told my mom, and she said that I got the same one. We argued until she realized that she forgot to give us all of our presents. She was hiding them because we would open them and seal them back up. She forgot where she hid them, we teased her for years about this. I have kids now and I've done the same thing, sometimes I forget where I've hidden the gifts."

- Guy from Boston: "My wife and I wanted to celebrate our son's birthday by bringing him to Myrtle Beach. We have three kids and my wife's best friend has two, but several people wanted us to take their kids and the three of us wound up with ten kids for the weekend." Me: "You should be getting a medal."

- Male: "I had just had a fight with my wife and then I went to a bar. A guy in his eighties gave me some advice. He said I should sincerely apologize and told me a whole list of things to say. I went home and said to my wife, 'I'm sorry I was stupid.' She interrupted and said, 'You're right, you were a stupid ass.' That was the end of the argument."

- I asked the couple in their mid- to late twenties who had been dating six months, "How did you meet?" They replied, "Our families arranged it. They knew each other and invited us out to dinner and didn't tell us the other one was coming until we were on the way. There were two open seats at the end of the table next to each other and when we talked, the table went silent."

- Young woman: "I moved to Denver two months ago and I was on business in Pensacola, Florida. My flight was canceled to Orlando, and I rented a car. I got the last one and there was a family going to Orlando, so I drove them there. Their two daughters in their twenties were planning on moving to Denver and my sister lives there too."

- Chicago businessman: "My friend owns a nice restaurant in Chicago, and when we heard there was going to be a protest rally there, about fifty of us grabbed our guns and knives and protected his place. We also had help from three police units, and it was safe."

- She told me that her sixteen-year-old brother named her Lexie. "My dad was happy since he was a big fan of wrestler Lex Luger. When my sister and I would argue, he would send us to two corners of the room, and he would do the play-by-play as we wrestled."

- He: "Five years ago I dated a really hot girl who loved to go with me and my friends to strip clubs. She would always be asked to go up on stage and dance, but I was uncomfortable with that. I can't believe I used to date someone so shallow that they wanted to show off in front of everyone."

- The couple walked out of the hotel, and I noticed that the woman's blue and white dress matched the guy's blue and white shirt. Me: "I'm guessing matching outfits was not your idea? I'm sure no one in the restaurant will notice." Dating only three months, he said, "We work in the same hospital, the same department, and we do the same job." Me: "You're not going to tell me you match at work too?" He laughed and said, "Yes."

- The two friends told me that they were both in the area of the Twin Towers in New York City on the morning of 9/11/2001. They ran out of two separate buildings and bumped into each other. "One of my cousins survived after being on the eighty-second floor. One of my friends didn't make it. It was his first day back from his wife having a baby that week."

- She remembers the morning of September 11, 2001: "I worked in a grocery store five blocks from the World Trade Center. That morning I had a dentist appointment, and I sat on the subway with my headphones on. I saw some people looking out the window at a fire in the distance, but it's New York, so I didn't pay attention to it. When my dentist was finished, he tried to scan my credit card, but it wasn't working, so I said I would pay him next time. I headed to work with my headphones on and I arrived around 10:30 a.m. [almost two hours after the first plane hit]. My boss could not believe I didn't know what had happened. We could only take cash, but when people were coming in dazed and full of soot, I broke down and cried. It took me three hours that night to walk home to Brooklyn and my mom was hysterical because I couldn't call her and tell her I was OK."

- Husband: "My wife has had some really bad luck the past few years. She was in our garage and a bat flew into her head, fell on her arm, and gave her rabies. The treatment caused her liver and kidney to fail and they had to be removed. Another time we were on a boat, and we hit a wave hard and her back broke. And another time, she backed into the open dishwasher and needed her hip replaced."

- She: "When I was nine, we didn't have a lot, but I found some presents with my name on them in my grandmother's closet. I opened them up and put them in my closet. I got whooped good by her and she gave all my presents to my sister." I handed her a gift card and said, "This doesn't make up for all the presents you lost, but now when you tell the story it has a better ending." She was very happy.

- Him: "We fell in love during a billion-dollar wedding we were working at. I was playing guitar and she was playing the violin, and we were smiling at each other while we were playing. The wedding was for a well-known Chinese guy, and it was in the Indian Ocean."

o His mom, Sylvia, ordered the ride for him. I said, "My mom's middle name was Sylvia." He said, "Sylvia is my mom's maiden name." Me: "Her name is Sylvia Sylvia?" Him: "No, I mean it's her first name." (My wife later explained to me that my mom didn't have a middle name, but my dad wanted her to have one and so they came up with Sylvia.)

o His family was in an Airbnb when the hurricane hit recently in Florida. He said, "We were moving into our new house in a few days, but it was delayed. The roof was damaged, but we had one of the first houses to get repaired. The storm lasted twelve hours and we stayed in the Airbnb. The owner wanted to kick us out, because our lease was over, but with the State of Emergency we were able to stay. She lived in California and had no idea what was going on. She wanted to get the Airbnb ready for the next people, but the building was a mess."

o The woman staying here in the South temporarily after a big break-up said, "I'm not a techie. I need to get a husband to do these kinds of things for me." I told her that my wife is my techie and I pointed to her picture on our business card. "She does a lot of those things for me, and we've been married almost forty years." She said very enthusiastically, "I could be a sister-wife!"

Female Comments About Friendship/Family

- *One female to another: "How's their baby look?" Reply: "It was four weeks early and it looked like it could have baked in the oven a little longer."

- *"My son was born on July 4th. He came in with a bang and out with a bang."

- *She: "My grandmother used to say that red lipstick was for whores."

- *Young woman: "When I came out as gay to my family, my ninety-year-old grandmother said immediately, 'I wish I liked women, men suck!'"

- *The eighty-three-year-old woman just left her car of twenty-seven years at the junkyard. "My children will be happy that I won't be driving anymore, but I'm not going to tell them for a while."

- *She: "My ninety-nine-year-old grandmother is so stubborn. I said to her, 'You must have been an awful teenager.'"

- *Woman: "I have six tattoos on my body; four are dogs of mine I lost, one is my dad who I lost recently, and the other is an eye on the back on my head, my neck. I used to tell my three kids that I needed eyes on the back of my head, and I've had one for twenty years."

- Marine biologist: "My parents let me watch scary movies when I was four, like *The Shining* and *Jaws*. I've always rooted for the shark." Me: "Why?" Her: "Because people were in her territory."

- The bright, almost-seven-year-old girl had been in my car maybe five minutes when she asked her dad, "Why do all the drivers talk so much?" (Not me, of course.)

- Looking at her teenage daughter's choice of a Halloween costume, she said, "It was a sexy nurse costume with big boobs, and she doesn't have any."

- I asked the pregnant woman, "Is this your first child?" She said, "No, it's my last one." (She has one.)

- My uncle wasn't working and spent a lot of time hanging out next to a fence. He had to go to court and the judge asked, "What do you do for a living?" He said, "I'm just holding and leaning."

- Young woman: "I'm going to be two hours late for my sister's wedding brunch; do you think I can get a police escort, just this one time?" Me: "No."

- She: "My grandparents raised me that every day I wake up, I should thank the Lord."

- The eight-year-old girl asked, "Are we almost there?" Me: "Count to 5,000 in your head and we'll be there." Minutes later she said, "Are we almost there?" Me:

"How much did you count to?" Her: "4,000." Me: "Keep counting, we're almost there."

- One of the three women pointed at another and said, "My first ex was her second ex. We used to hate each other, and now we're going to a concert together." The third woman joked she was their daughter.

- Proud mom of two college graduates: "When my kids were in a crib, I used to whisper to them, 'You're going to college.'"

- She: "I asked my three-year-old niece, 'Is there anyone who knows more than you?' She said, 'No.'"

- He said, "When the kids moved out, we said, 'We're rich.'"

- Picking up a family of three at the beach, I said, "I need to make sure none of your suits are wet." Woman: "They're not, do you want to check?"

- Woman: "I keep telling my dad, who's sixty-seven, that he should retire, but he's told me that if he retires, he'll die."

- She was going to her brother's house: "I have a baked chicken and mashed potatoes in my purse for my brother—he sucks at cooking."

- She: "My mom was talking to my fifteen-year-old son about being around when he has his own kids. My son said, 'I can have kids right now.'"

- She said, "I have six children, eighteen grandchildren, and seven great-grandchildren. I came here to get some peace."

- Taking the mom and nine-year-old daughter to Wonder Works at Broadway at the Beach, I saw it up ahead and said, "There it is, the upside-down house. When you go in, you have to walk on your hands." The mom said, "Really?" Me: "No, I was trying to get a response out of your daughter."

- Me: "Yes sometimes families can be a challenge." Her: "Yes, yes, yes, they are all apples from the same tree."

- She: "When I had my first child, she slept through the night because I put in some breakfast food before she went to bed. I was told I had to wake her up in the middle of the night to feed her and I said, 'Hell no, I'm not waking her up.'"

- She: "When my daughter moved to the South, her son's elementary school teacher tried to get her son to slow down and told him, 'You have to slow your roll.' My daughter told her, 'Don't you tell my son to slow down.'"

- Mom: "My daughter started saying 'no' at nine months and she never stopped."

- On a bachelorette weekend, the girls had just become Shania Twain fans and were talking about "girl power." One girl in the back made her point saying, "We're basic bitches, sir."

- I asked the female college student what it's like to have six brothers and sisters, and she said, "As long as I get food, I'm OK."

- "I'm crashing the wedding with my girlfriend."

- Woman: "I was toilet trained when I was one by my older brother. Now I have to toilet-train my child." Me: "Have your brother come over and do it."

- The twenty-one-year-old girl when asked about her twenty-seven-year-old sister said simply, "She sucks."

- "We were trying to get our mom a Mother's Day present in the store the other day, but we couldn't get rid of her."

- I picked the mom and daughter up from the airport and they both said they were celebrating their twenty-first birthday. Me: "I'm going to have to sing you happy birthday." One of them said, "You do whatever you need to do, let's get this party started."

- She: "When I was a kid my mom idolized Tom Jones. When he came on TV, we all had to be quiet, and we saw a different side of mom."

- She: "When my twenty-one-year-old sister has a headache, she describes it as 'a little mouse running around in my head stabbing me.'"

- She told me, "I'm seventy-five years old and I have thirty-five grandchildren."

- She: "My brother's a whore. He thinks he owns my house."

- Female Air Force cadet: "My dad started teaching me to fly when I was two years old. There's a picture of me sitting on three pillows in a cockpit."

- The young female rider said, "All my friends are guys. I can't deal with girls and all the drama."

- She: "My mom at seventy-five is the coolest chick ever."

- Young woman on the phone: "My mom is weird; she does weird stuff." My rider had almost all blue hair.

- First time mom: "I can't wait until my two-year-old can walk and talk."

- One girl in her twenties said to the other girl, "Did you see her ring? It's huge and it cost $30,000. Who would want to put a $30,000 ring on their finger?" The other girl replied softly, "I would."

- Mom: "I have an eleven- and nine-year-old. It feels like I gave birth yesterday." Me: "If it was, you had a really long day."

- She: "My grandfather always told us that he brought my mom and aunt to Disney World and Disneyland several times, but when he got to Disney World, he said he had never been there before."

- Female: "My dog is like my daughter, and I call her dog-ter. My dad calls her grand dog-ter."

- "I went on a Facebook group called 'Wedding Disaster' and I felt better that I wasn't the only one."

- She: "If I had a girl, she would have been hell on wheels."

- She: "Moms always believe in you."

- Single woman raising six kids: "I would do anything to keep my family together."

- She: "My cousin in Georgia is painfully nice, you just can't seem to get it out of her."

- "My sister gave me my first cigarette when I was nine, but she still denies it today."

- Young woman: "I consider myself one of the boys. I don't hang out with girls; they are too nasty and there's too much drama."

- Dental hygienist: "A sixteen-year-old girl came into our dental office with a chipped tooth from basketball. Her younger sister had superglued it back on and the glue is toxic; there was a lot of pain."

- Her daughter is six. "I still remember the first time she gave me that 'what the f---' look."

- "My sister is an ICU nurse and she just appeared in the Sports Illustrated swimsuit issue."

- I asked the woman going into the Air Force, "How did you learn how to fly?" She: "Not on purpose. I was sitting next to the pilot and my dad asked if I wanted to fly. He gave me the basics and I did it for a few minutes."

- Young expecting mom: "I'm worried about giving the baby a shower." Me: "Don't worry, babies don't get showers, only a bath. You might be thinking of a baby shower."

- Three college guys and a girl: Guy: "The three of us are all in the fraternity." Girl: "Sadly, I am not in the fraternity."

- Young mom: "I have a baby-free weekend. I'm going to drink wine and watch *Grey's Anatomy*."

- She: "My family is all creative, we're a very right-brained family."

- She: "Our third child is our golden child; he just has this twinkle in his eyes like his dad."

- She: "This is a picture of my daughter; isn't she beautiful?"

- She: "My eight-year-old got her ears pierced yesterday and she now looks forty-one."

- She: "When I was eleven, I wanted a bathing suit, and my dad said, 'If you want it, go out and earn it.' I started working in a clothing store to get clothes, and at fifteen, I was running a small store."

- She: "My husband and I are sailors. We sold our house in Florida this summer and bought a sailboat. We are going to homeschool our three kids, four, three, and one, on the boat as we make memories for them [making] a life sailing."

- Woman: "My sister is 5'3" and I'm six feet tall. She's a lot like me though, but she's a little blond chick who's a savage."

- I told the woman about the rider who was the only rider I've ever had to stop from talking and she said, "You never met my grandma; she doesn't even take a breath when she starts talking."

- She: "I don't do well with rebelling children."

- Referring to her friend who we were picking up, I said, "your boyfriend." She: "He's not my boyfriend, he's my stupid friend."

- The mother of two teenagers said, "I'd like to see the internet go out for three months. Some people would be out of their mind."

- She: "My grandmother is a real spitfire. She just turned one hundred and she looks seventy-five and does a lot of independent things."

- About having two boys: "Their clothes are dirty and their room stinks."

- Me: "What do you do back home?" She: "I'm a stay-at-home mom without kids." Me: "When did the last kid leave?" Her: "Over a year ago."

- The woman reserved a hotel room for her son and daughter-in-law because "they need a break from their new baby." I said, "They should jump all over that, but if they don't, let me know."

- Female urologist: "I learned how to fly when I was kid and got my pilot's license before my driver's license. It was expected since both my parents were pilots."

- Woman living in Los Angeles: "I don't use rideshare in LA, I'm cheap. I don't drink so I'm Uber for my friends."

- She: "My dad is inappropriately funny. He says thing that other people are only thinking, and people laugh."

- "There are some mouthy southerners, including my daughter."

- "My daughter was born looking like a chimpanzee; she had hair everywhere."

- Mother: "My two-year-old has an Italian accent; she's saucy."

- One eighteen-year-old girl said to her friend, "Don't be a bitch in the car on the way home."

- Her fifteen-year-old daughter asked her, "Which end of the year dance recital should I invite grandpa [of Indian descent] to?" She: "The one where you show off the least."

- The two sisters each said that they were the funnier one. I asked the older sister to tell me something funny and she said, "Can you see my sister's face in the rearview mirror?" They both broke up laughing, but there was nothing funny about her sister's face—she could have been a model.

- "My daughter's reception venue wasn't going to let us have 250 people, so we spent $7,000 to flatten out our backyard to have it there. The venue came through and we could have 150. We sent out another set of invitations and cut a hundred guests."

- The two girls seemed to be a little annoyed that the guy had ordered an Uber about an hour early. I said, "I give you a lot of credit for planning ahead, it can be difficult getting a ride." His girlfriend said, "You don't have to hype him, he's his own hype-man." (He's in sales.)

o   The young woman told me how much she loves The Beatles and Queen, which are her mom's favorite groups. "My mom told me a long time ago, 'When you live in my house, you listen to my music.'" I convinced her to go home and tell her mom she's taking her to see the Beatles movie *Yesterday*. She said, "Thank you, you made my morning."

o   The two girlfriends had me laughing through two rides early in the morning. I asked, "Have you had any sleep?" One answered, "What do you think?" and the other said, "Do naps count?" When I said they were a great first ride, one said, "We aim to make every ride the best ride—we're wonderful." When one of them said she hates Monday, I told her it was my favorite day of the week, and she made me laugh all day by saying "F--- you!"

Male Comments on Friendship/Family

o   *The big Texan with a big cowboy hat got into my car with his wife. My side door is heavy to slide shut, so I told her to use both hands. She closed it easily, and I said, "Wow, you must be pretty strong." The husband said, "My wife is used to handling a whopper." The ride was only one minute long, and I never stopped laughing.

- *Male: "My sixteen-year-old daughter just told me that she has a boyfriend. She didn't want to tell me because she was afraid I would scare him. I just wanted to talk to him about guns and graveyards."

- *First guy: "I don't know why my finger hurts." Second guy: "You put it in my mouth at 4 a.m." First guy: "You bit my finger?"

- The Puerto Rican man said, "My dad, when I was young, had me pour salt and pepper on top of each other on a paper plate and told me to separate them. He said, "You can't separate the world that way."

- The male cook said, "My friend gave me mushrooms to try when we were working, and I had a bad trip. I sat outside for thirty minutes talking to myself."

- Him: "My kids say to me, 'Dad, you have to join this millennium.'" I say to them, "Send me a postcard."

- Him: "When I drink, my friends tell me I beat up the neighbors, so I stopped drinking."

- Older man: "My kids were worried about what I would do when I retired, and I joked, 'Maybe I'll be an Uber driver.' They didn't think I would, but I became an Uber driver for a month just to piss off my kids, and I loved it."

o Dad: "My little boy told me that I was better than a cartoon parent."

o First male: "I have to get gifts for my five kids." Male friend: "He never learned when to pull out." Me: "I'm not touching that line." First male: "I was really stupid; I have five kids with four women." Me: "I'm not touching that line, either."

o When I told the sixteen-year-old, unmasked male that we're really not supposed to drive sixteen-year-olds, he reassured me by saying, "I'm vaccinated, and I became a man when I was thirteen." (Probably not referring to a bar mitzvah.)

o He said, "My grandmother always sneezes three to six times. I wait until she's done before I bless her."

o Picking up his friends at a strip club, he dropped his wedding ring near my car. After a couple minutes he said, "I can't find it; it's OK." I got out of the car and said, "It may be OK today, but it won't be tomorrow." We did find it.

o The recently engaged guy said to me about first meeting his fiancée, "She has rich parents, which kept me interested for a while." (Joking.)

o My rider was renting a car and taking his wife and two kids on vacation to Disney World. Afterward, the kids were staying with their grandparents. I asked him, "What are you going to do then?" He said, "I'm going to work to pay off the vacation."

- I picked up several members of the bachelor party and asked if any of them were getting married. One replied, "He's been missing for twenty-four hours."

- Him: "I'm an Uber driver to my grandchildren. I take them wherever they want to go."

- Him: "I'm twenty-seven and I give relationship advice to people. I hit rock bottom and lost everything due to drugs and decided to change because I saw how it was affecting my mom."

- Male: "My grandmother is a gamer. She used to buy and play all these games years ago and still in her eighties, she burns out a tablet every year."

- He said, "I've seen a lot of people chase happiness but lose their soul. The most important thing for me is to be a good father and husband."

- "My friend and I were at a bar in New York, and we looked online and saw that we could get tickets for the Michigan game for only twenty dollars. We got in our car and drove to Michigan without telling anyone. My girlfriend made me sleep on the couch for two weeks."

- Male with young kids: "The greatest thing about having kids is reliving your life and experiencing their joy."

- Male: "My dad taught me how to fly when I was nine years old, and I was sitting on a telephone book in the cockpit. I got my pilot's license when I was fifteen, before my driver's license."

- Male: "Our two- and four-year-old are handfuls, but they are so freaking cute."

- Him: "Our kids are grown; they don't want anything to do with us."

- Grandfather: "If I could have had grandchildren first, I would have."

- Talking about a male friend, he said, "He has a lot of confidence with women, for no real reason."

- Him: "We were celebrating our twenty-two-year-old daughter's birthday. Doing shots with a twenty-year-olds is a tough job."

- He is the only male in a family with seven women: "They talk about nothing and expect me to comment."

- Male: "I have six children and only one grandchild—they're losers."

- "My dad always told me that old age and treachery will always outlast youth and exuberance."

- Male bartender in his early thirties: "My seven-year-old daughter is the best thing I've ever done."

- The family from Connecticut told me what they named their dog. "It's an Aussiedoodle and he's Sir Oliver George Flat-White the First."

- He: "When I was twenty-two, I had a few days off and we wanted to get pizza in New York. The five of us drove from Charleston to New York and stayed overnight with someone. The next day we got two pies and drove home."

- "One day when I was younger, someone threw sand at me, and it got in my eyes—part of the reason I wear glasses. Many years later, my sister told me that she threw the sand."

- The man said, "A father died in the house I'm living in. That red cardinal is always around and when someone yells, 'Hello Charlie,' it always turns around."

- The man said, "When I retire, I'm going to get on my son's nerves, because he gets on mine now."

Female Comments on Dating/Marriage

- *Two women from Indiana: "Our husbands are so needy. They don't even know how to feed themselves when we're away."

- *The female attorney said, "Paul McCartney was my first crush when I was three. He's the only eighty-year-old man I would trade for my sixty-year-old man."

- *"We were watching the movie *He's Just Not That Into You* and I said, 'I'm not desperate to get married.' He said, 'Would you marry me?' I said I would, and we've been married six years. He was the sixth man I was engaged to." (By age twenty-five.)

- *The woman said her husband was an introvert, and after the one-hour ride she said, "You've said more words on this trip than my husband has in seventeen years."

- *A woman in her twenties said, "All girls are crazy, but you just need to find *your own* crazy!"

- The woman told me, "I'm taking my three kids on a year-long trip around the world." The kids were 6, ten, and twelve, and she wanted them to see the world. It was a tribute to her mom who had visited all the African countries in her life.

- Young woman: "Do you have any advice on how to find a rich guy in New York?"

- She asked, "Why are you living your best life?" Me: "For one, I'm married to an amazing woman for thirty-seven years."

- She: "We were friends for thirteen years, and one day I had a glass of wine and now we're together."

- She: "Why do men call you so much? They are so clingy."

- Wife: "The first time he cooked for me, he put Italian dressing in the pasta sauce. It was horrible." Husband: "I didn't have enough sauce; it was delicious."

- Wife: "When a man offered to help me carry out two cans of paint, my husband said, 'She can handle it. She had a baby come out sideways and had no problem.'" (Not true.)

- Female: "I met my husband in the hospital; he was my patient. He was in a terrible accident, which left him a paraplegic. We're married and building a house, and he has said that he's glad the accident happened."

- I mentioned that the husband laughed a lot and the wife only sometimes. She said, "He laughs for me."

- She: "In a relationship, you have to make sure the shoe fits before you wear them."

- I told the woman who is used to being single, "I don't know what it's like to be single." She replied, "I'll tell you, it's fun."

- Speaking with a couple who both worked with numbers a lot, I asked, "Who is better with numbers?" She said, "He likes people more than I do."

- About to celebrate their first wedding anniversary, he said, "We're going black bear hunting in Canada, and it was her idea to go hunting." I asked her, "Why did you suggest going hunting?" She: "We went hunting on our honeymoon."

- Woman in her early fifties (?): "Young men on these dating sites are looking for 'sugar mamas.'"

- I asked the couple, "How did you meet?" She said, "I saw him walking across the street; he had a cool walk and big white eyes. He was looking good."

- Young woman about getting engaged: "I don't want to get engaged on a holiday. I just want it to be a normal day."

- She: "We're looking for a house, but right now we're living with his parents, and it's a lot of fun. They enjoy hanging around us."

- I asked the young couple how they got away for a ten-day vacation. He said, "She convinced me. She is pretty cute." Her: "It really helps to be cute sometimes—maybe he'll propose here?"

- Young women: "We just climbed out of the first-floor window; our boyfriends are on house arrest."

- Wife: "Don't listen to the backseat driver." Husband: "Don't listen to her, listen to me." Me: "I'm going to enjoy listening to all three of you give directions." (Referring to the GPS.)

- Wife: "I don't roar unless he needs to be roared at."

- Me: "I've been married for thirty-eight years." Young woman, "No effin' s---, that's my dream."

- Getting out of the car, the man almost shut the door on his wife. She said, "He's trying to get me to stay with you."

- Talking about her boyfriend who is shorter than she is: "I do love that little man."

- She: "I walked up to him in a bar and asked if he was friends with one of my friends, and then he couldn't take his eyes off me."

- She said, "My boyfriend is a gem; he wouldn't even take me to work."

- The young couple had been dating for five years. Smiling, I said to the guy, "You know, five years is a good amount of time dating; some people would say it's time to pop the question." Before he could answer, she enthusiastically said, "Oh, yeah!"

- The former Uber driver said, "[I] had a young guy in Boston that wanted me to help him pick which one of five women he was going to go to that night. I let him talk about them and narrow them down to two, and then he picked the one and I took him there."

- I told her that "my wife cooks and I eat." She said, "You should make dinner for your wife. Make her curried chicken."

- She: "My sister called me and said that she found my soulmate, but he's with someone else. Two years later I met him at her barbecue, and it was love at first sight—we ignored everyone else that was there."

- She: "We bought this expensive older house, because my husband wanted to gut it and rebuild it. He never gets anything, so I went along with it, and now I get a new kitchen."

- The woman came from Brazil to Charleston for a three-week vacation and decided to stay. Me: "What do you like best about Charleston?" Her: "My boyfriend."

- The woman used to be in a difficult relationship, and she would see this guy around the apartment complex. "His friendly greeting was the only kind words I heard all day." (They're married today.)

- Young female: "I'm studying marketing, but I hate it. I don't want to work." Boyfriend: "She wants me to pay for everything." Girlfriend: "What's wrong with that?" (Dating only eight months.)

- The woman was married thirty-eight years with three kids like my wife and I, but she had eleven grandchildren. Me: "No wonder I have no grandchildren; you have them all." She said, "You're going to have plenty of them. I'm already speaking it." Me: "I'm pretty sure that's not the way it works."

- After getting a pierced nose, she was pleading with her boyfriend to get some cream from the drugstore. "I don't want my nose to fall off."

- Probably after a drink or two, she said, "My kids hate me, because I'm so loud." Her husband added, "Anyone who drives her should get double pay."

- Young woman: "You've been married for thirty-seven years? How do you do that?" Me: "One year at a time."

- The woman walked out of the pub in the afternoon barefoot and her boyfriend put his jacket on the ground for her to walk toward my car. She said, "My feet aren't dirty; I cleaned them in the bathroom sink inside. I've done that my whole life."

- She: "My significant other has bad karma and he's an awful driver."

- When I told the woman that I had another woman say, "Our husbands are so needy; they don't even know how to feed themselves when we're away," she replied, "Did they come home to dead husbands?"

- Talking to his wife about raising their young daughter, he said, "Once that tree fully grows, you can't bend it at all."

- She: "I bought the house without my husband seeing it. He says he trusts my taste since I married him."

- Females about their boyfriends: "They met us at a stripper joint." (Not really.)

- I said to the funny couple, "How about you stay in my car and make everyone laugh the rest of the day?" She: "Why don't you come with us on our summer road trip this year?"

- She: "We worked at the same company, and he had to quit his job when we got married. He opened up his own business and now we make a s---load of money."

- She: "My husband and I don't ever talk politics because I'm a Democrat and he's a Republican."

- The couple had just come out of the two-hour timeshare seminar and said, "They were good at their job. They even said that we needed to buy timeshare so we could get away and help our marriage so that we wouldn't wind up divorced."

- She: "I'm a chaotic person. I attract chaos." Boyfriend: "I always bring calm and peace to a situation."

- She: "Getting back to dating at age thirty-six, I got some good advice from a friend. She said to go on thirty dates as quickly as possible, and you'll know." He said, "We're celebrating our one-week anniversary dating. This is our fifth date this week." I said to him, "I think you're doing pretty well."

- Getting in the car, I said to her, "You must be Amelia. He doesn't look like an Amelia." Amelia: "Not tonight, he doesn't." Me: "I don't need to know any more about that."

- I asked the woman who has been married for forty-five years, "What is the secret to a successful marriage?" and she said, "Hard work and patience."

- The couple was celebrating twenty-one years of marriage; I asked them how they met. She: "He was my chemistry tutor in college." He: "I got her grade up from an F to an A … We went out to celebrate, and then I scored." She: "We did not do that!" (He misspoke.)

- Married for forty years, I asked them, "What's the secret of a successful marriage?" She said, "Commitment and trust."

- She: "I want to make today special for my boyfriend since today is Sweetest Day, which we celebrate in the Midwest. It's important to me, since Christmas is coming and then my birthday."

- I asked the couple dating how they met, and she said, "I was getting a tattoo from my cousin who was learning how to do it and he walked into the house with a beer. I didn't pay any attention to him." He added, "I got a beer tattoo and now sometimes she pays too much attention to me."

- She: "I try my very best every day with my five-year-old and three-year-old, and cocktails help.

- I picked up a couple at a Fuddruckers and drove them close by to a private airport where they were flying home. I asked how long they were in town, and he replied, "We just came in for dinner." The wife added, "He loves Fuddruckers and so we flew in from North Carolina since there are no restaurants close to us." He also had leftovers in his hand.

- 2020: "We drove through the West and Midwest in our motor home from February to August this year and we didn't kill each other. We didn't eat outside our motor home until we got to Montana, which had everything open since they only have eight people living there."

Male Comments on Dating/Marriage

- *My rider showed me a picture of his wife, and when I showed him a picture of my wife, he said with a thick British accent, "Our wives have something in common—they have abominably poor taste in men."

- *"My wife had to kiss a lot of toads before she found her prince. I married the first person I kissed; I didn't think it was going to happen again."

- *Older man: "I've been married fifty-one years. My wife says she been married sixty-one years, because I've made it seem ten years longer."

- *Me: "How did you two meet?" Him: "It's a funny story. She ran a stop sign and drove into me. We talked about the damage to my car for a couple weeks and I finally said, 'How about I drop everything if you let me take you out to dinner?'" (Together six years, married one.)

- *"I can't tell my girlfriend this, but a few years ago, I made out with Jenna Bush, George W. Bush's daughter. The Secret Service wasn't happy about it."

- *I said to the couple who'd been dating for five years: "So you're in the dating stage?" Him: "We're actually in the married-and-just-want-to-kill-each-other stage, we're just not married yet."

- *The married couple of ten years was celebrating his birthday and I said it was more significant than me celebrating thirty-nine years of marriage the next day. He disagreed, saying, "Anyone who suffers the pain and torture of a woman for that long, it's more." His wife added, "She may not be as bad as me."

- Me: "How did you two meet?" Him: "She's been stalking me since she was two."

- The two men got in the car, far, far back in a neighborhood, and I said, "I'm sure the GPS can get me out of here, but just tell me what to do and I'll follow whatever you say." He replied, "My wife needs to hear that seminar."

- Husband: "We have three kids, twenty-two, twenty-three, and twenty-four." Me: "You certainly didn't fool around. "Her: "We did, that's the problem." Husband: "It's not funny, it was expensive."

- "My dad has twenty-four brothers and sisters, all from the same parents, and I must have a thousand cousins. I just want to go somewhere where no one knows me."

- The husband said when his wife uses the bathroom, "Even if she just pees, it's twenty-five minutes."

- He got in the car in a good mood and told me he'd just taken his name off the credit card that he'd shared with his wife of three years. "She bought a $9,500 Prada purse to get back at me. It's her responsibility now."

- The intelligent and creative guy explained about a woman he used to be with: "I fell in love with all the moons that circulated around her."

- He: "I hate locking doors, so my wife locked me out of the house twice and I kicked in the door and repaired it. The third time, I sat outside and waited."

- Putting their luggage in the trunk, I asked if there was anything else. He said, "Is there room for her in there?" I said to him, "You better be nicer to her, otherwise I'm the only one who's going to be nice to you today." She quickly added, "Don't spouses often disappear on a cruise?"

- Husband: "I don't Google, I have a wife."

- Married for fifty-five years, I asked the couple from Tennessee, "What's the secret of a successful marriage?" He replied immediately, "Yes, dear." His wife said, "Doing things together."

- Him: "My parents met when my mom at the age of twenty-one picked up two male hitchhikers who had been drinking. They hit it off immediately."

- The couple was married thirty-six years, and I asked, "What's the secret of a successful marriage?" and he said, "Tolerance," and she agreed and said, "You have to give your spouse a break sometimes."

- I asked the couple about to celebrate fifty years of marriage, "What's the secret of a good marriage?" He said, "Putting up with her." They both laughed a lot; I think they're going to make it.

- I asked the couple from Long Island, New York, who'd been married for fifty-four years, "What's the secret of a successful marriage?" I watched the wife grinning, and she said later it was because she was afraid of what her husband would say. He said, "Fight every day, because it doesn't matter anymore."

- I asked the couple married fifty years, "What is the secret to a successful marriage?" He said, "You can't give up when the road gets bumpy."

- I asked the couple married thirty-six years, "What is the secret to a successful marriage?" He said, "Don't worry about nothing. If you're working seven days a week and doing everything you can, it will work out."

- I asked the couple, "When did you get married?" The guy answered, "Nine months ago. It's been the best nine months of my life."

- "I walked up to him in a bar and asked if he was friends with one of my friends, and then he couldn't take his eyes off me."

- He retired and then unretired: "When I retired, my wife thought that all my downtime was hers."

- I told him that one middle-aged man said that he likes going to Walmart to pick up women. The other middle-aged man said, "It's better in the frozen food section of Publix."

- He explained why he went to law school one year after his wife: "We like to make bad choices together."

- The older man admitted, "I'm juggling two or three women, and it's a bit of a mess."

- He explained, "In high school, I worked very hard to lose my virginity with my girlfriend, but it just didn't work out."

- I asked the couple who'd known each other for twenty years, "How did you two meet?" He said, "I used to sell weed to her ex-boyfriend."

- The young couple met in a bar, and I asked the guy, "Did you have a pick-up line?" He said, "She wanted to bring me home the first night."

- He said about his girlfriend sitting next to him, "She thinks everything I say is funny. She's the only one."

- Man about his wife who was sitting next to him, "Everything she says is unusual."

- Husband of ten years: "I'm still trying to make my wife into what I want her to be."

- The young guy said, "Having one girlfriend is a lot of work."

- Him: "My fiancée is graduating law school in May and we're getting married in June. She's impressively crazy."

- Couple on their first date in their forties: Him: "We met on SugarDaddy.com. [Not really.] She stalked me on Facebook after not seeing me for five years. [Not really.] Bambi is her striptease alter ego. [Definitely not.]"

- Him: "Don't get rid of your old lady, it's expensive."

- Young couple dating three years: He said, "She asked me recently what I love about her, and I said, 'You're pretty, beautiful, and I love your glow.'"

- Him: "I didn't ask my wife out on a first date. She was my bartender, and one night after we both finished bartending at different places, she called at 3:30 a.m. and asked if I wanted to come over for a swim."

- I asked the friendly couple who have been dating for four years, "So when are you getting engaged?" He said, "When she pops the question."

- Taking the young couple to get their marriage license on Jail Road, they discussed which one of them would be more likely to be arrested. Me: "So, did you come to any conclusion?" Him: "I think she would."

- Woman sitting next to her husband: "We've been married twenty-five years and every minute has been wonderful." Husband, "It's difficult for anyone to say 'every minute.'"

- She: "My husband was bawling at our daughter's wedding." The husband joked, "I was bawling because it cost me $40,000."

- She owned a spa, and he did all her marketing. I asked, "How long have you been married?" He said, "Not yet; I have an ultimatum for December 31st, but I may wait until the last minute."

- With his wife next to him, he said, "Ghost shopping is when your wife stays at home and shops, and no one sees nothing." Me: "I understand why they call it ghost shopping; when the bills come in, they're scary."

- He: "They say you want to be sure you marry the right person. We thought dating ten years was the right timing." (To be married in a few months.)

- Him: "I crashed my car when I had a seizure." Girlfriend: "I was there, and it was terrifying." Him: "It wasn't terrifying to me; I was having a seizure."

- 6:30 a.m. on a Sunday: "I haven't gone to sleep yet. My bro and I met two girls, and I'll let you use your imagination." Me: "Do I have to? I'm driving."

- Groom: "My wife and I right now for our honeymoon are just going to an island for a couple days. She calls it a 'mini-moon.'"

- Me: "How long have you been married?" Husband: "Thirty years. It's time for parole."

- Husband: "My wife finds me truly riveting." (She wasn't in the car.)

- "One of my retired friends told me that a retired cop was stabbed to death by his wife because they were spending too much time together."

- He said, "My wife just ate a lot of lobster crab—there's still some on her shirt."

- "I told my wife all my awful stories when I was younger, and she still hates me."

- At 6 a.m. Sunday morning, he said, "I can't sleep. I have to get something to eat. I got married last night." Me: "Did you get any sleep last night? Oops, I shouldn't have asked you that."

- "I was married seven and a half years—I'm not going to do that again."

- As I opened the trunk, the husband, with dozens of small Walmart bags full of food after the wife had gone shopping for the family of six from Minnesota, said, "That had to cost at least fifty dollars." It cost $300.

- I asked them how long they were dating, and she said, "Three years." He replied, "Three going on thirty." Me: "You better be nice to her, or she'll start hitting you."

- Him: "To save money during the pandemic, my girlfriend had the idea to buy a cow. We bought a large freezer and we've been eating the meat for six months."

- Married for nineteen years, he was out with the guys and texted his wife, "Feeling a bit of loneliness without you."

- My rider Paul texted me, "I'm wearing a lime green dress." When I arrived, I said, "You said you were wearing a lime green dress, what happened?" Him: "That was before, it looks better on my wife."

- He was a Walgreens store manager, and he said, "My wife helps the world [a social worker] and I make money off it."

- Running out to my car, he said, "You know how it's like, women always want one extra kiss."

- "Our first date was at a Mexican restaurant, and we spent six hours there talking. The staff wasn't too happy with us."

- Him: "After my last divorce, I made a list of about ten things that a woman I dated in the future could not be and she [his wife] has four of them."

- Male: "Due to us having to quarantine together, my wife and I have a better relationship."

- He: "My dad told me when I was young, 'Whatever you do for work, even if you're shoveling fishhooks, you should shovel more than anyone.'"

- Me: "Are you married?" Him: "No, we've been dating for two months, although we've known each other for a long time. She wants a ring." When they got out of the car I said to him, "I've been married almost thirty-eight years; it's a good deal."

- Picking the couple up from an amazing house, he said, "We don't use Uber much when we go out for dinner, but we're trying not to be a--holes."

- "I dated my fiancée's best friend for two years a long time ago and we're still friends."

- A couple maybe in their forties said, "Can you tell us the best strip club to go to? When we travel, we always go to one in each town."

- Me: "I've given five thousand rides in this car." Him (with his girlfriend next to him): "I've given five thousand rides too."

- He: "When I was in my mid-twenties, we had a contest on who could sleep with the oldest woman. I slept with a sixty-year-old, but I didn't win."

- I rescued a married man early in the morning from a million-dollar house from a lonely widow who he drove home because she had too much to drink. He said, "I put her to bed. She wanted me to get in bed with her. She was beautiful, but I told her I had to go."

- He was exhausted when he got in the car and said, "I only had five hours of sleep." Me: "I had less than that." A few minutes later, he was on the phone with his friend and said, "She was hot, we had fun. I'm probably embarrassing myself in front of my Uber." I said nudging him, "No, I'm not listening."

- Male: "My wedding was postponed in July [due to COVID-19] and now is scheduled for January 1. However, it does not look promising to have over two hundred people there. We will get married that day, but if we have to, we will reschedule the reception for July."

- On his twenty-first birthday, he told me, "I lived in Maryland and my girlfriend suggested we go on vacation in Charleston. I said no, because I didn't want to spend the money. Two weeks later, a good friend asked me to move to the Charleston area with him, and I did, without my girlfriend." I said, "You probably shouldn't tell that story to your next girlfriend."

SOUTHERN HOSPITALITY IS REAL

It is not a myth. People in the South are incredibly friendly. Southerners train their children at an early age to be respectful and friendly. When people like me move from the Northeast to the South, we have to adjust to a slower pace of life and how incredibly friendly Southerners are. This is how a rider explained his experience to me a few years ago:

"Sickeningly Nice"

The rider from New Jersey had been in Myrtle Beach for six months. The best line I've ever heard about Southern hospitality came from him. He said, "The people down here are sickeningly nice." He meant that in a nice way. I have repeated that line hundreds of times and people in the South enjoy it as much as people who are visiting the South. The same rider told me, "I was in a Walmart and there was one woman in front of me, and she was talking to the cashier, and they wouldn't stop. I kept thinking to myself, 'Please God, I just want to go home.'" He also told me this: "Every time I come out of my condo with my puppy, all the neighbors come out as if they had never seen a dog before."

Over the past five years, I have collected many Southern hospitality stories that I've personally experienced and I've shared many of them with my riders. I'm only going to share my two favorite stories, because we have a lot more stops to make before we reach your final destination.

Personal Story #1
The first night that my wife and I arrived in Myrtle Beach after moving, and we ran out to Publix, the big supermarket in the area. We were only going to get a few things before it closed. As we walked up to the register, there was a young man of maybe twenty who was the cashier. (My wife remembers him as the helper.) He asked if he could take the items out of our cart and put them on the conveyer belt. We said yes, but we looked at each other and had no clue as to what was going on. After everything was scanned and bagged, he asked if he could wheel the cart out to our car. I was laughing at this point, but we agreed. At the car, I popped the trunk, and he asked, "Can I put the bags in your car?" I said something like, "If you put them in the car, you're coming back to our place and putting everything in the fridge." I did it, but we were amazed at the service we got on our very first night. We were not the only Northerners to be amazed by Publix.

Personal Story #2
I was working as a courier delivering packages and I pulled into a neighborhood I had never been in before. Up ahead, I saw there was a guy in his driveway, but it didn't mean anything

to me. As I got closer, I could not believe what I was seeing. The man was washing his car, his back was to me, and he was waving at me behind his back. I wanted to pull over and say, "Can't you let me drive by in peace? You don't know me, you can't see me, and you're never going to see me. What am I supposed to do, honk three times or wave at your ass?" I kept driving and shaking my head. People in the South wave a lot.

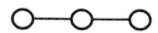

○—○—○

Below are the two very best hospitality stories you will probably ever read, and afterward are many reactions and comments on Southern hospitality. If you've never been to the South, you need to visit just to experience Southern hospitality.

The Ultimate Southern Hospitality Story

It doesn't get any better than this. The twenty-one-year-old woman from Minnesota told me an unforgettable story that she'd experienced the year before. When I heard she was from Minnesota, I told her that Minnesota was just rated the friendliest state in the country in a travel survey and that South Carolina finished third. She said, "Oh no, people in South Carolina are friendlier," and then she told me her story. She was driving in Columbia, South Carolina, three hours away from Myrtle Beach. Her car broke down and she thought that she needed coolant. She walked two miles to a gas station and bought the coolant.

Standing outside the store, a man was pumping gas into his car. He looked at her and said, "Do you need any help?" Being from Minnesota, she was used to people being friendly, so she told him she could use a ride back to her car. He drove her there and put the coolant in, but it didn't work. He decided to pay $150 to have her car towed and then drove her three hours back home. He refused to accept any money. She wanted to know why he did it, and he said, "I thought God was telling me to help someone, and you were standing there." It was incredibly generous of that man, who went far above what anyone could have expected. I hope one day he reads this story and knows that I have told this to a couple hundred people.

The Steak Dinner

The woman told me this great family story of how they try to get together every few years despite living in many different states. She said, "My ten brothers and sisters and I met at a nice steak restaurant in Georgia along with a few spouses. The older couple sitting at the next table loved the fact that we were all family and having such a good time. The woman told me that she hadn't spoken to her two sisters in a long time, and one of my brothers said that he would pray for her that it would work out. When it came time to pay, we were arguing about who was going to get the big check and the waitress told us it was taken care of by the older couple. They even paid the tip." I am pretty sure that family will always remember that night because of that couple's generosity.

The Perfect Fit in the South

The woman told me that her husband had a successful business, and they had just purchased a house in New York when the pandemic hit, causing them to lose the house. For their anniversary, her husband put her in the car and drove to South Carolina without telling her what they were doing. They bought a house in Mt. Pleasant, and she said, "The transition to the South from New York was easy, I fit right in here. It fit like a glove." She found out that her outgoing personality and friendliness was the same thing she found in South Carolina.

Comments

- *He said, "It is difficult adjusting to the South from the North. You have to adjust to people waving five fingers at you instead of one."
- *I asked the woman from New York who'd been living in the South for two years, "Have you gotten used to how friendly people are here?" She said, "I'm not there yet. Just this week the cashier at Publix asked me what I was making for dinner. Do I tell her I haven't made a home-cooked meal in ten years? When we first moved in, a neighbor left a pie on the front porch and I told my husband, 'Don't you even think of eating that, it could be poisoned.'"
- Female professor: "When you go to Hall's Chophouse [in downtown Charleston] they hug and kiss you—it's the most action I get all month."
- *The young woman from New York was living in the South three years. Me: "Have you gotten used to how friendly people are here?" Her: "Yes, and I don't like it. I prefer rude people, where I can give more right back to them."

- The woman from Connecticut told me, "My first day at work in Charleston, I walked into the elevator, and everyone was talking to me. When we got to the second floor, some people got out and some got in and they started talking to me. I thought they had all been drinking."
- She is a business owner in Connecticut and a homeowner in the Charleston area. I was talking about how friendly people are here. She was having trouble getting people to work on her house and do a good job and she said, "I wish people would be less friendly and more efficient on their job."
- She: "My sister was visiting down here from New York and all the salespeople were talking to me. She got angry and said, 'Stop talking to them and making friends, I don't want to talk to them.'"
- Male from Philly: "When I first came down south, the people were so nice, I thought they were mocking me."
- Me: "Have you gotten used to how friendly people are down here?" She: "Ugh, I was so put off by it."
- Me: "What do you think about people being so friendly in the South?" He: "It's kind of weird, but good."
- "We couldn't believe the woman here who walked out the door in front of us and then came back and apologized for letting the door shut and opened the door for us. In New York, she might have spit at us."
- Woman from New York living in the South: "I'm usually pretty patient down here, but every once in a while, my inner New Yorker comes out."

- From Ohio: "We come here for the Southern hospitality."
- From New York, he was trying to adjust to the South. He said, "When someone would approach me with a big smile and say, 'Hello,' I would first think of where my wallet and phone were, because I didn't want to get robbed."
- When I told him about the guy waving behind his back, he said, "If that had happened in Detroit [where he's from] or New Jersey [where I'm from], he would have been cursed out."
- Young woman from Philly living here: "I still force myself sometimes to say hello to people."
- Him: "People in the South are just living in a different time frame than people in the North. You may have five slow cars in front of you, because someone is looking at a cool bird."
- The woman from the North: "Getting used to the friendliness of people down here is exhausting."
- She was from the Northeast and was frustrated by the service in a very nice restaurant. "The waiter did not stop talking to us and I was thinking, Don't you have something better to do? At another place, the bartender kept complaining it was so busy instead of just pouring my wine, it was frustrating."
- She is from New Hampshire: "It's a little weird walking down the street and saying hi to each other here."
- From New York, she said, "When I first came down here, I would go into a gas station and people

would ask how my day was going. Up North, people don't even look at you."
- He was from New York: "I was genuinely struck with how friendly people were in the South my first day. I left my wallet on the counter of a store and a guy came running out after me. In New York, that would have been gone."
- Woman from the South: "When I come into work I say 'good morning' to everyone. If they don't say anything to me, I say, 'Is your mouth broken?'"
- She moved from New Jersey to Vegas and then moved to the South: "I probably would have died if I moved straight to the South. Being in Vegas prepared me for the friendliness in the South."
- She: "I had been in South Carolina only a couple months and could not go home for Thanksgiving. I was at a bar and started talking with a couple on Thanksgiving and they invited me back to their house for their Thanksgiving dinner, and I had a great time."
- She was going to church on Christmas Day with several bags and wrapped containers: "I have ninety-six chocolate cookies for people." Me: "You couldn't make another four to round it off?" She: "I was up all night. I have to make more for people who aren't getting any."
- She: "The transition to the South from New York was easy; I fit right in."
- Trying to adjust to the South from New York, he had someone here say, "Have a great day and be kind." He couldn't understand why they said that.

- "The people here are much nicer than in Philly."
- Visiting from Boston, he said, "People are like in slow motion down here."
- From the North, the woman said, "People down here walk too slow."
- Young New Yorker: "I love it down here. It's so quiet and calm."
- Young woman raised in the South: "If I didn't show respect when I was a child, I got spanked. I sometimes say 'sir' and 'ma'am' to people only a few years older than me."
- Me: "Have you gotten used to how friendly people are here?" The young man said, "Not really; I'm a pretty private person."
- Woman from New Jersey about living in the South: "I love it when people say, 'Have a blessed day.'"
- He: "When I moved from Texas to Massachusetts, I thought people were cold, rude, and impersonal." Me: "Other than that, they were pretty nice?" Him: "Yes."
- He was living in the North: "I was sitting in an airport in the South and this guy came over and stuck his hand out and introduced himself. The first thing I thought of was, 'I don't give a shit who you are,' and then I remembered I was in the South, and I was the one with the problem."
- Older man: "I've lived in the North and South in three different countries, including here, and people in the South are always friendlier because they are outside more since the weather is nicer. However, people in the northern parts of countries are more

loyal and have closer relationships with people, since they are inside more."
- The young woman who works in New York but grew up in the South said, "People in New York think I'm insane for smiling so much."
- She: "When I first started at Publix, I was taking a cart out of the store for a couple from New Jersey. They said, 'What are you doing?' When I told them, they said, 'This is crazy; we're not used to this.'"
- "People are way nicer in the South."
- "The South taught me to be nice."
- "In the South, it's a more respectful society."
- Me: "Have you gotten used to how friendly people are here?" She: "I may never get used to how friendly they are."
- "People are too friendly here, especially at restaurants. Sometimes I'd like to go to restaurants that the people are rude."
- He grew up in Spokane, Washington, and was very independent. He married a girl from South Carolina but could not believe how friendly people were in the South. "My in-laws were constantly asking what they could do for me. I had to get used to how people talked to me."
- "Moving here was a culture shock. Even fast food is not fast."
- "Uber drivers are a lot friendlier here than they are in Michigan."
- Woman: "I made a plate of food at a barbecue for my boyfriend, who was from the North, and his mom could not believe I did it. She expected her

son to make his own plate, but that's how we do it in the South."
- Former New Yorker said, "Being down here now, I don't know how I was raised in New York."
- Him: "I think how friendly people are in the South is a myth; however, they are much friendlier than in the Northeast."
- She: "When I moved to the South from the North, it was a big change. I was in a bar and a guy accidentally hit my arm and spilled my entire drink. Just on reflex, I cursed at him, and he apologized completely. He said he'd get me another drink, but I was surprised when he came back with it. Then, he asked me if I wanted to dance. I said to myself, what is going on here?"

9

DRIVING IN CHARLESTON, SOUTH CAROLINA

About seventy miles south of where I live in Myrtle Beach, South Carolina, is the beautiful town of Mt. Pleasant. It is a very large suburb of Charleston and it's a very scenic area that has around a hundred thousand people living there. The entire Charleston area has over eight hundred thousand residents. On the way to get to downtown Charleston from Mt. Pleasant, you have to travel over the very large and modern Ravenel Bridge. It was built in 2005 at the cost of $500–$600 million dollars. Downtown Charleston is one of those special places that is a major tourist and wedding destination. It is known for its history, architecture, and food. Charleston is one of the oldest cities in the country; it was founded in 1670 and is 353 years old.

Downtown Charleston is the home of the College of Charleston, which was founded in 1770 and is the oldest educational institution in South Carolina. It has over ten thousand students and for many years has had a demographic as high as 70 percent women who go to the school. I joke that women have a torrid love affair with Downtown Charleston, but it's not far from the truth. Why? The history, "the vibe," shopping, the weather, and of course the food. Also in downtown Charleston is The Citadel, which is a military college of a couple thousand men and woman. Since 1922, it has existed downtown on its three-hundred-acre site.

About one third of my rides have come from the Charleston area. I've been fortunate to have met some incredible people who live there and people who were just visiting. Of my fifty top rides, twenty-four of them I met in Charleston. Many stories and comments throughout the book are from the Charleston area, but I'm going to focus on the Ravenel Bridge and the College of Charleston, which have provided me with some amusing and interesting moments. I have added in some comments about Charleston after these two main topics.

The Ravenel Bridge

It's an amazing bridge, and I would regularly see people walking, jogging, and biking on the bridge as I drove over it. Many riders told me how much they enjoyed going over the bridge, so I decided to do the same thing. In the spring of 2020, when I was not Ubering on the weekend due to the pandemic, I drove down to Charleston early on a Sunday morning. I did a little jogging and some walking, and I took some pictures too.

What Was the Ravenel Bridge Built to Look Like?
The bridge was built in 2005 and it replaced two bridges that people considered scary. One day, a rider, who was an architect, told me that he studied the bridge and "it was made to look like two sailboats in the distance and has 128 cables on it." I thought it would make an interesting trivia question, so I started asking my riders, and below are some of the answers. The second picture below was taken during an accident on the bridge; I was looking straight up to the top.

The bridge looks like:

- "The golden arches."
- "A toaster."
- "Mountains."
- "Two birthday hats."
- "A Christmas tree."
- "Diamonds."
- "A slice of pizza."
- "A fish."
- "A pair of old, long pants."
- "Another bridge."
- "A whale; the scales on the side of a whale." She showed me a picture on her phone and she's right.
- "Missouri." She really meant the arch in St. Louis.
- The woman in shipping said, "A bra." Me: "You see a bra on that bridge?"

- The man was with his adult daughter in the car, and I told him that a woman thought it looked like a bra. He said, "They look like pointy nipples."
- When I told the woman that I've had a few women who could see that the Ravenel Bridge looked like a bra, she said, "I've never had a bra like that; they must not have any boobies."
- When I asked the two couples what the bridge looked like, the two women who had been drinking said, "Boobs."
- After telling her that a guy said the bridge looked like the golden arches, the woman got upset and said, "What part of math did he not understand? The golden arches are round, and the bridge shows two triangles!"
- Female nurse: "The bridge doesn't look like a bra; if anything, maybe misshapen boobies, and I've seen a lot of them."
- After correctly guessing that the Ravenel Bridge looks like two sailboats, I told her that she was the first local person to guess it. The young geology major replied, "That's because I'm a smarty."
- **The Accountant That Changed Her Life:** My Favorite Ride #33 is in an earlier chapter. In the story, I explained that I asked her the trivia question, "When the bridge was built, what was it built to look like?" She didn't know, and when I told her, she said, "I was the first one to go over the bridge. When I was in third grade, I entered a contest where I drew a picture of the Ravenel Bridge and I won. I represented the elementary school and there

was a winner for middle school and high school, and I rode with them over the bridge in a limo on opening day. The limo then drove me to school."

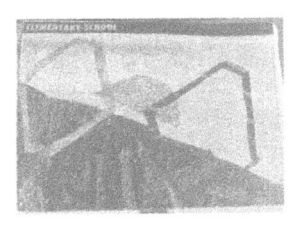

This is her drawing, and it is on my visor, so when I go over the bridge, I see her picture and the bridge. Riders really enjoy the story, and below is her picture from the newspaper:

- **Two Women and the Ravenel Bridge:** One of my very first rides I had after putting the above picture in my car took me completely by surprise. I was going to ask the young woman my trivia question about the Ravenel Bridge, and I said to her, "You know the Ravenel Bridge?" She said, "It's my last name." Me: "Your last name is Ravenel?" She: "Yes; R-A-V-E-N-E-L." Me: "Are you related to Arthur Ravenel, who the bridge is named after?" She: "Yes, he's my uncle. He's ninety-five, and I was just with him for Thanksgiving." (He passed away one month after this conversation.)
- With the very next rider, I had to tell her the two stories, and she added to the story by telling me this: "The bridge had to be named for Arthur Ravenel because he fought for twenty years to get it built. The weekend before it opened, they had the roads open for pedestrians to walk across it." She walked across the bridge for her family. She said that she watched the bridge being built since her house and the family store was right

next to the bridge. She said the whole neighborhood was bought out for the bridge, but one guy would not sell. "They actually took the roof off his house and then he decided to pack up and leave. As a child, I saw the two bridges before that, when they were built in the sixties." She is writing a record of her old neighborhood so her family will have a history of it.

The College of Charleston

It is located in historic downtown Charleston. It was founded in 1770 and it is the thirteenth oldest educational institution in the country. On one of the first days I drove in the area, I had four female freshmen in my car, and I asked, "I'm not familiar with the school; what is it best known for?" I didn't get the answer I expected, but it started another hilarious topic for conversation. She answered quickly, "There are a lot more girls here than guys." After I stopped laughing, I learned that the student population was about 70 percent women and 30 percent men.

Why would it be so slanted? There are a couple possible reasons, but one of them has to do with how much women love downtown Charleston. Here are some of the best comments about the College of Charleston:

I asked several male students, "How are you managing with the seventy-thirty ratio of women to men?"

- *"I have five girlfriends. I'm doing the best I can to keep everyone happy." Showing me a picture of an attractive girl, he said, "This girl wouldn't give me

the time of day at most schools, but here it's slim picking."
- *"It's the best thing in life. The girls are making us smarter."
- Taking him to the airport to see his girlfriend, he said, "It's not fair; in chemistry class, there are four beautiful blondes all around me and I have to concentrate in that class."
- "I like to think I handled it with grace and aplomb."
- "I'm taking full advantage of it."
- "I'm not complaining about it.
- "I think that 60–70 percent of the girls at the College of Charleston are blond."
- I asked the former male student at the College of Charleston, "Why do so many girls go to school there?" He said, "I think their mothers want them to go so they can visit Charleston regularly."
- The three male College of Charleston students explained, "When we were recruited, the college representative called us over and said, 'The school is 70 percent women.' We had spent eighteen years living in Charleston, and another four years couldn't be too bad."
- When I asked a woman about the seventy-thirty ratio, she said, "It's annoying."
- Asking the female student, "What is the College of Charleston best known for?" I was surprised when she said, "The clap."
- There's a Facebook site for women at the College of Charleston and it's called, "Are You Dating My Boyfriend?" You have to be approved to get on it.

- One female student said, "I saw my ex on there, but I didn't make a comment."
- The male college student had transferred to the College of Charleston only three weeks ago, and discussing the number of women there, he said, "If I had a daughter, I wouldn't let her go here."
- A woman who lives nearby said, "There are a lot of Peter Pans here; this is like Neverland."
- As I drove through downtown, I told the three males visiting about the ratio at the college and one of them said, "It looks like they are coming out of the sidewalk." I agreed and said, "Yes, sometimes it does look that way."
- A male coach at the College of Charleston: "I taught some guys here how to have a steady girlfriend, instead of just being casual as many of them want."

The Ultimate Downtown Charleston Lover

My two riders on Sunday morning, October 30th, were from Staten Island, New York. The mother and daughter were going to spend the next three days in Charleston, and it was the mother's first visit. The daughter, a hair stylist in her twenties, was making her second trip to Charleston. Her first trip was on Thursday, October 20th, ten days earlier for a bachelorette party. She loved the town so much; she told her boyfriend to come down to spend a few extra days with her. She left on Tuesday, October 25th, five days ago.

Her mom had three days off, so she convinced her to go to Charleston, and she came with her to show her around. She said, "I love King Street." She enjoyed the shopping and great restaurants. I said to her that she's probably thinking about having her bachelorette party here one day and she said, "I'm thinking about my wedding." I look for her every time I drive in Charleston; you never know.

o—o—o

- The young woman said, "I love living in Downtown Charleston. It gives me accessibility to life."
- Female professor: "When you go to Hall's Chophouse, they hug and kiss you—it's the most action I get all month."
- Couple who used to live in Charleston and was back visiting: "We think Charleston is the best city in the country."
- Me: "Why do women love Charleston?" Woman: "It has character."
- Male: "Downtown Charleston is nice, but when I walk down King Street, it doesn't look clean. I feel like it could use a really good whitewash; maybe a weekend of whitewashing."
- Personal injury attorney: "I was driving over the Ravenel Bridge today and my car started shaking. As I headed off the bridge, I saw my tire roll down in front of me."
- Taking him to work on his second day at a fancy restaurant in Downtown Charleston, the young man said, "I work with a lot of beautiful women, and they are not wearing much either."
- Visiting from New York, the couple told me, "We couldn't believe the woman who walked out the

door in front of us and then came back and apologized for letting the door shut and opened the door. In New York, she might have spit on us."
- "If you call a restaurant in DC and they are busy, they hang up on you. That does not happen in the South."
- Visiting Charleston, the female artist said, "If I lived here, I would eat, drink, and paint my way through Charleston."
- The woman from West Africa said, "It's always been a dream of mine to live in the United States." Me: "How did you end up living in Charleston? Her: "I googled it. It's not too hot and not too cold here."
- I asked the guy, "Do you miss living in the Northeast?" Him: "Hell no, I'll defend Charleston in the next Civil War."
- I was raving about the magnificent houses around the golf course on Daniel Island and the older man said, "It don't suck."
- Visiting from Boston he said, "People are like in slow motion down here."
- Young man who lives locally talking about Mt. Pleasant: "I was in a liquor store and girls were wearing see-through shirts. That's how they are in Mt. Pleasant." (I'm positive I've never seen this.)
- The woman in Downtown Charleston said, "There aren't any men in this town."
- I asked the young attorney to explain to me what the very popular Southeastern Wildlife Exposition was in Charleston, and he said, "It's great; there are a lot of exhibits, shotguns, girls, and alcohol."

- She: "I love Mt. Pleasant; I think it will be my final destination."
- Woman from Indianapolis: "I'll take Charleston over an NBA game every time." (Indiana is known for loving basketball.)
- Me: "Do you like living in the Charleston area?" Him: "I didn't when I was young, but as you get older, you appreciate it more." (He's twenty-one.)
- "We used to call the town 'Plasticville.'" The woman had lived near Mt. Pleasant and commented on the number of women who had plastic surgery.
- Male: "I wrote an urban novel about Charleston, and I've sold about five hundred copies out of my store."
- Professional woman from Los Angeles: "People are so happy and hopeful here. That's why I moved to Mt. Pleasant from LA." (A few months after visiting for a bachelorette party.)
- Driving in Daniel Island, the guy in his twenties looked at the beautiful houses and asked, "What do they do?" I replied, "They don't do anymore, they did it."
- Male: "Sometimes I think the people down here have had their brains melted by the sun."
- I picked up a woman at Charleston airport arriving from New York City, and she said, "I love the air here. It smells better here."
- She: "Here in Charleston, if you spit on the street, it floods." (Rain does wear down the roads quickly.)
- "My mom and I have a tradition of walking the Ravenel Bridge early in the morning on my

birthday. The only problem is, it's early in the morning, and I'm not a morning person."
- If I stopped at the wrong time on King Street, the woman would have said, "Please officer, don't castrate my Uber driver for dropping me off here."
- When I told them how the horse carriage is directed through town, she said, "I can't even maneuver my car well."
- I said to a guy dating his girlfriend less than a year: "You should take her to Charleston." Him: "Maybe for the honeymoon."
- Bartender: "Sometimes it's hotter here than a doorknob in hell."
- "The best way to describe Charleston is hot and flat."
- Woman: "There aren't enough restaurants in Mt. Pleasant." (Trip advisor says there are 502.)
- The four guys in Charleston had been drinking on a boat. Arriving downtown, one of them said, "Look at that truck. It's got no tires and it's up on blocks—we should steal it." I said, "If you do, I'm going to take a picture of you doing it and hang it up here in my car for everyone to see."
- "The scenic view of Charleston is the best in the country; I fell in love with it."
- She: "We're going to a wedding here in Charleston for the son of friends we saw married here forty years ago. The wedding is in the same church."
- Guy in his mid- to late twenties: "I'm a compulsive liar. When we go to Hall's [steakhouse in Charleston], we always celebrate an occasion to get

a free bottle of champagne. The last time we were there, we celebrated my fifth promotion."

She Bought an Island

My rider's great-grandmother bought an island in the 1940s, maybe thirteen acres, in Charleston. She paid $30,000 and her husband asked if she could get the money back. She started her own restaurant and it's still popular today. My rider helps run the restaurant with her dad. There are only a handful of houses on the island, and most of them are owned by the family. The island is worth a lot of money, and they've turned down substantial offers in the past.

"I got cut badly and was bleeding, but I'd do it again."

The young woman told me this about her visit to The Pounce Cat Café in downtown Charleston. You pay an admission fee and can drink and pet rescue cats which are up for adoption. She "absolutely loved it, really."

Selling Real Estate

The real estate market in Charleston is oversaturated with six to seven thousand realtors. I asked one of the realtors how they succeed with all the competition. She said, "The way you overcome that is by doing things others won't do and focusing on being the best you can be. Realtors are already complaining that January is slow, but I have four listings in the first five days."

Working In Charleston

He said, "I lived in Myrtle Beach and was asked by my contractor to take an assessment for Boeing in Charleston to test my skills and knowledge. They paid me to do it, and then Boeing offered me a job. I spent six years working in Charleston and going back to Myrtle Beach [two hours away] on the weekends to be with my family until we bought something in Charleston."

When You Come to the Fork in the Road

Driving in Downtown Charleston is definitely challenging. The road conditions are difficult, and your car is constantly going up and down as you drive, like an amusement park ride. In addition to that, there are one-way streets, horse carriages, bicycles, and tourists walking everywhere.

One day, I came to a fork in the road, and I took it in the tire. The salad fork was still in my tire, and it destroyed the tire. This is how it looked when I tossed it away.

10

MOTIVATION AND INSPIRATION

I have been fortunate to have many rides that have motivated and inspired me. On the other hand, I have had some rides where I was the one who did the motivating and inspiring. Sometimes the ride had to do with a personal situation, and sometimes it involved someone who had overcome adversity or achieved significant success in their career. About fifteen of these rides are listed in my top fifty rides, and the asterisk next to the title indicates it is motivational or inspirational. Below are twenty-two more stories that I will always remember.

Riders That Inspired Me

The Future College Student
I had no idea she was in high school, because she spoke and carried herself as if she was older. I was heading home, and my last ride of the weekend was clearly my best one. It turned out that this was her very first Uber ride and I told

her it was going to be her best one. I got a laugh, but the ride changed when she told me that she was the only thing her mom had. She said, "My mom is my hero." When she was a baby, her dad and brother both drowned in a boating accident. "I want to go to the University of South Carolina for fashion design and make my mom proud." She told me she was struggling with public speaking, and as a former public speaker, I was able to give her some tips. I told her that she spoke very well, and I wished her well in school. As she got out, she said, "Thanks for all your advice; I'll never forget you." She was the first rider to inspire me when I was relatively new to this—I haven't forgotten her.

Inspiration Was in His Voice
He has a joy for life. Even if I hadn't seen him get in my car, I would have known he was special. The ride was filled with optimism and enthusiasm, and it was his and not mine. I did see him get in my car, unlike any other rider. He was in a small wheelchair. The double amputee put himself on the ground and took the wheel off his chair and then folded the chair and lifted himself up into my car. When he was six, twenty-one years ago, he was stricken with meningitis and was put into a coma. His two legs were amputated and some of his fingers. He told me that he was lucky it happened when he was six, because he has no memory of using his legs. They were never able to conclude where the meningitis came from.

In high school, he became a wrestler and a two-time state champion, and he was in great shape. He said, "It bothers me when people say they can't do something. I try to figure out how to convince them that they can." He enjoyed working as a counselor in a camp for disabled people, since going to that camp had previously been helpful to him. We had a terrific conversation, and he was willing to share a lot of details about his life. I know he had a good time, because he surprised me with a very generous tip when I dropped him off. The ride was unforgettable and worth a lot more than the money I made.

Turning Fifty
What are the odds this could happen? A woman ninety days from her fiftieth birthday had a list of ninety things to do that she'd never done before. She got picked up by a driver who had a list of sixty favorite foods he was working on eating before he turned sixty. It really happened, and she was my last ride of the day; she was spectacular. A social worker from Pennsylvania, she was in Myrtle Beach for a three-day fishing trip with a male friend of hers. It was her friend's dream to take this trip, and when he wound up with an expensive extra ticket, he asked her to come. After she boarded the plane, her friend was not allowed to board, since his driver's license expired six hours before the flight took off.

She was still determined to go on the trip, although she now had no equipment. I picked her and her equipment up at Walmart. She was excited but a little nervous, since she had never done this before and did not know anyone, either. We had plenty of laughs and I got her in the mood for her big challenge. With a great personality, I knew she would be fine, and we enjoyed talking about our unusual birthday quests. She said, "One of the things on my list is skydiving, but I'm afraid of heights." When I dropped her off, she was mentally and physically ready for the challenge, but she's on her own when she's ready for skydiving.

She's Running in Every State

It was a short ride, but very inspiring. The sixty-four-year-old woman from Minnesota was in town to run a half marathon. She said, "It takes me two-and-a-half to three hours to complete the 13.2 miles." She was running six more in the next three months, with the last one being in Hawaii in January 2023. Her goal, along with her brother and a friend, was to run a half marathon in every state, and they will be celebrating in Hawaii when they complete that goal. She will have accomplished this goal in about two years' time. She retired last year after a long career in social services. I didn't have time to ask her what her next goal is, but I'm sure it will be something special.

A Brave and Determined Mom

I was impressed and inspired by her. I know people go through all kinds of difficult struggles, but as a father of three, this ride took a lot out of me. As a single mom at the age of nineteen, she found out that her little boy was diagnosed with a rare disease, which caused him to have fifty seizures as a baby. The seizures had already caused a lot of damage to her son, who at four years old, could not walk or talk. She told me, "He's a happy child and he is always smiling." She watched him die twice and he was brought back to life. He is on special medication and has been doing well for the past two years.

He has already passed his life expectancy and she believes he is going to make it. She's doing everything she can to help him. I didn't need to be convinced, because I heard it in her voice; "I'm strong," she explained. She works full-time as a medical assistant, which she has always wanted to do. Her mom helps her a lot with her son. A few years ago, she had a very odd experience. She was in a mall with her son and a woman came over to her and said, "Has your son had seizures?" She said, "Yes," and the woman told her, "He's going to be all right, and you'll get through this," and then she walked away. I thanked her for sharing her story and wished her the very best. She has gone through a very tough four years and hopefully the worst is behind her.

The Christmas Gift
For Christmas weekend in 2022, I decided to give out five-dollar Dunkin' Donuts gift certificates to four riders who had the best holiday story. I wasn't disappointed, and this was the best one. She used to be a server at Waffle House and said, "I always spent time talking with my customers. It was Christmas Day, and I was talking with an older woman, and we were sharing some of the personal things we were going through at the time. She told me that every Christmas Day she goes to another Waffle House and eats chocolate chip pancakes, because that's the last meal her son had before she lost him. When she was leaving, I said, 'I'll see you next time,' but she said, 'You won't see me again.' I thought maybe she was really sick, or she was my guardian angel. Her bill was on the table, and she left me a seventy-five-dollar tip. I kept the bill." She texted it to me an hour later and I would have published it here, but it has the woman's name and credit card number on it. It says next to tips "$75.00," and in big letters across the receipt, it says this: I'M PROUD OF YOU!

Tragedy and Inspiration
She was about to graduate in psychology and pre-law and was then headed to law school. A relative of hers inspired her

to pursue law, but in a very unusual way. The relative was studying one night to improve his test scores to get into law school when he made an awful mistake after drinking. He got in a car and hit an oncoming vehicle on a bridge, killing two members of a family and injuring another one.

At the trial, the grieving family pleaded with the judge to be lenient since the drunk driver had a spotless record. The judge agreed and sentenced him to one year in prison, and for two years, he agreed to be a public defender. Her relative is an attorney today and has helped many people after his experience, which still haunts him today. My rider is determined to succeed as an attorney to help other people in need as her relative has, and I have no doubt that she will.

The KFC Chef
He used to be a divorce lawyer with four offices before he sold everything and moved to the South to care for his very sick son. After several years of caring for him, his son passed away. After a period of mourning, he went back to work. He got a job at KFC since cooking is something he loves to do. He has a wonderful personality, and he is very good at cooking. Customers regularly call up the store to see if "Chicken Matt" (not his real name) is working that day, because his chicken is better than anyone else who cooks it. He may be happier today than he was when he was a lawyer. He is passionate about cooking and his life. He is a true inspiration.

The Bodybuilder
When I think of a bodybuilder, I usually think of someone with bulging muscles and a very large physique. My female passenger told me she had just competed and finished fifth

in a bodybuilding competition at the age of fifty-four. She was thrilled with her results, because "I was the only one in my class who did not juice." She started competing at the age of forty-eight. She's a fitness trainer with twenty clients and she's raising three children by herself. I asked how she was able to accomplish so much, and she said, "It's all time management; I plan everything in advance." She keeps in shape by exercising religiously for only one hour each day. I was inspired listening to her, and I did notice that she didn't look a day over forty. She didn't have superpowers, but I think most people would agree that she is a Wonder Woman.

The Positive Guy
When I picked him up from the hotel in Myrtle Beach, he had only two quarters in his pocket. A friend set the ride up for him. He was in a good mood, but he had just had a rough night. He was at a wedding and lost his wallet with $300 in it. The wallet had not turned up. He told me, "There's nothing I can do, so there's no reason to be upset." He had spent the day relaxing at the pool. He can't get on a plane because he has no identification. He said, "If I have to spend two more days here, so be it. I love it here."

Earlier this year, he was in a motorcycle accident. He explained, "A car hit me, and another car ran over my ankle." The doctors told him he was going to lose his leg, but they were able to save it by putting a plate in it. He is a construction worker in Long Island, New York. I asked him about his positive attitude, and he said, "I got it from my dad, but my brothers are not positive like I am." If you were having a bad day, this story should cheer you up.

The Recovery
Four years ago, the twenty-one-year-old woman was a passenger in a car that was hit by a drunk driver in a truck. She was the only person injured in the accident and she was airlifted to the hospital. The doctors did not think she was going to make it. It took her two years to learn how to walk and talk again. She also had to work on regaining her complete memory. She had the side of her face reconstructed also. You could never guess any of this by looking at her; she's completely recovered. She's hardworking, friendly, optimistic, and very grateful to be given a second chance. She's also very determined and said, "Don't tell me I can't do something—I'm going to do it."

A Great American Success Story
We have all heard about people who come to America with nothing and achieve success, but how often do you get to talk to someone who did it? She had a beautiful accent, and she was from Romania (east of Hungary and south of Ukraine). She was excited to see I had a bill from Romania hanging in my car. She arrived here over twenty years ago "with only a backpack and shoes." She did not speak any English, but was helped a lot by watching cartoons on TV with captions. She was on a college visa, but after a month in New York, she decided to work and make something of herself. She said, "I was working at times for three dollars an hour. I worked my ass off. I was not going to give up."

Today, she is an executive assistant, married with two kids and living in suburban Chicago. She works for a very important executive and due to confidentiality papers, she could not tell me the company she works for. She loves her job, because "every day is a different challenge." When she first came to a local office in the South, she told everyone what she needed, and she learned very quickly that things move slower in the South. She was a delightful person to talk to and hopefully she shares her inspiring story with many other people.

The Dedicated Worker

We all have worked with people who have trouble getting to work on time. Some people are just always late, or they just aren't reliable, but my rider was remarkable. At forty-one years old, he was working at a Longhorn Steakhouse, and he was making quite an impression. He was restarting his life after making a big mistake as a kid and spending several years in prison. He had to get a starter's permit to drive, since his driving records were too old, so he rode his bicycle to and from work. He rode it ninety minutes each way, six days a week, and some days, after he had worked a twelve-hour shift. Trying to be optimistic, I said, "at least you get some good exercise." He replied honestly, "It sucks." When he had major problems with his bike, the managers at Longhorn all chipped in and bought him a new bike. I was bringing him to work after heavy rain the night before. I was impressed with his dedication and wished him well in his new life.

A Victor, Not a Victim

You can just tell that some people are going to do amazing things in their life, and this twenty-three-year-old woman was certainly one of them. She had just been in a bad car accident where her car was totaled, and she lost two teeth. She had a couple teeth replaced and did not seem fazed by the experience. She had three bartending jobs and was a manager of a retail store. She grew up in foster care and was the valedictorian of her high school class. She said, "I believe in being the victor, not the victim." After working as an intern at a funeral home and "embalming 1,500 people," she wants to own her own funeral home one day. She wants to move out west and described herself as "a planner." I'm sure she's going to accomplish whatever she wants in her life.

An Amazing Woman
This was a different kind of inspirational ride. I thought I didn't understand what she said, and I asked her to repeat it. She told me, "I'm taking my kids on a yearlong trip around the world." Her kids were six, ten, and twelve years old, and she had planned out the first six weeks of the trip. Her husband had a remote Wall Street job, and he was going to visit with them during the year. Her kids were going to attend school online and she was going to make this trip with them all by herself. She wanted to teach her kids about the world. The trip was really a tribute to her mom, who loved to travel and had visited all the African countries. She said, "I've already started a blog to write about this." I told her that she just made my blog with her ambitious plans.

The Artistic Dentist
He had had a twenty-five-year career as a dentist, having his own practice and currently working for someone else today. The most interesting part of his career is that he became a dentist at age forty.

He had started college many years ago, but he didn't finish it. He worked on several kinds of jobs—a tour guide, a painter, and many others. He took out his phone and showed me three paintings that really looked like pictures; they were extraordinary. He said, "I sold the last one to my sister for $2,300." Just trying to find his way, he went back to school and graduated with a 3.7 GPA. A professor told him that he could do anything he wanted and suggested he go to dental school, which would fit in with his artistic nature. He told me it was very hard, especially with only one other student around his age.

He'd been happy with his career, and he was fascinating to talk with. When he got out, he said to me, "It was a pleasure driving with you; you should charge extra for psychological counseling." I certainly didn't do any counseling, but his life experiences I have shared with other people. He'll be the one doing the counseling, just through my mouth. And, he's already had twenty-five years of experience doing great work in other people's mouths.

Can I Do Anything at All for You?

It was a short ride from his house to CVS for his heart medicine and then back home. In that short time, he surprised me and inspired me a great deal. When he got in my car, he was overwhelmed by the foreign bills I had hanging in my car, because he'd been travelling and collecting his own foreign bills. He said, "You gave me goosebumps, you put a smile on my face." He has stage 3 congenital heart disease. At the next stage, he would need a new heart. He had lost several people in his family to the disease. He told his doctor, "I refuse to bend to this disease." He'd been travelling with his son, but this week was a difficult one for him. I surprised him by giving him an extra Malaysian bill and he said, "Can

I do anything at all for you? I just hope I can ride with you again." He made my day, and this ride will always be one of those special short rides that I'll never forget.

The Single Mom
I thought she was in her mid-twenties until I found out that she had six children. The most striking thing about her was her bright pink hair, which reminded me of Julia Roberts in *Pretty Woman*. She was putting on her makeup and explained to me that she was raising her kids by herself and that she was thirty-six years old. She was only getting some support but was making money by selling creative things on Facebook and at a local store. She was overcoming some disabilities she had and had big plans for her business. She said, "Whatever it takes to keep my family together," as I dropped her off. I wished her well; she had me believing that she would succeed.

Riders Who I Inspired

The Couple Who Really Needed Sunshine
The sun was fighting to get through the clouds when I picked the couple up as they sat on the curb. The ride was only a few minutes long, and I asked them how they were doing. He replied, "You wouldn't believe me if I told you." He said that they had had a string of bad luck that week including their car breaking down. They went out last night and had a friend bring them home, but something went very wrong. They spent the whole night in the police station and hadn't slept much and were obviously down. I told them it was a good thing I picked them up since my business name

is "The Sunshine Man." I told them a couple of quick and funny rider stories and encouraged them to have a positive attitude. He said, "I heard a good attitude and a smile will get you somewhere." As I turned onto Ocean Boulevard, I said, "Like to Ocean Boulevard," and they both laughed.

As I pulled up to their hotel, the sun came out at the perfect time. I gave them my card and said, "If you ever need some help or someone to cheer you up, you can call me." I got out of the car to clean my mats and the guy got out on the other side and walked around to me. He shook my hand and said, "Thank you." I've gotten a lot of very nice compliments and tips over the years, but that moment was priceless. I knew I did a great job in only a few minutes, and I knew it meant a lot to them.

The Future Chef
When I picked the twenty-year-old woman up, I thought she had come out of a doctor's office, because she looked sick. I didn't realize that she was depressed because tomorrow was her last day at the restaurant. She was holding her headphones and told me I could listen to my music, but somehow, I got her to talk as she sat next to me. She was leaving her job as a dishwasher because they wouldn't give her a chance to be a chef. She had gone to cooking school, but the school suddenly closed. She wants to own a restaurant with her brother and knows that she can cook. "I have no real friends, only online," she told me.

She was working on a long-distance relationship with someone who came from a very different background than she did. I praised her for knowing exactly what she wanted to do, since so many young people don't. I encouraged her to keep working toward her goal and we talked a lot about relationships. I told her it was important for her to speak to someone about her depression. She was a lot happier getting out of my car than she was when she got in it, and I think we were both better off not listening to music and instead listening to each other.

The Server
I have picked up a lot of servers, but this is the one that stands out more than any other. I had had a challenging morning, but this ride changed my day for the better. I picked her up at a restaurant where she thought she was on the schedule, but she wasn't. She was quiet until she was able to reach her boyfriend. She had the call on speaker, and she started to cry. It sounded like she had cheated on him, and he wasn't ready to come home or talk to her. He needed time to "reflect" and he would be home when he was ready.

At the end of the ride, I shut off my app and tried to calm her down. I told her that he was obviously upset because he cared a lot about her and that he needed some time. I told her that most guys do not find it easy to talk about how they feel, and she had to stop calling him and spend time getting herself ready for when he came home. I gave her several suggestions, like getting some exercise or fresh air, taking a bath, putting on some music she liked, or cheering herself up however she could.

I told her that after being married thirty-seven years, it's important to realize that the other person in your relationship is not you. They don't think the way you do due to their previous experiences, and they handle things differently. They also don't always agree with you and that's OK.

She did calm down and thanked me for "being a good guy." Later, she gave me a very generous tip of twenty dollars, but whatever problem I was having that morning didn't seem important anymore.

The Panic Attack

As I pulled up, I could see that she was in trouble. The young woman, maybe around twenty-five, was in a hurry. She had been with her friends and suddenly she had to leave. She was having a panic attack and needed to get home quickly. I spoke with her calmly and asked her about her life and what she did for work. She was very personable, and I could tell she did well selling computers. "I've had to deal with panic attacks my whole life; it's hereditary," she told me. By the time I reached her place, she was much calmer, and she thanked me for getting her home. Unfortunately for her it was just another day dealing with her illness—I'm glad I was there to help her.

11

WORDS OF WISDOM AND ADVICE

I've been impressed with the lives my riders have had, their sense of humor, and the advice they've given me. Putting this chapter together, this is some of their advice. (Marriage and relationship advice is in the relationship chapter.)

She Said This

- The woman had met several famous people and treated them just like anyone else. She said what we really need today: "All you need is manners."
- Woman who has had a long, successful career: "You don't sell yourself in an interview, you sell yourself every day that you work."
- "Those who know don't tell, and those who tell don't know."
- "If you believe in your heart that you should do something, you should do it."

- Female rider: "I feel very blessed to have met so many wonderful and unique Uber drivers. I think God puts people in your life for a reason."
- She told me: "My friend Paul Farmer, who's a global health pioneer and recently passed, said, 'If you can't find the solution, be the solution.'"
- I asked the successful account representative what her secret for success was and she said, "Whatever challenge I have, I figure out how to get it done for my customers."
- Positive flight attendant: "We have to keep positive people together; you don't want that spirit to die."
- The overworked accountant was told by her last Uber driver, "Don't set yourself on fire to keep someone else warm."
- Woman: "If someone tried to pay me for doing a good deed, I would say, 'Don't block my blessing.'"
- The twenty-four-year-old woman said, "I'm just riding the wave wherever life takes me."
- She: "My grandmother taught me this: 'Work with excellence.'"
- She turned down a management job because "you can't raise a store if you're raising a family."
- Female bartender: "I believe in being a victor, not a victim."
- The woman said, "Laughter is better than Xanax."
- Woman: "I tell my employees not to bring their work home and [not to] bring [their] home to work."
- Woman with third child going to college: "It's not where you go to college, but it's what you do there."

- After losing her best friend to COVID-19 the day before, the positive, older woman said, "God puts good people in my life. I'm trying to make this a great day."
- Woman in her forties: "It gets better every year."
- Woman: "We need more love in this world."
- She said to me, "The world doesn't spread enough kindness."
- "It's important to smell the flowers and blow out the candles." (On letting things go.)
- "To have a friend, you have to be a friend."
- Woman: "My advice is, never work for a fast-food place when you're pregnant." Me: "As a sixty-one-year-old male, I'm going to follow that advice."
- Her mom had had a stroke in the past year after constantly watching the news and worrying about the virus. She said, "The news doesn't add anything to your life."
- Her two favorite quotes are, "Die with a memory, not a dream," and "Time is a commodity you can only spend once."
- "The world needs a little sunshine."
- The woman from Chicago said, "Laughter is food for the soul."
- Female flight attendant: "It's up to you to create your positivity and attitude."
- "Life is one big test."

He Said This

- My favorite quote is, "A closed mouth does not get fed." It means that you have to go out and get what you want.
- He was in Coast Guard law enforcement: "I treat each person like I would my father until they give me a reason not to."
- He said, "Small things go to a giant."
- He said, "When you open yourself up to the world, you make things happen."
- Him: "When I turned thirty, I did not care what other people thought."
- "Go out and do what you need to do—get it done, there are no excuses."
- He explained, "The most important thing that young people should spend money on is experiences."
- "My family believes that everyone has a purpose and that the world has a plan for you."
- Him: "You can't let chaos stop you from your goals."
- Finance guy: "Numbers don't lie, but people do."
- Wealthy man: "When you have money, you don't want to have the money in your name."
- Speaking about the virus, he said, "There's a lot of good that comes out of bad."
- His advice from his dad, "He told me when I was young, whatever you do for work, even if you're shoveling fishhooks, you should shovel more than anyone else."
- Male: "A woman does not make you smarter unless you're with one."

- Young man in his twenties: "When you have a passion for something, you'll get it done. You need to have the mindset of getting it done."
- Male: "I don't talk about work at home. I've already lived it once and I don't want to re-live it."
- Him: "I believe that you have to shine your light on the world."
- He told me this well-known phrase: "God gives his toughest battles to his strongest soldiers."
- "Finance is not essential; money is."
- Tax consultant: "You always have to look for opportunities."
- "I live by three principles: logic, fact, and sense."
- Robotics consultant: "The most important thing today is to be passionate about what you do and have people be able to see it."
- The pastor said, "The world needs more kindness."
- Sales manager: "I'm not sure where I got it from, but when I talk about enthusiasm, I tell people that the *-iasm* [stands for] 'I am sold myself.'"
- The Mexican chef who loves making pizza said, "If you don't love what you do, do something else."
- Sales manager: "I think if you do the right things, the universe puts you in the right place for things."
- I asked the man about his smile, and he said, "I've been through a lot of things in my life. If I'm not smiling, they win."
- "If you torture the numbers enough, they will confess to anything."

- Male engineer: "I tell my kids and any young person—whatever you're going to do in life, get an engineering degree first."
- Recovering from brain surgery: "You have to talk about what you want. It creates the belief and attracts what you desire."
- Me: "How do you slow down as someone newly retired?" Him: "I don't let anyone put me on their schedule."
- Recovering alcoholic: "If you have enough pain, you can overcome anything. A bottle is not worth prison."
- "A dog can't bark and bite at the same time."

Someone Said This

- My parents told me that I wasn't raised to bitch and moan. "If you have a problem, solve it."
- "Nobody can fix you; you have to fix yourself."
- "The secret to being successful is passion and commitment."
- "You don't want to be promising the world to someone when you don't have it."
- "The problem with communication is the illusion that it has been achieved."
- "A fish wouldn't get in trouble if it kept its mouth closed."
- Jamaican proverb: "A little laughter is better than a quarrel."
- "Technology is where all the possibilities lie."

12

FUN MOMENTS

With over ten thousand rides, there have been a lot of fun moments, and it would be impossible to cover all of them. Below are twenty-one rides that were special for different reasons, but the most common thread they all had was that they were really fun.

Enjoying the Meal at Outback

It was a perfect setup. I pulled up at the local Outback Steakhouse and I knew this was a very short ride, less than a mile. It was 5 p.m. I was hungry, and I had eaten everything in my car. I saw the older woman (in her seventies or eighties) slowly walk toward me, and she was holding one of those very large leftover bags that they give you. She looked like Robin Williams dressed as Mrs. Doubtfire, and when she got in my car, she kind of sounded like him.

I had never met her before. We said hello and I said, "Could you do me a favor? It's five o'clock and I have another hour to drive before I go home for dinner. I'm all out of food; could you not tell me how wonderful your meal was?" I was wearing a mask, but she could hear my smile and she delivered one of my all-time favorite replies in a very sweet voice: "Oh, that's really too bad; I have a lot of extra delicious ribs that I could share." She paused and added, "And I love to lick my fingers." Her house was across the street, and I was still laughing when I pulled into her driveway. I said, "Thanks for not telling me about your delicious meal." Getting out of my car she said, "I do have a mean streak."

The Four-Year-Old

His father was an emergency room doctor in San Francisco, California. He had a big car seat, and it was impressive how his father talked with and took care of him, trying to keep him awake so he would sleep on the plane. I asked if he could count to ten, and his dad said, "I don't think he can." I showed the boy my ten fingers and he counted each of them for us, maybe for the first time. I told the dad to grab one of the brochures and he pulled out the one with the pirate show, and the dad asked his son, "If you were in that picture, what would you do?" The boy replied, "I would help them with the fire. I want to be a fireman." I don't know what that little boy will do for work in the future, but I'm absolutely positive he's going to be a pretty impressive man one day.

All About the Dog

I had a great opportunity to interview the local anchorwoman about her job; however, her dog made it impossible. She had a little basket, and inside she had a Papillon puppy. We talked about having a dog since my wife wants to get a puppy and I've never had a pet. She told me that the dog was "her best friend" and that she takes her everywhere, including on a patio at a bar. She's also done commercials with her puppy on her television station. She told me the dog is very smart and can wave and I heard her say, "Wave, wave." I looked in my rearview mirror, and sure enough, the puppy was waving at me. I would have gotten a picture, but I was driving. When they got out, I took a picture of the puppy, but she wasn't waving at the time. I did get my finger in the picture, but I never thought I'd have a dog waving at me.

Visiting Bojangles

The twenty-two-year-old needed to get some biscuits at the local chicken place. While we were in the drive-thru, I could tell he was eyeing the girl in the window. When she was putting his order in his bag, I told him that she dropped her phone number in his bag. For a split second, I had him believing it might have happened and then we broke up laughing. He said, "I am going to go back there." I have no doubt he will.

The Bus Ride

He was upset when he got in my car. He was trying to get to work, and he was an hour late. He had been on a bus with six people about an hour and a half ago. A woman sitting in front of him had pulled down her mask to take a drink and the bus driver yelled to her that she had to keep it on. The passengers defended her, and the bus driver stopped the bus and called the police. Everyone was told to get off the bus. Not only was he late for work, but he lost two dollars on the bus fare. He was told he could get it back if he called the bus terminal, but he wasn't interested in it. He said, "What are they going to do, send me a two-dollar check?"

I said to him, "You've had a rough morning. Look at the sign above me that says, 'If You Can't Find the Sunshine, Be the Sunshine.'" I added, "Don't worry about it, you're even." I reached for my wallet and handed him two dollars, and he smiled and said, "Thank you." I said, "One day you'll get a chance to do something totally unexpected for someone and you'll remember today." I finally had a chance to tip a rider and I enjoyed it. He will tell that awful bus story many times in his life, but now it has a "sunny" ending.

Not Scott

I was picking up Scott from his home in the Charleston area and a woman came out of the house jogging and grinning. I knew immediately that I could have fun with her, so as she approached my car, I said out the open window, "You're not Scott." She got in the car saying, "Yes, I am." I replied, "No, you're not Scott." Her answer in between laughing was, "I am; why can't Scott be a girl's name?" I told her, "Because Scott is my brother's name—you're not Scott." Finally, she admitted that her husband's name was Scott, and I said, "Don't even tell me what your name is, I'm just going to call you, 'Not Scott.'" Several times during the ride, I called her "Not Scott," and when we said goodbye I said, "Goodbye,

Not Scott." I have told this story to dozens of riders who got in my car when someone else had set up the ride and I always get some laughs with it.

Encouraging Retirement

The woman from Minnesota told me that her and her husband may eventually move to the Charleston area, possibly the Isle of Palms, a beautiful area. Her husband, sixty-seven, has been a dedicated optometrist for most of his life and has been thinking about retiring for years. Having talked with many retired people, I discussed with her the hobbies he has and options such as working a day or two a week or volunteering in retirement. She was enjoying the conversation and I asked if she'd like me to write him a note, and I did: "Your wife was delightful to talk with. Start retiring and spend the rest of your life with her. The Uber Driver." She was very happy I wrote the note and I hope to pick them up when they move there and hear his reaction when he read a note from an Uber driver about his retirement.

She is Me and I am Her?

I regularly tell people that 98 percent of the people who get in my car have not been drinking since I drive during the day; this ride represents the 2 percent of the other riders very well. The four women were visiting Charleston on a girls' weekend, and they were enjoying their visit. I told them that I brought my shovel from New Jersey to South Carolina in case I needed it. One woman from Pennsylvania, said, "You should come to Pennsylvania and shovel my snow."

The woman was a fourth-generation children's shoemaker and a business owner, but when I asked, "Who said that?" her reply was, "I'm Jeffrey, the Uber driver." She said that she was me and I was her. I asked, "How am I going to explain this to my wife?" To add to the silliness, her boyfriend's name is Jeffrey. I told her I was from Phillipsburg, New Jersey, and she said excitedly, "I've been to the Chick-fil-A there." I replied, "How many drinks brought that comment on?" I enjoyed being part of their group for a few minutes and I sent them a copy of the story I wrote about them.

The Hair Lady

How do you turn a ride into a fun ride? You could just say this was a weird ride, but I did have fun for a couple moments. My rider was annoyed immediately since I was looking for her on the other side of a building. She said almost nothing before her first of three stops, but I did see her fixing her hair. When she went into the store, I got out to clean the car quickly and the picture below shows what I found on the back seat:

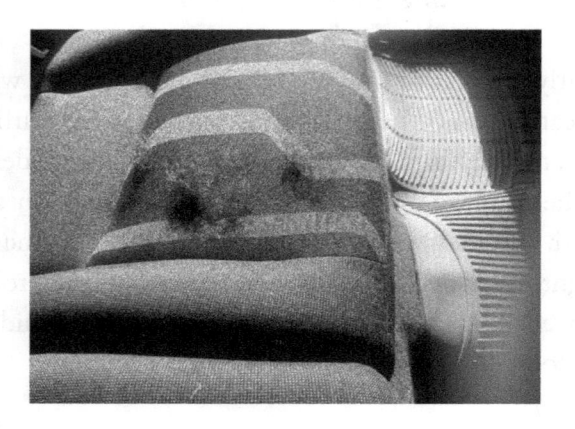

Looking at the three clumps of hair, I knew this was my chance. I snapped the picture, and when she came out, I said with a smile, "I was just cleaning the car and found this on the back seat. I'm guessing you don't want them, but that's more hair than I have on my head." She did smile and took her hair back, but she was still unhappy. I had a pretty good time and I'm still enjoying that ride right now.

Singing Opera

She was a college student locally and a music major. She had just won a singing contest singing opera. I asked her, "Would you sing a line of opera so I could hear your voice?" She did, and she had an amazing voice. When she got in the car, the sun was shining. Now, as she got out, it was cloudy. I said to her, "Remember, even if the clouds are out, your voice will always make the sun shine for others." It was a pretty good line and she loved it.

The Ark of St. Louis

It is pretty common for drivers to complain about short rides, but some of my most memorable rides were very short rides. I was in Downtown Charleston picking up a college student. She started to flag me down like a cab and I immediately started laughing. She sat directly behind me, and this three-minute ride was full of laughs. I asked, "Where are you from?" She replied, "St. Louis," and then she paused and said, "St. Louis, Missouri." I was laughing again and asked, "Is there another St. Louis?" She told me, "No, some people don't know where St. Louis is." I quickly added, "It's in Missouri." We were both laughing now.

She said there wasn't much to do in St. Louis, and then I added, "What about the ark?" I laughed harder and said, "Now, for the rest of your life you can talk about the Uber driver who asked about the St. Louis Ark." She got out of the car laughing; little did I know that there really are college students who think St. Louis has an ark and not an arch. One guy even told me, "I've had people ask me if I've gone in the ark."

Teaching McDonald's History

There are two different things about McDonald's I have taught people. I have asked a number of riders this question: "How did McDonald's make their fortune in the beginning?" I did have two people guess the right answer after seeing a show on the company. They made their fortune in real estate. The individual store owners had to rent the store property from the company and the company cleaned up, but not with food.

Secondly, I had four women in my car from the Midwest and two of them worked for the McDonald's corporation. I asked them if they knew what the most famous McDonald's commercial was of all time. They had never heard the jingle "You Deserve a Break Today." It was written in 1971 by future music star Barry Manilow. I started to sing the beginning, "Get a bucket and mop, scrub the bottom and top," and they played the jingle on their phone. One woman said, "That's pretty catchy."

"Yes, that's why it's their most famous commercial."

In case you didn't know, the rest of it is, "Tell me what does it mean, that McDonald's is clean. You deserve a break today, so get up and get away, to McDonald's."

Promoting the Movie Yesterday

As a big Beatles fan, I could not wait for the movie *Yesterday* to come out. I had been promoting it in my car to many riders because it was such an original idea. (You should see it, it's a fun movie.) Finally, after many months of waiting to see it, I was going with my wife on Sunday, and I could not wait. My last ride on Saturday night turned out to be a couple from New Jersey (where I'm from) and I told them Beatles trivia and other info to get them ready to see it. The guy said, "Why don't you come see it with us?" I would have loved to, but his wife made me laugh when she added, "I'm more excited about you seeing the movie than I am about me seeing it." I hated to turn them down, but how could I explain to my wife that I went with people I didn't know instead of her?

The Wicked Witch and Snow White

I picked up a woman at a hotel who had had a long day working in housekeeping. I was driving her to her second job for another five-hour shift. She told me that she hadn't had anything to eat since breakfast. I started to give her fatherly advice that she had to eat, and then I remembered my apple. I told her that I had a big, delicious apple that I was going to give her, and she had to eat it. She started to laugh and then she accepted it and was devouring it. She told me that her husband usually checks with her to see if she ate. I had to tell her to slow down because she was also laughing. I said, "If you choke, how am I going to explain this? I'm the wicked witch and I gave Snow White an apple and she choked on it? "She enjoyed the apple and the laughs; I can't remember if I ever washed that apple. Please, don't tell her.

She's in the 2 Percent

I usually tell riders that 98 percent of the people who get in my car have not been drinking. Since I drive during the day, it may be 99 percent, but the point is that almost of my riders are pretty normal and sober people. I went to pick her up at a Mexican restaurant and she was with a friend and her husband. Immediately, I could see that she had had a lot to drink, so when she got in the car, I said, "You're part of the 2 percent!" I explained it to her, and she thought it was very funny.

She asked me to take a picture of her and hang it up in my car near the picture of the Super Bowl ring from another rider. She said, "If you do that, I'll give you points." (Whatever that means.) She asked me to stop at a liquor store, and as she walked out holding her beverages, I snapped the picture. It's been hanging in my car for many months; she's a big hit, and she's wearing that same smile she had on when I picked her up.

He Doesn't Talk Too Much

The retired man from Michigan made an impression on me immediately. He was seventy-five years old and had been retired from social services for twenty years. When I got out of my car, he became only the third person to tip me before the ride. He was about to celebrate fifty years of marriage, but he told me that his wife and daughter tell him that he talks too much, and I told him that it wasn't true. It had been a great ride and I told him I was going to help him out. I wrote a note on a piece of paper that said, "I loved talking with him—he doesn't talk too much. The Uber Driver." I told him to give my note to his wife and daughter and I'm sure he did. How much fun did he have on this ride? Later, I realized that he tipped me two more times on the app to become the only person to ever tip me three times for one ride.

"Happy Birthday to You"

On back-to-back days I got to sing "Happy Birthday" to young riders celebrating their birthday. On a Saturday morning, a dad and his nine-year-old son were my first victims. When I found out it was his birthday, I asked him if I could sing "Happy Birthday." He said that I could, and his dad asked me if I was a singer. I told him I wasn't, and he joined in with me to sing to his son.

The next day a mom and her seven-year-old daughter were celebrating her birthday. I told the girl about my singing yesterday and although she was a little shy, she said I could sing to her, and her mom joined me. I told both kids that this was probably the last time an Uber driver would sing them "Happy Birthday."

Driving Mary Poppins

She really wasn't Mary Poppins, but she had a delightful British accent and was wearing a big hat. Originally from Ireland, her and her boyfriend were now living in New York City. I called her Mary a couple times, and we talked about two Disney movies, *Mary Poppins* and *Saving Mr. Banks*. She was enjoying our conversation as much as I was, and then she sang a few bars from "Supercalifragilistic." I told her a few of my British stories and this was one of those rides that was full of laughs for everyone.

The Woman Who Does a Chicken Dance

Chicken is my favorite food, and I've had a number of "chicken rides" where my rider and I talk chicken. One day I picked up a local woman who works the "chicken bar" at the deli in the local supermarket. She told me that when the rotisserie chicken is ready, they yell out, "Yeehaw, come and get it!" and one worker comes out from behind the counter and does a chicken dance to music. Customers take pictures and sometimes they join in. I have to see this, and I might join in if she's dancing.

On another ride I gave her, she told me this: "I have six tattoos on my body; four are dogs of mine I lost, one is my dad who I lost recently, and the other is an eye on the back of my head, my neck. I used to tell my three kids that I needed eyes on the back of my head, and I've had one for twenty years." She said she's had quite a life and has considered writing a book about her life. I asked her what the title would be, and she said, "Oh My God, What Now?" She has made me laugh a lot; wait until I start writing her biography!

The Note to My Daughter

My daughter created a podcast for people in the technology industry. She gave me a hat for my car that says, "Proud Podcast Dad." From time to time when riders are in the tech field, I tell them about her podcast. I was driving with two guys, and I brought up the podcast. One guy asked if I had been on the podcast and I laughed and said, "I'm really technically deficient; I can use the Uber app though." He said that my daughter should interview me as someone who is deficient in technology but is able to use it effectively to get people where they are going. I laughed and said, "How about you write her a note?"

He wrote: "I, Michael, recommend that your dad joins your podcast as a guest discussing how Uber is connecting someone who is technically deficient with people across the globe.

Kindly, Director of Finance

I could not wait to give it to my daughter, but I was never invited on her podcast. I wonder, with a published book, do I have a chance now?

The Ride to Atlanta

It was an unexpected moment and it happened at midnight on a Saturday evening. I was driving on Saturday after 5 p.m. I had already driven ten hours that day and I was planning on finishing around 6:30 p.m. I accepted a very long ride to the Atlanta, Georgia, area from Myrtle Beach. It was about five hours away and three hundred miles. The rider needed to get home and he gave me a fifty-dollar tip before the ride to take him.

The actual ride was uneventful, and we stopped a couple of times for gas and food. I pulled into his driveway and said goodbye, and a moment later the app told me I had made $408 for the ride. I was tired, but after seeing the amount I made, I was wide awake and drove another hour or so before I stopped to get some sleep. I took the next day off and arrived home before noon. It is easily the most money I've made on a ride and $458 will always be a special number for me.

13

GREAT QUOTES

There are interesting, unusual, and funny quotes throughout this book. I have split these quotes into a bunch of categories. The quotes that have an asterisk are rider comments that made my lists of favorite comments over the past four years.

Animals/Insects/Pets

- *The young woman said, "I'm going to a reptile convention. I help rescue exotic animals and right now I'm helping a tarantula."
- *Same young woman a year later: "I rescued three tarantulas and the first day, one of them got loose and my sister found it crawling up my back. I was screaming and gave them all to someone else that night."
- *Him: "When I first came to South Carolina from the west coast, I saw a seven-foot gator on the golf

- course. I picked it up from its tail and it started hissing." Me: "What did you do then?" Him: "I put it down and ran."
- *"Geese don't poop in the air."
- Male: "I'm an animal lover. I've had a pet tarantula, lizard, rats, and others. Rats are very smart; you can call for them and they just jump into your lap. I have roommates now, so I only have cats."
- "My dog [a boxer] doesn't know he's a dog. We were getting our motorhome ready to leave and left the door open and could not find him. After looking for a while, we found him, sitting in my driver's seat ready to go."
- The twenty-year-old guy said that he has about two hundred pets. "I have about 140 fish and another sixty assorted pets." I asked if he had a zebra and he said, "Unfortunately, no."
- The older woman told me, "I have two large dogs that are over one hundred pounds." She started doing impressions of how they sounded; it didn't sound very good.
- If you want to put someone down, he said this was a Midwestern saying: "May an elephant caress you with his toes."
- The man said, "A father died in the house I'm living in. That red cardinal is always around and when someone yells, 'Hello, Charlie,' it always turns around."
- "My dog is just larger than a hamster; she's barely a dog."
- She: "Years ago at work, we all brought in food to share. Two younger women wouldn't eat my food

because I had a cat, so I told them that the cat sits on my shoulder and helps me cook."
- "We need a bigger backyard for our six pets and so we can get more pets."
- She told me, "On my bucket list is that I want to visit all the best zoos in the world. I love animals. I want to build a very large animal shelter, like a hotel without rooms."
- Man: "I like dogs better than people."
- Woman: "My seventy-pound dog picks his own bandannas to wear."
- She: "I used to have a crazy dog. The boxer was a killer. He had five skunks under his belt, and we had to get rid of him after he got loose, broke into a neighbor's house, and killed the cat."
- She: "I'm obsessed with animals. I grew up with eight dogs, five cats, and eight fish in a fish tank."
- Woman: "I'm not going on a safari here with all the mosquitos. I hate them, but they love me." Me: "Who has better taste?"
- "My husband and I wanted a new hobby during the pandemic. We had two dogs and a cat already, so we got five quail."
- Him: "I ride my bike four to five miles with my dog running with me." Me: "How did you do it in the beginning?" Him: "She really didn't like it at first."
- I asked the female dog-sitter this: "What advice can you give me on how to get used to having a dog for the first time in my life?" Her answer was, "Remember that a dog thinks like a dog. People take what dogs do too personally."

- Dog trainer: "Dogs need structure and training first and the affection for the actions you want them to take."
- I asked the two women in their twenties, "Did you have a good time here?" She said, "It didn't suck, we had a blast." Passing the wax museum, which has King Kong hanging on to the Empire State Building, she said, "Shit, look at that ass."

Food

- *At thirty years old, he'd finally accepted that he was unique, and he explained it this way: "A good bowl of pasta has a lot of pasta that looks the same, but you have to have spice in that bowl." Me: "So you're the spice in a good bowl of pasta?" Him: "Yes."
- *When he made pizzas in the Virgin Islands, he would be asked why his pizza tasted so much better, and he would say, "Happy dudes make happy foods."
- *A woman said, "Paula Dean has killed more people with her recipes than anyone."
- *The large man said to me, "I didn't get like this by exercising."
- She: "I don't eat any sweets—no cookies, candy, or cake. I never have, I don't like how they taste." Me: "Has not eating any sweets your whole life made your teeth good?" Her: "Hell no!"
- Woman in her thirties: "When I was three, I had a dream that I was eaten by a chocolate Kiss, and I became an almond—my parents laughed their asses off."

- Picking the hotel employee up at 7 a.m. from working the night shift, we talked about how her favorite meal in the morning is pasta. She said, "If you haven't had pasta at 7 a.m., you don't know what you're missing."
- As the woman got out, I said, "Make sure you have everything; if you leave food, I'll be eating it in five minutes." She replied, "What if I poisoned it?"
- Female: "I started eating uncooked pasta as a kid and I still eat it now; sometimes I just snack on it."
- Young woman: "My ride-or-die is chicken." (She loves it, and I do too.)
- Male: "I've eaten uncooked noodles, but they'll kill you when they come out."
- Young guy: "I had the worst pizza in my life late last night. I ordered it and it was cold, and I threw up all night. I threw up pieces." Me: "You wouldn't happen to have any pictures, would you?"
- First words from a rider: "So you don't like salad?" (?)
- She: "If I could eat sushi all day, I would."
- "We flew in from North Carolina for a burger at Hamburger Joe's."
- She: "Ice cream is like magic for me." I added, "You make it disappear?"
- Talking about her favorite chicken from college, she said, "It's uber, uber fresh." Me: "Did you just tell an Uber driver that something is uber, uber fresh?"
- The male college student seriously asked me, "Is there a place that has buffets on four floors?" Me: "Did you think that up when you were awake or sleeping? I think it's a great idea."

- I asked the two couples how they liked the restaurant that serves a lot of meat and the vegetarian said, "I don't like meat, but the meat was very good."
- "There's different crap at different restaurants."
- She: "I hate all the food down here in the South; I mainly eat sushi and salad."
- "I don't like buffets, because people's arm hair can get in the food."
- Man in his early fifties: "I only eat one meal a day, for dinner. When my body starts feeling sluggish each month, I fast for four days straight, only drinking water."
- When I told the guy that a female rider said that after working the night shift, her favorite meal is pasta at 7 a.m., he said, "7 a.m., 6 a.m., 5 a.m., 4 a.m.—anytime is good."
- She was a starving dance contestant and said, "I could eat a cow now." I doubt she ever had a hamburger.
- "I love pizza, but it can hurt you."
- "I may have to eat ramen the rest of my life."
- Female agreed with me: "I would eat barbecue now." (7 a.m.)
- He said, "Why would a roofer risk his life going up on a roof when Chick-fil-A is offering a one thousand dollar starting bonus and paying twenty dollars an hour?"
- While eating Hamburger Helper for breakfast, the rider said, "If it's in the fridge, I'm eating it."
- She told me, "On a job interview in college I was asked, 'If you were an item on the McDonald's

menu board, what would you be?' I was a vegetarian and I completely froze. I couldn't think of what was in a McDonald's; I hadn't been there since I was a child."
- He's from Texas: "My brother and I make expensive bourbon and I'm going to talk about it at Greg Norman's Australian Grille. We always joke that maybe we'll make enough money one day that we can eat at one of these places. We usually stop at a convenience store on the way home from them."

Drinking Something

- *She'd lived in Myrtle Beach twenty years, and I asked, "Where are you from?" She: "I'm from my mom." (Drinking alcohol.)
- *On New Year's Eve, she said, "You should hit one of those deer so I can skin it and have deer sandwiches."
- *First guy: "I don't know why my finger hurts." Second guy: "You put it in my mouth at 4 a.m." First guy: "You bit my finger?"
- *He bought me a Gatorade because "It's important to hydrate." Me: "After I drop you off, I'm going to dehydrate at a gas station." Him: "Well, I live on a dirt road, and you can dehydrate all you want there."
- *"Uber was created so I could go out at night and drink mimosas."
- Sitting next to me, the young woman had had too much to drink and suddenly touched my arm, which made me jump, and she said, "It's probably

a good idea not to touch the Uber driver." A few minutes later she said, "I have to fluff my boobs."
- The morning after she had been drinking, she said she was still recovering. I had no idea until she said to me, "Are you a triathlete?" I was wearing shorts; maybe she was looking at my legs?
- The engineer and the department head of a college had had a few drinks, and after joking with them, the department head said, "Alcohol is OK for this week, but it's not a part of our curriculum."
- She: "I hate coffee, especially the smell. I just got off work six hours ago and I must go back in. I just have a big glass of wine and I'm good."
- "My English teacher told us that her and her friends were drinking and one woman got a tattoo of a bowl of mashed potatoes on her stomach."
- The coffee store manager said, "People enjoy the irony that coffee makes you go."
- I asked him, "What is your favorite sport?" He said, "Day drinking."
- She had been drinking when she looked at a carriage ride brochure I had and said, "I want to kill some of those horse carriage drivers." (She was against cruelty to animals, but not people.)
- Young woman: "We were celebrating her birthday and we did drink a lot. We weren't drugged, mugged, or raped, but I did shake a tree."
- Female bartender: "I told the guy that his girlfriend needed to go home, and a few minutes later, she started peeing on herself. The clueless boyfriend tried to clean it up with a cup."

- The female college student sitting in the middle said, "You can't even tell I drank the most wine. We're twins [referring to the girl next to her], but she's one year older."
- Man: "I just got a DUI. I've been driving fifty years drunk, and they finally caught me."
- Coming off the casino boat where she had some mimosas, the young nurse said, "If I jumped off the ship, I could have been a mimosa mermaid." Hours later, I told a female bartender about this, and she said, "I'm going to make that the drink of the day—the Mimosa Mermaid."
- "I'll go into Starbucks to order; I have to show them a video of what I want."
- I picked up the two couples at 5:30 a.m. from a closed bar. Me: "Closing down the bar?" Him: "No, we were doing some landscaping." Two of the landscapers had to be helped into the car.
- The sleep-deprived young woman on Sunday morning had been drinking the night before. She said, "I'm an effin' academic weapon."
- When she found out that I write about stories riders tell, the young woman who had been drinking said, "If you want a sex story, I'm about it." (I wasn't.)
- Male: "I used to have a $68,000 truck, but I had to cut it loose after the DUI."
- The twenty-five-year-old woman said at 8 a.m. on a Saturday morning, "I'm going to stop partying tomorrow."
- She had been drinking, but she was discussing what would happen if she got in a fight. "I would

probably get in a fetal position and suck my thumb."
- "My twin daughters had just turned drinking age and they got an Uber and went out and got drunk. My son went out hours later and the Uber driver asked, 'Do you have two sisters?' They'd puked in his car and did the same thing in another Uber."
- The two bartenders had too much to drink on their day off. I put their white cooler, which looked like a medical container, in the trunk. Halfway home, one of them yelled out, "I forgot the cooler." I replied, "No, it's in the trunk. I have it and you're going to get it back as long as there's no chicken in it." (My favorite.) He answered immediately, "There's a human kidney and four Coors Lights."
- I told several guys in their mid-twenties on a Saturday who were here for a bachelor party, "If you're going out tonight, demand and prices will be high for riders." Him: "Oh no, we're going to be in our rooms studying the Bible." Me: "I'd like a picture of that." Him: "We can send you a lot of pictures."
- The two women had too much to drink, and they wanted to go to the nearest convenience store. The destination on my app said Berlin and it was ninety-three hours away. The women said, "We are not going to Berlin," which was true. Fortunately, the app could not give me a route to take them to Berlin, Germany, so I just took them up the road a couple miles.

Transportation

- **Best Comeback By a Rider:** Picking up the two women at the hotel, the tall one had a very tall suitcase and the short one had a very small suitcase. As I started to move the tall one, I looked at the tall woman and said, "Did you take any furniture from there?" Her reply was quick: "No, it's a body."
- *Female: "I hate driving. If I'm driving, you're going to get hurt." Saying goodbye to me, she said, "I hope no one hits you."
- *Young woman: "I had a male Uber driver who spent the whole twenty-five-minute trip telling me about his Beanie Baby collection. It was painful. I nearly jumped out of the car."
- *"You should do Uber at the border; you won't have to travel far. You can call yourself, "Sunshine Coyote." (My business name is The Sunshine Man.)
- *She said, "You swing both ways with Uber and Lyft?"
- She said she missed her flight because "I was stuffing my face at an all-you-can-eat buffet. God wanted me to have one more day of fun."
- She: "Sometimes the GPS doesn't let us be great."
- Woman: "You have ten thousand rides, so if you made just $1 for each one, that's a lot of money!"
- After telling them I was going to take a bathroom break, but decided to take one more ride, she said, "Your bladder is more important than us getting to the airport earlier, so you can stop if you need to." When I dropped her off, she ordered, "GO EMPTY YOUR BLADDER!"

- Defending the fact that drivers in South Carolina say that Ohioans are bad drivers here, she said, "If you take drivers from South Carolina and put them in Ohio in the snow, I'm pretty sure they would be bad drivers too."
- Picking up the family of three from the beach, I said, "I need to make sure none of your suits are wet." Woman: "They're not, do you want to check?"
- She told me, "My rental car was stolen. I left the keys in the car and the car unlocked."
- "I don't like going on a cruise; it's like going to Golden Corral with a bar."
- Two Romanians had just gotten off their ship and told me, "We have fifteen thousand containers on the ship."
- Male: "I was at the DMV yesterday and I failed the eye test twelve times; I couldn't get the last letter."
- Former Uber driver: "I used to tell people they should sign up for Uber in case they have an emergency. If you can't pay your rent three days before it's due, go out and drive."
- She: "I'll sit up front. I don't want you to be subservient to me."
- Young guy: "I sold my car one night in a bar because I was bitching about it. Funny thing is, he's only seen the car at night."
- Me: "How long did it take you to get used to your Tesla driving you?" He said, "Five minutes. You're supposed to have your hands on the wheel, but I hooked up a weight so my hands can be free."

- When a woman's car moved into my lane and cut me off, the young man said, "I wish I had a milkshake to throw at her."
- Him: "It was such a nice day I decided to walk to the airport." (From North Myrtle Beach twenty miles away; he gave up after an hour.)
- Him: "I've had some really neat things happen in my life. I once got a free trip to Mexico to purchase tequila."
- I asked the two Mustang enthusiasts: "What's the best thing about Mustangs?" One of them said, "Everything," and the other said "Nothing," at the same time.
- He was flying back to New York because the sewer had overflown and destroyed the apartment he was renting out. I wished him luck, and he said, "Well, it's going to be shitty for a while."
- The sign in the window said, "Kids up in this bitch." I asked my female rider what it meant, and she said, "I think the driver is more confused than we are."
- She: "On my flight home, a very large woman sat next to me and spilled her coke all over me. They didn't have much to dry me off, so I sat all wet for three hours."
- The young woman said, "When I get my car back, I'm just going to Billie Eilish my way to work every day."
- Male: "I had a really bad motorcycle, but it was a blessing in disguise."
- After the GPS said to turn left when it was clearly right, my female rider said, "That bitch makes my

- life miserable every single day." (Her townhouse is difficult to find.)
- The young woman said, "I want to go on a cruise, but I'm afraid of water."
- She: "If I had my druthers, I'd never drive again."
- Woman: "I was in Columbia, South America, when I accidentally got into a cab that was a fake cab—I was a little kidnapped."
- The female limo driver said, "My nephew is a limo driver, and he was giving a wine tour in New York and all seven people gave him a hundred-dollar tip."
- Woman: "Two years ago, I told the company who owned my car to come pick it up. I'm now saving $700 a month."
- He said, "After a very close call on a plane, I could not fly without knocking myself out first. Finally, one day six years later, I just got on a plane and said, 'If it goes down, it goes down.'"
- Young guy: "My boss is paying me forty dollars a week to go ten minutes in an Uber and drop off another employee's check." Laughing, I said, "Since I'm driving you, I should get a cut of that." At the end of the ride, he tipped me twenty dollars.
- Her Uber driver kept staring at her, and then asked, "Are you dating?" The woman in her early sixties, who has been mugged seven times (in New York) said, "You better pull this car over right now; I know how to break a nose in three places."
- Male sales manager: "I called American Airlines' customer service and chose the option for them to call me back when someone was available. They

said it would be twenty-four hours. It turned out to be less time, but I missed the call because it was 3 a.m. on a Saturday."
o After telling him I had three people in my car today with serious medical problems, the seventy-year-old man said, "I can add to that. I was hit on a motor bike in the middle of an intersection. I was in the hospital for seven weeks and broke almost everything on the upper right side of my body. I broke my ribs, and a stint was put in for my heart. I've been out five weeks and I have no pain."
o "I rented an Acura from Avis out of the DC Airport, but it was an unusual car with tinted windows all around it. I had all the information to pick it up and I went to the gate, scanned the info on my phone, and left. When I had to change plans, Avis could not find my reservation—there was no record I had a car. Two days later, I went back to where I got it, parked it, and left, and never got charged. We think it might have been a car that was repossessed, but it wasn't in their system."
o He bought a $60,000 Audi electric vehicle and drove it twelve thousand miles in a year and a half. "Three days before I was going to sell it for a nice profit, a big red light came on saying, 'Exit the car. Do not park near a building.' The dealership told me to let it cool down and drive it to the dealership, it might explode. They couldn't give me a loaner [they had none], could not get the parts, and finally, the parts showed up in pieces to fix it, but they

didn't have the tools. It's been four months and I'm going to get it now."
- He: "When I was twenty-one, I went to a party at midnight. I drove into a large neighborhood with only one gate you can get in and out of. I couldn't find the party and didn't have a phone number, but I couldn't get out of the neighborhood. It took me six hours to find the gate. I almost ran out of gas."
- Two couples visiting Charleston on business were out on the water with other business associates and had a horrible experience. Woman: "I saw it. Something hit the second mate and knocked him overboard. The Coast Guard found him twenty minutes later, but it was too late."

Communicating

- *The four women from Nashville were dressed and perfumed up for Saturday night. Me: "There's a lot of perfume in this car." Her: "Do we smell good, or do we smell like a whorehouse?"
- The female rider explained the other rider's comment, "Do we smell good, or do we smell like a whorehouse?" by saying, "In a whorehouse, there are a lot of smells, some good and some not."
- *Young woman: "I love corny jokes, so I got a tattoo that says, 'corn,' and it's just above my knee." Me: "It says 'corn'?" She showed it to me—*corn*. (Corn-knee.)
- After telling this story to another woman, she said, "She's not as corny as ethanol."

- *"We can't see you, we're in the parking lot. We are three medium- to large-sized humans."
- *She: "When Jeff and his wife move to Charleston, we're going to be doing a nightly stand-up routine."
- *He made his point when he said, "Sometimes you just have to get the stupid out of people!"
- Me: "How are you today?" Male: "I'm amazing." Me: "Why are you amazing?" Male: "I'm always amazing. I decided a few years ago that I was tired of being negative; life is too short." Me: "What did your family say when you changed?" Male: "'Who the f--- are you?'"
- She: "They call me crazy because I speak my mind."
- On the phone she said, "If you know where we are, come get us—I'm cold."
- I told him that he had a great sense of humor and he said, "I don't need anyone to tell me how great I am, I do that every day."
- He was on the phone with his airline and said, "If they don't let me check in when I get there, I'm going to flip over the counter and then call you back." Hanging up politely, he told me, "I have been escorted out of an airport on a golf cart."
- The Southern girl in her twenties told me, "I don't have a Southern accent because all my family are English teachers. I can't even try to talk Southern."
- I was picking up Tiffany, and a rather large man walked up wearing a mask. Me: "You're not going to tell me that your name is Tiffany, are you?" Him: "No, I'm not until I put on my makeup." (I did not react until he laughed.)

- Me to the woman: "You have a great laugh." Her: "I do?" Me: "Don't tell me no one has told you that before." Her: "They usually tell me to shut the f--- up."
- When she asked Siri (her phone dad) to call someone, Siri said something like, "One moment." She replied to me and said, "Siri is late, just like me."
- The British guy insisted on hearing my British accent when I told him about the British race car driver. He laughed and said, "Americans trying to sound British do 'hoity toity English' like you, or 'posh English.'"
- She: "I like the idea of people, but when they open their mouth, I know why I need to have alone time."
- I thought he said, "May your day be ever painful," but he really said "pingful." (The sound on the app when I get a ride.)
- He was trying to say he didn't want to be too positive or rah-rah and said, "I don't want to be too woo-woo."
- Young man: "I don't ever talk that much." (He talked almost the whole trip, and I listened.)
- She was telling a joke about Dubai, and I misheard the punchline. I thought she said, "fun stuff" but she really said, "Flintstones." She lectured me: "It's funnier when you hear the joke the first time."
- Male: "I'm a great conversationalist, but today I'm off my game."
- Male: "I believe in C. F. Stupid ['can't fix stupid']. I have a t-shirt that says, 'I'm a mechanic but my wrench can't fix stupid.'"
- The woman in her late twenties told me, "I don't have a family or kids and when I'm on vacation I like to wear a bikini, but I felt a little uncomfortable around a

bunch of kids; do you know what I mean?" Me: "I've never had that exact experience, but I understand." She: "I like to curse too, and I had to tone it down."
- She: "When I win the lottery, I'm going to fund my cell phone invention and one day be on the cover of Forbes magazine."
- Male: "I had a number of things that I needed fixed around the house, nothing major. I had someone come in and then they texted me an estimate of $30,000. I texted back, 'Is that $30,000 or $3,000?' They said it was $30,000, but they could do it for $28,000. I got someone else who did six days work for $6,000."
- She: "When I came down here, I was trying to find a doctor's office, and I asked a man on the side of the road. He told me to turn after the 'Horse Trader' sign, so I was looking for it. I finally gave up and called the office and told the receptionist what he said. She put me on hold and then had the entire office on hold listening to me telling the story again. They all burst out laughing. The man with the thick Southern accent had said 'Harris Teeter' [a store], not Horse Trader."

Health

Below are some health comments and then a section on comments on the pandemic.

- A woman who was recovering from drug addiction told her boss at the barbecue place, "If I could

- smoke meth all day and do nothing, I can certainly smoke meat. I'm going to get a t-shirt that says, 'I smoke meat, not meth.'"
- Her: "What changed my life and made me more positive was being in a terrible car accident. I broke both hips and it took me two years to recover while I was raising my autistic child."
- Him: "It takes thirty days to get rid of a parasite. It's not fun."
- After surviving pancreatic cancer and two surgeries while she was pregnant, the woman told me, "I wake up every morning trying to make the day better. Nothing bothers me anymore because I know it could be a lot worse."
- When I told her the wait time was two minutes before Uber started charging her, she said, "I can't even pee in two minutes."
- "When my twenty-one-year-old sister has a headache, she describes it as 'a little mouse running around in my head stabbing me.'"
- Male: "I was in rodeo for ten years and did not get hurt, but I was on a sled with my young daughter and I broke two bones in my back and was laid up for six months."
- She: "One of my friends years ago fell from a crane and broke almost every bone in his body, but he lived."
- He: "We would have walked to the restaurant, but I'm having a problem with some gout. They are about to cut my foot off."

- Male in his early thirties: "I lost over one hundred pounds. I got a stomach virus working in a school cafeteria, and then a cold, and then I was dehydrated and got pneumonia. I was sick for two months and have never gotten my old appetite back. I can go four days without eating."
- Young male: "I'm the kind of person who craves chaos."
- "I've done the walk on the beach for five minutes and that's enough for me."
- Young woman: "If I'm going to be sick and alone, I'd rather be sick and alone on the beach."
- "I'm as balanced as an elephant on a tightrope."
- "My doctor said he doesn't lecture me about being overweight because I'm very healthy due to a lot of exercise."
- "My dad has a rare illness. If anyone around him is sick, he gets it and spends 24–48 hours puking. He has no immune system."
- Me: "What do you for fun?" Him: "A little streaking sometimes." (Joking.)
- She: "I don't like rain, because I don't have any control over it."
- Woman: "I've been drug-free for four years and I've helped fifteen other women with God's help remain drug-free."
- The man explained, "When that balloon [from China] was flying over our area, it had chemicals that came out of it, because people started sneezing a lot afterwards."

- Woman: "I try to throw out ten things each day in my house. When you throw things out you don't need, you feel better."
- Male: "Life hasn't started taking shit away from me like my memory and health."
- She said, "Anxiety is my copilot."
- Taking him to the hospital, he told me, "I may have broken my elbow. I dived into a pool at my bachelor party and it wasn't deep enough, and I put my arm up to protect my head."
- The young woman told me, "I cured myself in six months of having severe anxiety by eating small doses of psychedelic mushrooms."
- She: "I like to be happy; doesn't everyone?"
- Woman: "Every time I was making a big change in my life, I would have the same dream that my teeth had fallen out."
- She: "My dad has written down his dreams every night since college. One night, he had a dream about a guy that he hadn't seen in many years. The next day, he got a call that the guy suddenly died giving the eulogy for his mom."
- Thirty-six-year-old man: "The forties are the best times of our lives." (How would he know?)
- "The doctor said my brain was scrambled in the accident."
- He: "I was hypnotized on the phone by someone who is helping me overcome my faults, and it's helping me."
- Woman: "Adults only laugh about four times a day, and kids laugh about four hundred times a day."

(Actually, it's seventeen and three hundred, but who's counting?)
- The man with stage 3 degenerative heart disease said, "I refuse to bend to this disease."
- Male: "If you make me laugh, I'm going to have to piss in your car."
- "After my car accident, the EMT told me to squeeze his hand while they gave me pain killers for my other broken hand. Later at the hospital, he told me that I squeezed his hand so hard he was getting X-rays, because he thinks I broke his hand."

Pandemic Comments

- *The older woman was angry that she had to wear a mask in my car and did not talk during the ride. Getting out, she said, "I hope you don't die with that on, it gave me pneumonia. I usually tip extra for this, but not when you do something like this."
- *Woman in her late twenties: "The COVID vaccine is the only vaccine I've ever had. My boyfriend convinced me to get it due to my health. When I was a child, my mom didn't believe in vaccines. She worked in a doctor's office and forged all the vaccine paperwork."
- Woman in her twenties: "When I had COVID, I felt great; never felt better. I was in quarantine for two weeks, had no symptoms, and I didn't have to get up to go to work at 4 a.m."
- "They make the virus sound like your skin is going to bubble up."

- "If we're careful, the virus allows us to do new things."
- The young man told me, "The pandemic gave me a chance to change my way of life."
- Him: "When I first got tested for COVID, it was like they were pushing up to my brain and swabbing my eyeballs through my nose."
- She said, "My aunt is a CEO and she refused to get vaccinated. She believes COVID is made up."
- He: "During the pandemic, the AA Zoom meetings were very important, and they are still going on today."
- Her: "I'm going to get my lips done. When I stop wearing my mask, I want people to see something different."
- Male: "I was recently traveling in Mexico as a special guest, and I wore a mask; I didn't want to pee in someone's cornflakes."
- Woman from Maryland: "At the very beginning of the pandemic, I was in a Dick's Sporting Goods store with my son, and I got a call from the Department of Health. My son's French teacher was exposed to the virus, and they wanted to know where he was. I told them he was with me, and they told me to get out of the store immediately."

Famous People

- Jeffrey told me this: "When I was in college, they thought it was funny to call everyone named Jeffrey 'Jeffrey Dahmer.'" (The serial killer.)

- Quoting comedian Rodney Dangerfield, he said, "What's the difference between an oral and anal thermometer? They taste different."
- Female: "When I worked at a concession stand at Yankee Stadium as a kid, I got a fifty-dollar tip from Denzel Washington."
- When I told them that I've written a lot of songs, he said, "You must be writing anonymously for Justin Bieber and Maroon 5."
- The only woman to ever talk about Hugh Hefner: "He must have had a bad childhood."
- He: "I once did a charity event where I was bartending with boxer Joe Frazier. I wasn't too happy that we had to share tips with him."
- "We bumped into actor Bill Murray, and he told my ten-year-old son, 'Don't tell anyone you saw me, or I'll bite you.'"

Holidays

- The morning after a Halloween party, she was still dressed in costume and said, "I'm a Playboy Bunny, but I've lost my ears."
- Male chef the day before Easter: "I wanted to cook rabbit for Easter, but several people said it would traumatize the kids."
- *I called him on the phone and asked, "Where are you?" He said, "We are across the street from a large Jewish-like candle thing." Me: "I got it; I'm Jewish, and it's a menorah." His name was

Christian. (Below is the picture of the menorah in the middle.)

- Mom: "It took me three nights to wrap all the presents and my three kids unwrapped them in fifteen minutes."
- Young woman: "Last night I was celebrating my birthday, but I was arrested and accused of being drunk."
- I said to a female rider on Valentine's Day, "No woman should have to work on Valentine's Day. You should tell your boss." She replied, "I did, and he didn't go for it."
- Young man: "My Christmas gift this year was not going to jail."
- Taking her to her company Christmas party, she said, "Last year at the party, I was new, and they pulled names from a hat and gave away money, up to $5,000. I won $300."

- She: "When I was seven, I was concerned that Santa wouldn't be able to visit since we didn't have a chimney. My mom said he would come through the fire escape, but I didn't believe her."
- "I got no gifts for Christmas but the chance to see 2023."

Sleep/Aging

- *Working in the nursing home, she said, "The oldest person we have is a man who is 108 and he drives his own truck every Sunday and just got a girlfriend."
- *I told her about my male rider who said at 6 a.m., "I haven't gone to sleep. I hope you're not a narc." The woman laughed, snorted three times and said, "Sorry, I'm so embarrassed that I snorted, but not like the guy did in your story."
- The young man got in my car and said, "I woke up this morning and my voice is deeper than when I went to sleep. How long is puberty?" (six to twelve months—maybe he was seventeen?)
- She: "I've been getting up early my whole life." (She was twenty-five years old.)
- She said, "When I turned twenty-five, I got tired."
- She knows a woman who is 106 and the woman said to her, "I didn't get to be 106 by accident. It was from eating well and being active."
- She: "I usually get about five hours of sleep. I have three cases of Red Bull at home, and I drink three cans a day."

- Young guy early in the morning who hadn't slept: "I think you've been in a movie. You have a very soothing voice—you can put a person to sleep. I mean, in a good way."
- He said, "As you get older, you have to get your bones working. If you need to put WD-40 on them, do it."
- Male: "I can't sleep eight hours and keep my body stationary—I usually get three to five hours of sleep."
- Male: "There's a fine line between Friday night and Saturday morning."
- She: "If you're not aging, you're dead."
- Her: "I turned forty-one yesterday, but I was seventeen the day before." Me: "You had a really long day."
- "Lots of people don't know the difference between fifty and fifty-nine years old." Me: "Nine years?"
- The older woman was not happy with how she was aging. She said, "As men get older, they look more distinguished."
- He said, "I'm thirty-one, but I'm really an old soul."

Retirement

- As the couple got in the car, I asked, "How are you tonight?" The man, who turned out to be a retired cop from New York, said, "Good. I haven't had the urge or desire to kill anyone today." (Joking.) Laughing, I said, "Is it urge or desire?" Him: "That's open to interpretation." (He had an annoying confrontation with someone yesterday at his house.)

- The twenty-three-year-old worked two full-time jobs, and he told me, "I'll have plenty of time to rest when I retire."
- Male: "I don't miss the stress, but I do miss the people."
- Him: "I love retirement more than I loved accounting."
- "When I retired, I was an Uber driver for one month just to piss off my kids. They didn't think I would do it, but I enjoyed it."
- He: "When they stopped listening to my ideas, I retired."
- I asked the seventy-five-year-old man, "How long did it take you to get used to retirement?" He said, "It took me one day. The old football coach Bum Phillips once said, "I'm not planning on doing nothing and I'm not starting until noon."
- I asked the woman, "Was it an easy transition when you retired five years ago?" Her: "No. I went into therapy and I'm still there. If you're waking with nothing on your schedule to do, it's depressing."
- I asked him, "How are you adjusting to your first year of retirement?" He mumbled and all that came out of his mouth was something like "bbrrtt-bbmm." (Probably having a tough time.)
- The retired female cop from New York was wearing a shirt that said, "If you pinch me, I'm going to punch you." She said, "My coworkers made that for me because I used to say it at work all the time."
- Me: "How are you adjusting to being newly retired?" Him: "I don't know; I'm taking a lot of naps."

- The man said, "When I retire, I'm going to get on my son's nerves, because he gets on mine now."
- Retired female school administrator: "I don't care if I never see another child the rest of my life."

Music/TV/Movies

- *The female attorney said, "Paul McCarney is the only eighty-year-old man I would trade for my sixty-year-old man."
- Telling her about the above comment, she said, "I prefer George Clooney." She knew the month and the year he was born.
- My rider was raving about IPTV and telling me what I needed to get. I said, "Before I do that, I have to get something important—my wife and I never bought a TV here." Shocked, he said, "A TV is like having a fork in your house."
- Me: "My wife and I decided again not to buy a TV [after five years without one]. He said, "It's un-American, even people in third world countries have TVs." Later, I said, "I like to finish driving and head home between six to seven p.m." He: "Why go home? You don't even have a effin' TV!"
- The very busy executive, now retired, said, "I didn't watch TV for thirty years. I didn't even know what ABC and NBC were."
- He said "*Sesame Street* and *The Electric Company* are responsible for me having a perfect Midwestern accent."

- I was told on the show *Sister Wives* there is "a guy who is a stay-at-home thinker; he reads a book a day and then tells his wives what it was about."
- Having lived in Colorado for thirteen years, he said, "I've seen five hundred shows at Red Rocks. There's nothing like it in the world. If you have the chance, you have to see a concert there. Just do it."
- Female in her twenties: "I'm unique. I enjoy reading Shakespeare while I listen to classical music."
- Woman: "We saw The Beatles last night; I mean, a cover band of The Beatles."
- "The Three Stooges were really stupid."
- Me: "If you were stranded on a deserted island and could listen to only three singers or groups, who would they be?" The former DJ said, "Bob Marley, Biggie Small, and The Temptations."
- I asked the couple how their experiences were with Uber drivers on this trip, and he said, "Is this *Undercover Boss*?"
- "Phish is the most popular band that no one has ever heard of."
- He watches the television show *Blue's Clues* with his daughter. "The theme song is so catchy I find myself singing along and I can't get it out of my head for hours."
- He told me, "This is my 294th Phish concert."
- "My Uber driver said he had been offered a role in the movie *Black Panther* three times, but he turned it down because he doesn't like attention."
- "I was performing bluegrass music with a band for a State Department cultural program at an upscale

ceremony in Saudi Arabia. A very official-looking guy came over and asked, 'Do you know "Country Roads" by John Denver?'"
- Me: "Have you ever seen a swing bridge?" Her: "You mean like the one in *Indiana Jones and the Temple of Doom*?"
- He said, "I'm upset today because I fell asleep watching a series of shows where people play cards to save the world. Now I don't know where I left off."
- The rapper told me that when I write songs to known music it's called "jackin' the beats," which I did not know. I said, "Do you perform somewhere, or do you just rap for friends?" He fell asleep next to me. My next rider, a woman who was very tired, heard this story and said, "I guess he was rapping too hard last night."

Education

- *Teacher: Her name is America and she ordered the ride for her sister, who told me America always wanted to come here from Costa Rica. She lives here now in South Carolina and her students call her Ms. America.
- The older man was very impressed with the Uber app and said, "I know everything about you, even your sex life."
- "I would have had straight A's in grammar school, but they decided to grade spelling."
- "Liberals are more about the optics, how things look, and conservatives are more about how things are."

- The woman who had not been drinking said, "I go to Wake Forrest." Me: "What are you majoring in?" Her: "Philosophy, but I graduated." Me: "When did you graduate?" Her: "Last week. I forgot. It's fresh in my mind."
- She just graduated the day before with a political science degree. She said, "Political science doesn't have to be one side against the other; we are all Americans."
- She: "I was president of my sorority. I went through a lot of s---, but I'm a better person for it."
- Female college student: "If my life depended on it, I would not go back to being in high school."
- I asked the guy in his early twenties, "Did your strict upbringing give you a strong work ethic? Him: "Absofuckinglutely."
- He: "Whenever I get in an Uber, I learn something."
- "My friend, who is fifty, is the smartest person I've ever met, and he loves to read. For years we've asked him if he could read *War and Peace* in one day. Last Saturday, he read 1,200 pages and finished by 4 p.m. He said it was slow reading."
- The twenty-one-year-old told me, "I think I've read a few thousand books in my life. In high school, I read two hundred books in one year, and they put a picture of me up on the wall for reading the most books."
- "The largest manufacturer of tires in the world is Lego."
- "I'm giving a presentation today in my college class on people who like Jewish people for the wrong reasons."

- "My wife is a pre-K teacher; she brings all the diseases home."
- The sixteen-year-old college students told me, "I started kindergarten when I was three, and when I was four, I opened up our home computer to see what was inside."
- The female teacher in her first year said, "The best thing about teaching is the impact you have on a life."
- The female teacher explained that one day, a six-year-old boy approached her with a closed hand, and she thought he said, "I have a small penis for you." I asked him to repeat it, and he opened his hand; he had peanuts for me."
- The eighth-grade teacher in her first year said, "The best thing about teaching is the impact you have on a life."
- The female professor said, "Students are more entitled today. I told them that I would not accept late work, and one student said, 'You can't do that.' I told him I could."
- The teacher went to sit down at the hotel pool an hour ago and said, "It felt like hot coals. When I got up, a wasp flew out and I yelled out the F-word, because I was in a lot of pain, and my beer went up in the air and spilled on me. I tried to apologize to the people in the pool and the child, but they spoke another language." Me: "Did you tell your husband already?" (He was not there.) She: "I sent him a picture; I have a big welt."

Miscellaneous

- *The two women had about eight shopping bags from the outlet mall when I picked them up. I said, "What did you get me?" The younger woman said immediately, "A speedo." She paused and added, "Do you know what that is?"
- "I'm selling my blood for $600 a month and my rent is $1,000 a month. I'm almost living off my blood."
- Male: "I don't talk about work at home. I've already lived it once, and I don't want to relive it again."
- I asked him, "Do you have any plans for the holiday weekend?" He said, "I'm going to be lazy." Me: "Are you any good at it?" He: "I'm the best."
- The woman from Texas said, "I have a sign in my bedroom that says, 'Even when it's cloudy, I still believe in the sun.'"
- Eighteen-year-old male: "I found out that life is expensive."
- "I love people. I believe in their existence."
- Woman: "I'd live in a shack if it was only a couple hundred dollars a month."
- The group of girls had not been drinking yet that morning when one saw the sign that said "House of Jerky" and asked, "What kind of jerky is at that house?"
- "I know a lot of miserable rich people."
- He was talking about Masters, the Gentleman's Club, when he said, "Masters is a first-class organization."

- The very unique woman accurately said, "You'll never meet anyone like me."
- Woman: "My life is a comedy."
- "I have a beard and dark hair; I already look like a criminal."
- She: "I bought a positive cube on Amazon, which has something positive on all sides. When I come into work, I toss it up in the air to see how the day is going to go."
- The woman had a rough year, which included a divorce. She said, "2022 can f--- a duck." (Probably an original comment.) She's going to publish a children's book next year and added, "I'm going to kick ass in 2023."
- "I hate Mondays. I remember the smell of Monday from my childhood."
- He said, "The former President was a real butthole, but he did do some very good things for the country."
- A few guys in their twenties asked me, "Are there any hot girls you can refer us to?"
- He said, "I think I would have been very successful in [Ancient] Greek times."
- "The highest state-paid job in every state is a head football coach."
- She told her supervisor, "I can control my mouth or my face, but not both."
- He tried to sell to me: "You should invest in my business, you're the kind of person who can invest."
- Me: "What are you going to do when you get back in the job market?" Young black woman: "I want to

promote how important it is to breast-feed." (We then talked about breast-feeding.)
- "If you ask any more questions about my job, we're going to have to kill you."
- "I think if a job title has more than five words, it's made up."
- Me: "You look very familiar." Him: "I'm just really good looking."

… 14

RIDES FROM THE TWILIGHT ZONE

If you have seen the old television show *The Twilight Zone*, you know that the shows were not normal shows; something was just not right in them. Many were written and produced by a brilliant writer, Rod Serling, in the 1960s. Many famous actors and actresses appeared in the show, and the episodes were known for a surprise twist at the end.

In over ten thousand rides, there have been a handful of very, very unusual rides. Since I drive on the sunny side and my enthusiasm and optimistic nature leads to many fun rides, there are times that I came face to face with the other side. Here are a dozen rides that just were not normal.

Rock 'n' Roll and Hitler

I've only worked one New Year's Eve, and it was a pretty good night with nothing strange happening later in the evening. However, the most bizarre ride came early, around 7 p.m., when my rider texted me that he'd be standing at the corner with a guitar. I could not miss him. He was tall, with a full beard, a big smile, and a guitar. The ride lasted about three minutes and I was taking him to a Chinese restaurant. It was a remarkable three minutes. He was talking quickly, and our conversation went something like this: I asked, "What are you doing tonight?" Him: "I'm going to play some rock 'n' roll music." A few seconds later he asked me, "Do you know where I can play some music tonight?"

He asked where I was from and I said, "New Jersey." Then, he asked if I was Jewish and I replied, "Yes." His reply was, "I can't understand why people hate those effin' Jews. I love Jews."

He then asked the strangest question I've ever been asked as a driver, "Do you want to hear my Hitler joke?" I was almost at his destination, and I was just trying to be pleasant for a little bit longer, so I said, "OK." His joke was, "The more I read about him, the less I like him." Whether I said "oh" or "OK," I'm not really sure. I pulled up to his destination and said goodbye, and as I pulled away, he waved and gave me a big smile. Moments later, he rated me a one out of five, either because I didn't laugh at his joke or because I was Jewish. I don't think he was drinking; I just think he had some mental health issues. My weirdest ride? Yes, this is it.

Navy Guys in the Twilight Zone

There have been several *Twilight Zone* episodes where military guys, astronauts, or regular people are going somewhere, and when they return, the world has changed. My two riders experienced this for real in 2020. They were on a submarine with 140 others on a special mission and had no contact with the world for a good part of a year. They did not know about the pandemic. Pulling into a foreign port, they were told to make a mask out of their t-shirt, and they were given a report on the pandemic for the first time.

One of them said to me, "I went to shake hands with someone and they said, 'We don't do that anymore.' It really freaked me out." We experienced the pandemic day-by-day, week-by-week, and month-by-month, but they were thrown into a completely changed world.

The Falling Refrigerator

I was driving my passengers to Folly Beach in the Charleston area. We were in heavy traffic and we were finally getting close to our destination. A few minutes earlier, I had told the four guys from the Northeast how friendly people are in the South. A pickup truck turned into the middle lane, put its signal on, and then cut in front of me. There was so much room, a second pickup truck did the same thing, but much faster. The turn was so sharp that a refrigerator tipped over in the back of the truck. The driver, a young kid of maybe eighteen, got out to pick the refrigerator up. He was staring at us, and he looked angry. We had been talking and laughing and we were completely puzzled why this kid was staring us down. A couple minutes later, he went to turn left and I passed him on the right. He leaned over to the other side of his truck and stuck his hand out the window and pretended to have a gun and shoot at us. None of us had any clue why he was upset—I got away from him as fast as I could.

The Saddest Ride

It was an unusual and very difficult ride. Honestly, it was an awful ride. I picked up an older man, probably in his seventies. He had been in Charleston a few days from Kentucky. His son had had a serious medical issue earlier in the week when his blood pressure hit the roof and somehow damaged his brain. There was still a lot he did not know, but his son could not move some parts of his body and at times he was acting like a child.

The story got worse because the son had recently lost his job, and two months ago his son had to bury his wife after a brain aneurysm. Two years ago, the son had to bury his only child who died in a car accident. I felt awful for this dad, and I told him I would say a prayer for him.

The Ride That Wasn't a Ride

How can a ride be recorded as a ride when the rider never got in my car? It's not easy to do, but I've done it twice. I was relatively new to driving and I pulled into the Marriott Hotel to talk to the manager with my app still on. I had a rider the day before leave a jacket in my car and I wanted to make sure they got it back. As I stood there talking to him, I got a ride, and the woman who ordered it was standing close enough to me that I could have touched her. We weren't close to the door, so I said to her, "I'll be with you in a moment," and I finished talking with the manager and turned toward the door. The woman was at the door, and she yelled across the lobby, "We're going to walk it," and she walked out. I had no idea that it was a place nearby, but she never canceled the ride.

My app froze and I could not end the ride. Being relatively new, I started the ride, ended it, and called Uber Support immediately so the woman would not be charged. It was taken care of except for one thing—it recorded as a ride, and she got to rate me. She probably got a message asking how her ride was and she thought I was trying to rip her off. She rated me a one out of five and she never knew that I made sure she wasn't charged because she didn't cancel the ride.

The Argument

I was not just driving for this ride; I was in the audience for this intense debate between a female chemist and a male engineer who probably worked for the same company. It would have made for great television. It was an early Saturday night, and they were arguing about work. They had had a few drinks, but they were able to have a reasonably intelligent conversation as they went back and forth. She said, "We don't need people like you to come in to solve our problems." She later added, "I want to kill you." (Not that reasonable.) She wasn't dangerous, just very passionate. Toward the end of the ride, he said, "I wish I was more aggressive in this argument; I know I could win this." I told him, "After thirty-six years of marriage, I know that by sometimes not winning the argument, you actually win it." She replied hysterically, "That's what every effin' man in this country needs to learn." I asked if they were together, and they said they were "friendly, sort of." She gave me a hug for my one comment when we got out of the car.

The Negative Ride

When I dropped him off, I had two thoughts: I felt sorry for him, and I felt like I needed a shower. I would have liked to help and encourage him, but all I could say to him was, "Sometimes the best thing is to move somewhere else and start over." He had lived here in Myrtle Beach for five years with his wife and dad. His dad passed away a couple years ago and his wife left him, and he was bitter. He was willing to talk, and I let him vent. He said about living here, "The people suck, the wages suck, the politicians suck, and the weather sucks." I had this ride before the pandemic, so I hope he got a fresh start somewhere. I won't forget this ride, but I'd like to.

The Very Angry Woman

The pandemic has been extremely challenging for everyone and one thing Uber drivers needed to do is follow the rules that Uber had about wearing a mask and having your passengers wear a mask. I gave over four thousand rides following those guidelines and only two women had awful reactions. As I pulled up into her driveway, the woman was standing there, and she was probably around sixty years old. When she saw me wearing a mask, she said, "You're not going to make me wear that, are you?" I calmly said, "It's Uber's rules." Visibly angry she replied, "They don't work. I'll wear it, but you're the first driver to make we wear it." (It was early 2022.) As she got in, I calmly said, "When you ordered the ride, you agreed to wear it, and when I start driving in the morning, I agree to wear it, and then when I drop you off,

Uber asks me if you were wearing it." She replied, "I don't want to talk. I'm going to the BMW dealership."

I was silent for twelve minutes, and as I went to drop her off, I said nicely, "Have a nice night." Her reply was unforgettable: "I hope you don't die with that on. It gave me pneumonia. I usually tip extra, but not when you do something like this." She walked away believing that she made me angry and that she had won. Her words clearly said a lot more about her and her problems.

Going the Extra Mile

When you move from New York to South Carolina, it's a big step, but what if you're legally blind? I accepted my final ride of the day that took me about an hour in the opposite direction I was going. The twenty-nine-year-old woman had a sixteen-year-old cat and she'd already had a truck move some furniture for her. Her mom had come down to help her get settled, but unfortunately, she moved into an apartment complex she called, "the projects." She didn't stay there very long, and when I met her, she still had a few more things to get over to her new place, twenty-five minutes away. When I pulled up, she said, "You've got a lot more than you bargained for." I filled up my van with stuff, including a litter box that did not stink, and we were on our way. She was very nice and told me she moved to "get a change of scenery." We arrived in the dark and I had to point her in the direction of the back of the building. I made about six trips bringing everything upstairs for her.

She had said I should leave everything on the curb, but I'm not leaving a legally blind woman in the dark to carry a bunch of stuff around a building and up a flight of stairs. The ride turned out to be fifty minutes all together and I believe she had her parents in New York give me a forty-five-dollar tip for my efforts on the app. It was my final ride of a long day, and I got some serious exercise.

Like the old *Twilight Zone* episodes, this ride had a twist. I sent this story into a YouTube show about driving rideshare ("Show Me the Money") because it was such an unusual story; most drivers would have canceled it for many reasons. A few weeks later, I came up with the idea of giving out an award each month for a driver who went the extra mile. Along with The Rideshare Guy (a blog, YouTube channel, and podcast company that empowers drivers and helps them earn more money in rideshare), we are giving out a one-hundred-dollar gift certificate to deserving drivers who go the extra mile and it all started with this ride.

My Big Mistake

What happens if you're having so much fun and in such a great mood you don't dial it down for your next riders? It happened one time, and this is an example of what you don't do when you're driving. It was Super Bowl Sunday and the rides all day were terrific; I spent a good part of the day laughing. About 4–5 p.m. toward the end of my day, I picked up a couple at a hotel. The name on the ride was a name I had only seen as a male name, so as the woman got in the car I said, "I guess he's (that name)." I use this and variations of it all the time and I get a laugh from my rider. Sometimes, the rider will joke about it, and their line is funnier than mine. She told me it was her name and when I asked how she got the name, she said something like, "My parents were hippies. They're a--holes and I don't deal with them anymore." I laughed, but I wasn't sure if she was joking.

The guy asked why I wanted to know about her name, and I told him that I'm a collector of names. I told him my best name story and he said, "That sounds made up; did you ask his mom?" Then he asked me what Jeffrey means, and the woman said something that wasn't friendly, and I still did not get it. That's when he said, "Can you just get us to our destination?" I said "sure" and "I'm sorry," but I was stunned. I thought they were funny and were in a good mood like I was, but they weren't. Later, they gave me a one-star rating, and I deserved it. I wish I could have sent them a written apology, but this is as close as I can get to it. I am sorry.

Did the Pilot Move the Train?

The routine pick-up in Downtown Charleston to the airport should have been easy, but instead it turned out to be a ride I would like to forget. I could tell the rider was going to the airport by the distance of the ride. I had one main street to cross over before arriving at the condo where the rider was. There was heavy traffic, and right before I crossed over, a freight train started traveling across the road near the condos. I crossed the main street and stopped behind the train. I texted the rider that I was stuck. I could not tell if the rider was male or female, but they suggested I go to my left and try to get around the train. I gave it a shot, but when I turned toward the other side, the train was still there. Suddenly, the train stopped, and it started going backward!

I could not believe my good luck. It moved just far enough back, and as I crossed over the tracks, the rider was standing there and flagged me down. I asked him what time he had to be there, and he said, "Don't worry, I'm the pilot." We had a great conversation, and fifteen minutes later, I got a text asking me, "Why are you almost at the airport?" I had a very sick feeling. In my rush to get the rider after the train incident, I did not ask for the rider's name, and he never checked to make sure I was the right Uber. It was perfect for both of us, but it was a big mistake.

I apologized to the rider on the app and canceled their ride. The pilot canceled his ride and he felt bad and gave me $40 to work out the details with Uber. When I called Uber, they told me to keep the money and forget about it. I messed up and wound up with a very good ride and a big tip, however, there is no record of that ride. If I crossed the street before the train, none of this mess would have happened.

The Ride that Just Wouldn't End

My longest ride to Atlanta was six hours away, but somehow this ride seemed longer. It started on a Sunday morning as a sixty-five-mile ride to the Florence train station, which would take eighty-five minutes to get there. Two recent high school graduates were trying to get home to North Carolina. During the beginning of the pandemic, it took them an hour to get me. Their train was leaving in seventy-five minutes; I hoped it would be delayed. The pressure was on me—the next train was eleven hours later.

The train was delayed, but so were we, and we missed it by two minutes. I told them before we got there that I could continue the ride if needed, and I did. It was two more hours to the next station. Before we got in the car, we used the restroom in the empty train station. When I came out of the restroom, the girl was standing there with all the luggage. She looked upset, and we grabbed everything and headed to the car. At some point, she slapped her boyfriend, blaming him for missing the train. For the first hour, he calmed her down, and she fell asleep. He called his mom; he was crying on the phone, and she said she would meet them at the station.

When I arrived at the station, I got one of the biggest surprises of my life. As I took a bag out of the trunk, the girl said, "That's not ours; it was at the train station." I couldn't believe it. Somehow, I'd picked up someone else's bag in an empty train station! I was three and a half hours from home, so I called the train station and they said no one had been looking for it. Inside the bag were two names and addresses on a poster board and a few inexpensive pieces of jewelry or pins.

I drove home and showed everything in the bag to my wife. She also found some pot and something you vape with that was expensive. I sent out two messages on Facebook, one to a girl who sent the poster in the bag and the second one to the guy she sent it to. Two days later, my wife sent a message to the girl on Instagram, and she replied that she sent her friend (the guy) a message.

The never-ending ride continued and got stranger. I got a call from a guy named Jeff from New Jersey (yes, I am Jeff, also from New Jersey). His son had left the bag at the train station twenty-four hours before I picked it up. He was sending his son home to Pennsylvania, not too far from where I used to live. The father told me that his son had had some mental health issues and a heroin problem. Recently, the son had stolen his motorcycle and the dad knocked him out with a bat. He also said he harpooned him but didn't draw any blood. (Yes, I did say that he harpooned his son.)

A judge told him that his son could only get help in Pennsylvania since he's a resident there. He paid someone $100 to take his son to the train station with a bag of food. For some reason, the son walked through the train station parking lot into a hospital looking for food and they kept him for evaluation. The father said I could keep "his pot," but I politely declined. He told me the next time I was in the area I should stop by, since he has a large pool table. He had a friend in Myrtle Beach who owned a gas station/liquor store, and I could drop off the bag there. I left my house immediately to make the drop of the pot and the bag to another guy who was from New Jersey. My ride was over, finally, several days later.

15

MY FIRST UBER RIDE AS A RIDER AND MY TEN-THOUSANDTH RIDE

Two significant milestones happened during the past year. On May 17th, 2022, I took my first Uber ride as a passenger from Las Vegas airport. On Friday, January 13th, 2023, I gave my ten-thousandth rideshare ride in Mt. Pleasant, South Carolina (in the Charleston area).

Las Vegas, Nevada

I had given eight thousand Uber and Lyft rides and it was finally time for me to sit in the back of an Uber. I had been looking forward to it, but never would have guessed it would happen in Las Vegas since I'm not really a Vegas kind of guy. My brother was there for a vacation, and he invited me to come out for a few days. Once I agreed, I knew my first Uber ride was really going to happen.

After getting my suitcase in the Las Vegas airport, I went to the rideshare area. I was surprised to find it in the garage part of the building, and there seemed to be as many as sixty to seventy-five riders also waiting for a ride. I wasn't sure if this was the right spot, so I had to ask another rider. I was a little nervous, which I'm sure is amusing, but I wanted to make sure I found the right driver.

He showed up in five minutes and was very nice and opened the trunk for me. I told him I was an Uber driver from South Carolina, and I gave him a tip before the ride. I thanked him for the ride, and he appreciated it. I had at the time only been tipped before the ride twice, so this is not something that happens frequently.

My driver told me that he used to drive a truck across the country and drives Uber for three to four hours about five days a week. He said, "It keeps me away from the couch and TV." He had given ten thousand rides in three years; the rides in Vegas are typically shorter than I'm used to. He told me that he purposely drives under the speed limit "since people come here for a good time and I want to make sure they can do it." He was my kind of driver.

He was going to be sixty-five the next day, about three years older than I was. I wished him happy birthday and tipped him again at the end of the ride, thanking him again. He was a little confused by the second tip. He did a great job, and although it was a short ride, it was a very good one for my first ever Uber ride.

My Ten-Thousandth Ride

I knew the number ten thousand would be early in 2023. When I was a Lyft driver, I did 1,157 rides over a couple of years. Friday the 13th has always been a lucky day for me. On May 13th, 1983, I proposed to my wife, and on August 28th, 2023, we will celebrate forty years of marriage.

How do you celebrate a big number like this? One ride I'd had who was in marketing told me, "You should celebrate your ten-thousandth ride with firecrackers. Have your riders hold them." Her idea seemed a little dangerous, but it would have been good for some laughs. I asked some drivers online in South Carolina, and one said I should get a McDonald's license plate that said, "Over ten thousand served." The craziest suggestion was the driver who said, "Run naked down Ocean Boulevard near the Sky Wheel, then do a backflip into a split." I would have liked to see him do that. Other suggestions included that I should get large confetti for the car or a gift certificate.

I decided to do three things. I got a twenty-dollar Uber gift card for the rider, put up a gold banner with gold confetti hanging down around my car, and wrote on my side window, "Ten Thousand Rides Today." Below is the picture of my side window.

I bought a gold banner with attached confetti, and with my wife's suggestion, cut it in half. I hung it in the front of the car and along the two sides, pictured below. Originally, I tried to hang it from the ceiling, and I was taping it while I was flat on my back; it was coming down as fast as it went up. (Fortunately, no video of that is available.)

I had a lot of fun promoting this ride all day long. I had the gift certificate hanging up front and riders were pretty amazed about the ten thousand rides. I told the last couple of riders that they missed it by "that much" (holding my fingers slightly apart).

I drove from Downtown Charleston into Mt. Pleasant for my big ride. I took a break and cleaned the car up and picked up two guys in commercial real estate from Florida. The winner told me that the two of them had flipped a coin on who was going to order the ride and he lost. I'm sure my gift certificate paid for the ride, and he gave me a generous tip.

It was a short ride. The winner was originally from Westchester, New York, and he was a big New York fan like me, so it was perfect. I didn't tell him he won, but I had him read my note hanging from the gift certificate before I told him the good news. His friend took the picture below. There was a glare on the window, so the words on the window did not come out too well, but it was still a good picture.

I wonder what my twenty-thousandth ride will be like?

16

ME, MY CAR, MY GIFT, AND MY UBER SONG

How did I get to be an Uber/Lyft driver? I lived in New Jersey for fifty-seven years and my wife and I raised three amazing kids. We have regularly joked that whoever raised them did an unbelievable job. I went to college at Fairleigh Dickinson University in Madison, New Jersey, and majored in English and political science. I worked in middle management for several companies and visited high schools and gave presentations on careers in one job. I started delivering newspapers and circulars and then *USA Today*, my favorite newspaper. I worked full-time for them as a district manager and circulation manager and then did the same thing with *Auto Trader Magazine*. When they closed their distribution offices, I started my own business, Sunshine Man Distribution, in 2009. I distributed many magazines with independent contractor drivers and worked with many publishers in New Jersey and Pennsylvania and continued some of it in South Carolina.

Before leaving New Jersey, my wife signed up as an Uber driver and took one ride before we moved to Myrtle Beach, South Carolina, in December of 2017. I worked there for three and a half years full-time as an independent contractor courier. In July 2018, I signed up as an Uber/Lyft driver and started driving and picking people up, mostly on the weekends. I tell people all the time, I've delivered many things, but by far the best thing I've delivered is people as an Uber driver. In June 2021, I decided to semi retire after thirty-eight years of working full-time. I currently drive only on the weekends, three days a week, and just over one hundred days a year.

My Car

One month before we moved to South Carolina, my extended van was totaled as I sat at a traffic light. I decided to get a Ford Transit passenger van, because I had hoped to continue delivering things in South Carolina and I made sure I had four passenger seats in case I decided to be an Uber/Lyft driver. The greenish gray car, pictured on the back of the book, turned out to be an incredible asset. I enjoyed driving it, but my riders loved the legroom and headroom. I would regularly get compliments from my riders. Most people had never been in a car like it, and many of them had never seen one. They would say, "I've never seen a car like this," and I would reply, "That's why I'm here, just to show off the car."

After 7,500 Uber/Lyft rides and using it as a courier, it was time for another vehicle. I had to get another Ford Transit passenger van, but this one was special. The orange color is a tribute to my dad, who I had recently lost. His favorite color was orange. He never would have bought a car this color, but he would have loved to look at it. Secondly, with a business name of "The Sunshine Man," orange fits in very nicely with my name.

Below are some comments about my car:

- The pilot, who was quiet for the entire ride while I spoke with the other pilot, stood outside my car and said, "This is the best Uber vehicle I've ever seen."
- She: "This is the coolest car I've ever seen."
- "Perfect Uber driver and perfect Uber vehicle."
- About my car setup: "This is the coolest thing ever. I never had a better ride than this."
- Woman: "You have the coolest setup in your car. Don't tell anyone about your ideas." (Oops.)
- The male educator said, "This is the most perfect Uber vehicle ever built."
- "I've never gotten into a car like this before."
- "Your car is so cute."
- He: "This Uber car is perfect. I'm a big guy, but if I grew eight inches, I'd still be comfortable."
- "I love your van; it's really cool. I want one really bad."
- "I was feeling a little down when I got in your car, but after seeing your sign ("If you can't see the sunshine, be the sunshine"), I feel differently."
- Tracy, an Uber driver in Charleston, was taking a picture of one of my signs in my car when she said, "I'm not taking a picture of you, you're bald."
- My cars have been very important and extremely helpful as an Uber driver. In the fall of 2021, I picked up a woman who worked for the Kansas

City Chiefs and she pulled out her Super Bowl Ring at the end of the ride. The entire story is earlier in this book; she was my tenth favorite ride. Below is the picture of what was hanging in my car. I blew it up a little so people could see the stones; still, it's a big ring. Thousands of my riders have enjoyed seeing the ring. If you haven't read the story and the comments about the ring, you should. It will always be one of my best moments as a driver.

RIDER SHOWED ME

SUPER BOWL RING

$70,000 – MY FINGER

My Rider Money Museum

When a secret agent for our government came back from the South Sudan, he gave me a really cool bill pictured below and I hung it up. South Sudan is the newest country in the world, and I was surprised that some riders actually knew that. I thought other riders would enjoy seeing this bill, but I had no idea what it would lead to. I had a number of people take a picture of it, and then other riders started giving me bills from their country, and that's how my "Rider Money Museum" began.

I tell my riders that this is the educational part of their day and I frequently run through all the countries. Currently, I have bills from twenty-eight countries or places: South Sudan, Malaysia, Myanmar, The Philippines, Jamaica, Brazil, Scotland, Senegal, China, Chile, Venezuela, Italy, the Bahamas, Europe, Honduras, Argentina, Bulgaria, Peru, Canada, Thailand, Romania, Russia, India, Columbia, the Dominican Republic, Trinidad, Ethiopia, and Mexico. People of all ages have enjoyed looking at the bills. Recently, I wrote below or above each bill how they say "thank you" in each country. Now, riders see how unique the bills are and how different something as simple as "thank you" is around the world.

Below are some of the conversations that the bills have produced:

- A Mexican woman saw the Indian bill with Gandhi on it and said, "I love Gandhi. Would you be willing to trade it for Argentina and Italy?" I traded Gandhi, and she said, "If you ever want to trade more, come into the restaurant."
- Later that day, I told two couples that I traded Gandhi, and a guy said seriously, "My mother wouldn't have traded Gandhi."
- The professor of neuroscience was very enthusiastic about the twenty-four foreign bills in my car. On a call with his boss, he said to her, "Do you want to see the swag my Uber has in his car?" and then he showed it to her.
- She: "I've never seen anything like this." She then introduced me and videotaped me as I went through all twenty-five countries that had bills.
- He: "When I was in Zimbabwe, they were switching over to our currency, and you could buy their old money. I paid twenty-five dollars for a ten-trillion-dollar bill."
- She told me, "I collect Japanese coins. They have a hole in the middle of the coin, because a long time

ago, they used to put a string in their money and wear it around their neck."
- He spoke almost no English, but two minutes into the ride, the translator he was holding said, "I don't speak much English since I've been here a short time. I'm going to give you a bill from Chile."
- Me to the rider: "I guess you noticed all the money hanging in my car?" Her: "Where?" Me: "It's everywhere, the money." Her: "I thought you said 'bunny.'" Me: "If there was a bunny hanging in the car, you would have said something."
- She: "I'm impressed I got to see money from other countries."
- As the woman got in the car, she looked at my "Rider Money Museum" and said, "I'm so excited, I love it." She absolutely loved looking at all the money and hearing my money stories.
- He said, "Thanks for the museum."
- Talking about Gandhi, my rider said, "Isn't he the guy with a bald head and a robe?"
- He: "I'm sorry I don't have any currency for your car, but this South Carolina police patch can help you avoid a parking ticket."
- Older man: "I just gave away a bunch of old Belgium and Germany bills at my garage sale—I could have given them to you."
- After taking pictures of my foreign bills hanging in my car, the Korean woman said that through her app, "Only a hundred friends will get to see this."
- I told the woman that I had an extra bill from Argentina, and I could give it to her. She: "How

much should I pay you?" Me: "No, I'm going to give it to you."
- I told them that I drove from Myrtle Beach to Charleston just to pick them up. She looked at all the money in my car from other countries and said, "Did you go to all these places to pick up riders too?"
- She: "I like your schtick."

Pictured above on the right are two blue bills from Canada, and below that is Thailand. Next to Canada is Romania, and below that, the Soviet Union, and "thank you" in each country's language.

The Canadian Bill

One week after I received the beautiful Canadian bill pictured above, I picked up two golfers from Canada. One of them told me that "the bills are almost impossible to rip." He reached into his wallet and pulled out a hundred-dollar bill and tried to give it to me to try to rip it. I told him I was driving and his friend took the hundred-dollar bill and ripped it in half immediately. The three of us immediately started laughing. Below is the picture of the ripped bill, which I was told would easily be replaced by a bank.

My Gift List

When I started driving and meeting all these interesting people, it was very natural to write a blog post at the end of every month about the people that I'd met. I had been writing my blog, "Becoming a Southerner," since December 2017, when my wife and I started our journey to South Carolina. I wanted our children, my family, and a few friends to keep track of our adventures.

About a year after I started writing about my riders, I realized I needed two blog posts, one about their comments and the other being some short stories of my favorite people that month. There were so many good comments that at the end of my first full year, 2019, I wanted to give some of my riders a little gift. I quickly put together a list of eighteen comments from the year and printed it out. Immediately, I realized that I could only give it out as they were leaving my car, because everyone wanted to read it. I gave out this "holiday gift" through January to some of my riders. I also learned that women were more interested in reading it, and I was amazed at how excited they were. Below is the story of the most ridiculous reaction to my gift, and there is no way I could write about this without her story.

In 2021, 2022, and during 2023, I have given out a list from the previous year to nearly two thousand riders. It is so much fun to give people something they don't expect and something they can enjoy after the ride is over. I know of two riders who posted the list in their house and other riders who have given the list to others. All the comments on those lists are in this book. And now, you have to meet Ms. Enthusiasm.

Ms. Enthusiasm

By far, the best reaction I have ever had to my list of favorite comments came from a woman from North Carolina, who I have to call "Ms. Enthusiasm." I was driving her to a wedding that was just over the border of South Carolina in North Carolina. She was in her mid- to late-twenties and originally from Pittsburgh and a big Steeler fan. I entertained her with a few stories and told her my Immaculate Reception story, and she played the play twice on her phone since she didn't know what it was. She couldn't wait to tell her dad, and also her date, who she was meeting at the wedding.

We had a great time, and she did a lot of laughing until I told her I was going to give her my list of favorite comments, and her response was, "Are you joking? This is an Uber ride to remember!" I started laughing and had trouble stopping when she said, "This is the best day of my life." I pulled up in the parking lot where the wedding was, and I handed her my list. She didn't want to get out of the car. I said, "You have to get out, it's a wedding. You can read the list later, just fold it and put it in your purse." She said, "I don't want to fold it, I want to frame it." She had just started reading the list and I told her that I was writing a book about my Uber adventures, and she replied, "No way!" She put the list in her purse and got out of the car. Imagine if I told her that she was going to be in this book!

Below are some of the comments about my list:

- Male chef: "When you gave me your list of comments a few weeks ago, I hung it near my bed, and each morning I read one to get my day off to a good start."
- The three close friends, sorority sisters, were on a girl's weekend. One woman: "I don't think we've said anything funny [enough] to make your list of favorite comments." Another woman, pointing to the third woman, a lawyer: "I have it. We have known her [the third woman] for seventeen years and this is the first time we've seen her boobs."
- After giving him my favorite comments list for 2021, she said, "What a great way to start our vacation."
- She: "Your list was hilarious; it was great dinner conversation."
- When I asked the couple from New Jersey, "Have you ever gotten a gift from an Uber driver?" he answered, "This ride has been a gift."

- When she received my favorite comment list, she said, "This is my favorite thing!" Me: "Even better than ice cream?" She replied, "Yes!" I added, "It's not better than ice cream, I've eaten ice cream!"
- When I told him about my blog and my list of rider comments, he said, "That's effin' genius."
- Driving two older women in their sixties or seventies, I said, "I have a surprise for you." She: "Are you going to let one of us drive?"
- Me: "Have you gotten a gift from an Uber driver before?" Her: "Yes, a driver in North Carolina gave me pot, but I threw it out."
- When I told her about my list, she said, "That's fabulous."
- Mother: "Our two oldest daughters have been keeping a notebook for years on the things their younger brother says—they call it 'Comments from Cooper.'"
- Me: "Have you ever gotten a gift from your Uber driver?" Her: "No, just the gift of transporting me."
- She: "I can't wait to read your list; I make a list of comments that I hear people say."
- Her: "I was so excited at getting your list, I left my phone in your car."
- Me: "Can I give you an early Christmas present?" She said, "A puppy?"
- I told the couple I was going to give them a gift, but it was not paying for their breakfast. He replied, "That would have been a great gift."
- "This is our favorite thing to do; we're in marketing."

- After giving her my list of favorite comments for 2020, she said, "That's the nicest thing that's happened to me all day."
- The young woman was going only a couple minutes to a surprise birthday party for her brother's girlfriend, but she was bummed out that she had no gift. When I told her about my list of favorite comments, she got very excited and walked into the party with my list as her gift. I laughed for several blocks.
- Dropping them off in Downtown Charleston at a very nice restaurant and giving them my list, the guy said, "We'll take a look at it." His fiancée said, "I'm so excited to read this. We'll read it during dinner. Thank you."
- Complaining about the Uber driver who canceled on him due to traffic, I said, "Would you like a gift from your Uber driver?" Him: "No, it's not necessary." Later, he changed his mind, and as I pulled away, he was reading my list standing outside his front door.
- She: "We'll read your list when we go into the restaurant." Me: "Remember, you're going to be in a public place, so if you laugh too much, everyone will want to read it." She: "Don't worry, it will be for our eyes only."
- After giving her my list of favorite rider comments as a Valentine's Day gift, she said, "I wish I had something to give you." Me: "You did; you laughed at my stories and you're from New Jersey where I'm from. What could be better than that?"

- The woman was on a business call for 100 percent of the twenty-five-minute trip from the airport, and I had no conversation with her other than "hello." Taking her luggage out, I told her I was giving her my list of favorite rider comments for 2020. She said, "I hope I made the list for 2021." She didn't, but she made this book.

17

COMMENTS AND COMPLIMENTS

I've been very fortunate to have so many generous riders who have appreciated the effort I made to inform, educate, entertain, and of course, drive them on their ride with me. The best way of thanking them is with this book, but these are some of the comments and compliments I have received.

Comments

- The male designer from Los Angeles said, "Here's my card. When your book comes out, let me know. I want to buy it."
- Female: "Why did you move here?" Me: "My wife loves the beach and I love her, so we're at the beach." Female: "That's the best line I've ever heard."
- "You and your wife are tag-team Uber drivers."
- "Uber drivers are special because you have the opportunity to reach and touch people as they are going through life."

- When I mentioned that I write a blog about some of my riders, the woman yelled out, "We're going to be in the blog!"
- She takes seventeen thousand steps a day working in a parking garage. Me: "How about we switch jobs and I get some exercise, and you can eat all the snacks I have today?" She: "At the end of the day, you'll ask why I had no rides, because I'll just pull over and eat."
- She: "Where did you get your mats cleaned?" (I'd just cleaned them with water before she got in.)
- I asked the woman with long, bright pink hair if my hair was pink whether it would clash with my orange car. She said, "No, it would look great, you can bleach it."
- I started telling a story: "I had three women from Iowa yesterday—" and the guy interrupted and said, "You lucky dog." Me: "There is more to that sentence."
- When I told him that I was sixty-one, he said, "I thought you were forty-one." When I told this to two women later, one said, "I thought you were in your early fifties."
- "I love your bald head."
- "I'm surprised you're from the North; you seem like a Southerner."
- She: "I do hair and makeup." Me: "I really don't have either of them." She: "It's never too late to use makeup."
- "Your voice sounds like you've been a radio broadcaster."

- Me: "Would you like a trivia question?" Her: "Is this like the Cash Cab?"
- Me: "I'm from New Jersey." She: "I thought you were doggone Southern!"
- The barber said to me, "You earned your hair loss by living a long time."
- The young woman said, "Look at all the things you have hanging up there." Me: "Each one has a story; what do you want to know about first?" Looking at my business card, where I put an X over Lyft since I don't drive for them now, she said, "Why did you cross out 'Lyft'?"
- The mother from New York, a new Market Commons homeowner, was experiencing her first Uber ride with her future daughter-in-law, who she said "has a heart of gold." Getting out of the car, the younger woman said to me enthusiastically, "I love you."
- I told the thirty-one-year-old woman, "About 98 percent of the people who get in my car have not been drinking." She replied, "To be honest with you, I've had three drinks. Does that make a difference?" (Yes, you're in my book.)
- I told the story about the driver who tipped me twenty dollars for "not murdering her" on a three-mile ride. Getting out of the car, she said, "I'm looking forward to reading your list, thank you," and handed me a twenty-dollar bill. Me: "Is this for not murdering you?" She replied, "Yes, and opening the door too."

Compliments

The first four compliments below are on the back cover of this book, and they are as good as it gets. I have picked out another twenty that are listed below that. I've received many others, so I listed those a little differently at the end of this section. It is very humbling to have so many nice things said about me, and this is my way of showing my appreciation.

- "This man is a credit to the human race. I wish I could get more rides like this every time I get a Lyft."
- "I forgot I was in an Uber. It felt like a ride with a friend."
- "We had a magical evening ride, although it lasted only a mile."
- Woman from Indiana: "You are awesome! Love your zest for life! Thank you for making me laugh (a lot)."
- Young man from Kansas: "Of all the great things I'll remember from this trip, your good deed will be at the top."
- "Awesome person, need more people like you in the world."
- Favorite Ride #47, a young couple dating in Colorado: "You truly were an unforgettable person and we both appreciated your positive outlook on life. Please never change yourself, because you've reminded me that there are still people that look at the bright side and look for the good in people."
- Getting the woman ready for her interview for a manager's job at Publix, I had her laughing most of the trip. Getting out, she said, "Thank you. I'm

going through a divorce now and you have totally made my day."
- "I never leave reviews for Uber, but it was legitimately a pleasure riding with Jeff."
- *She got out of my car at noon after a three-mile ride and handed me twenty dollars and said, "This is for not murdering us. I have a fear of Uber drivers." Me: "Thank you, but you're wearing a black Friday the 13th shirt—I should fear you."
- "Thank you so much, you are my hero, Jeffro-no-fro."
- Male: "I really like the vibe you have in your car. You're the best Uber driver we've had. We need more people like you in this world."
- "One of the most entertaining and conversational rides I've ever had! Thank you so much for such amazing service!"
- *After a fun ride, he said, "You can blow sunshine up our butt anytime. I would have said 'ass,' but I thought I was on *Cash Cab*."
- From my Favorite Ride #5, the hilarious young man said, "I've never tipped an Uber driver, but I have to tip you."
- The owner of a limo business for twenty-five years looked around my car and said, "I like how you service your customers."
- The woman said she was a Diamond Uber Rider, which means she's taken a lot of rides. She said, "You're my best Uber driver ever."
- "I'm hoping some of your positivity rubs off on my four-year-old."

- She: "I love the title of the book you're writing. It could be a movie and you could play yourself." (Imagine that!)
- Getting out of my car, the communications manager said with a big smile, "This has been the best part of my Charleston vacation."
- As she got out of the car, the younger sister, who had not said much during my great conversation with her older sister, made me laugh out loud when she said, "I'm a better human being after taking this ride."
- Happy rider: "Does Uber know who you are, what you do?"
- He: "You are one of the nicest Uber drivers we've ever had." Me: "One of the nicest?" Him: "You even made the rain stop!" Me: "My business name is The Sunshine Man."
- "The man, the myth, the legend. Leaves before daylight, guided only by the mantra, 'People out there need rides.' The best South Carolina and New Jersey has to offer. Well done and congratulations."

Individual Compliments in Alphabetical Order

- "Amazing trip." "Awesome." "Amazing, amazing ride." "Attitude the best." "You were amazing."
- "Boyfriend loved the baseball stories, which took him down memory lane." "Brightened our morning." "Best ride ever." "Book will be interesting." "Best Uber driver ever!" "Bravo JEFFRO-NO-FRO!"

COMMENTS AND COMPLIMENTS

- "Chivalry is not dead." "Coolest thing ever!" "Changed my day." "Chivalrous way of going about picking up people." "Coolest Uber I've ever seen."
- "Delightful." "Don't want to get out of the car."
- "Excellent service." "Excited to be in this back seat."
- "Fan of yours." "Funnest Uber driver." "Feels like I learned something."
- "Greatest Uber driver in South Carolina!" "Great spirit." "Great personality." "Giving you ten stars." "Guy is effin' cool."
- "Historic Uber." "Hope I meet you again." "Happy you have a great rating." "Have never taken an Uber like this."
- "Inspiration to me, you don't have to be here." "I can tell you really enjoy what you do." "Interesting car." "Intriguing individual." "I like being in the happy car." "I know funny, and funny is you." I feel like I learned something." I love you so much, you're the best one ever."
- "Joy in everything you do."
- "Keep on doing a good job Ubering." "Keep doing what you're doing."
- "Like your vibe." "Love your energy." "Looking forward to reading your book." "Love people who smile." "Love how you decorated your car." "Love everything about this ride."
- "Most interesting ride we ever had." (From Malaysia.) "Most entertaining driver I've ever had." "My favorite Uber driver." "Most festive Uber I've ever been in." "Most passionate driver I've ever had."

- "Never had a better ride than this." "Not expecting this from my Uber." "Needed to hear from you today." "Nicest Uber driver I've ever had."
- "Pleasure meeting you." "Positivity, thank you for it."
- "Refreshing how passionate you are." "Ride is like Disney World."
- "So glad I got you to drive me." "Solid good people." "Special kind of person." "So happy. So glad our paths crossed." "Some amazing stories."
- "Thank you, Mr. Jeffrey. Tell your wife she has a lovely husband." "Thanks for making the ride better." "Thanks for talking to me." "Thanks for the normal conversation." "Talent for stand-up, you should do it."
- "Unforgettable ride!" "Unique car."
- "Vibe, I love yours." "Very enjoyable."
- "Wish we could put you on speed dial." "World needs a little sunshine." "Wonderful way of driving with Uber." "Wicked cool."
- "You're in the 1 percent." "You put a smile on my face." "You're a light in the world."

Comments About My Wife

- The woman was in her late twenties and was riding with her boyfriend. I told her that my wife has been hit on while she was driving rideshare and sometimes it was from guys in their twenties and thirties. Showing her our business card with my wife's picture on it, the woman looked at the card and said, "I'd hit on her too."

- The two young couples had been drinking. After telling them I had a thirty-three-year-old daughter, one woman said, "You look like you're thirty-two." Me: "I did just say I had a thirty-three-year-old daughter." She replied, "You never know." When I showed her a picture of my wife, she said, "She's beautiful; you got game."
- Thirty-year-old woman looked at a picture of my wife and said, "She's beautiful, what did she find in you?" After some prodding from me, she said, "You are cute."
- Saying goodbye to me after seeing my wife's picture on our business card, she said, "Make sure you tell your wife she is so beautiful."
- Looking at a picture of my wife, she said, "She's gorgeous, beautiful. You tell her I said she's 'beautimous.'" (At work, her and her friend came up with this word.)

My Uber Song

In high school, my good friend Larry wrote a parody of a song by The Who and he called it "Jersey Traffic." I thought it was the coolest thing to write other words to a song. He introduced me to the music of Allan Sherman, and I still love his parodies. I started writing songs or parodies in college and I enjoyed it. Over the years, I've written over three hundred songs, mostly to other music. I have written a few songs that are pretty good.

One early Sunday morning in Myrtle Beach, I was driving up Ocean Boulevard, and I was inspired. I wrote this song quickly, and it's to original music. I don't play an instrument, read music, or sing well, but I do enjoy writing. I had been driving with Uber/Lyft only a few months and I had no clue how much I was going to enjoy driving. It has become an important part of my life. In the song, I mention the mayor, my favorite ride, and the Egyptian Priest, who is listed as my twenty-first favorite ride.

The song below is a ballad, however, recently a driver heard my song and created some music to make it a jazz tune, which was very flattering. I added a few more words for the jazzy version, but the original words are below.

I hope you've enjoyed your ride as much as I've enjoyed giving it to you. We're heading toward our final destination.

"Ubering On a Sunday Morn"

It's an early morning Sunday
As I drive with my windows down.
I'm searching for my first ride
Somewhere in this town.

The breeze is blowing quickly
Through my head of hair.
The sun is rising slowly.
I can smell the ocean air.

It's an early morning Sunday
As the joggers make their run.
So many people still sleeping.
Not me, I'm having fun.

Who needs to go to the airport
And leave this peaceful town?
Me, I'm driving in circles,
Round and round and round.

I talk to people who I
Pick up from everywhere.
I learn a lot about life.
From each and every fare.

The Egyptian priest from Indiana
And the small-town mayor from PA.
I won't forget the words
I heard both of them say.

It's an early morning Sunday,
And it's another beautiful day,
I love driving with Uber
In Myrtle Beach today.

18
"AND IN THE END"

I'm a big fan of The Beatles, so the words "and in the end" can only mean one thing. The last song the four Beatles recorded together was completed in August 1969 and it was a short song called "The End." The one line in the song is this: "And in the end, the love you take is equal to the love you make."

This is our final stop on our journey together. I absolutely loved sharing with you this incredible experience I have had over the past five years. You can tell that I love being an Uber (and Lyft) driver, and I gave my riders my very best as often as I could. I have been very fortunate to have had so many of them share their lives with me and give me their best.

On the Uber app, I have a message that says, "I can't change your life, but I can change your day." I know that, for at least hundreds of riders, I was able to change their day for the better. I have always believed that one person can make a difference, and I know that so many riders have made a difference in my life and in many of my other riders' lives.

This was a special trip, and it has to end in a special way. When I started writing this book, I was thinking a lot about the introduction and the conclusion. How could I end this in a meaningful way? It was appropriate that I found my answer at a place whose slogan is "The Most Magical Place on Earth."

In March 2022, my wife and I had a terrific vacation in Orlando, Florida, with our family. As a huge Disney fan, one day I found myself in Disney World at Epcot Center in the Land exhibit. I was standing in line and I was reading the motivational quotes that were all over the wall. And there it was—my ending. I knew it as soon as I saw it.

"I may be only one person, but I can be one person who makes a difference." That ten-year-old girl knows what she's talking about. The ball is now in your court. I have done my very best to brighten your day and your life and I've used the words and lives of hundreds and hundreds of riders that I have driven.

Every single day, you can make someone's day. When you get in an Uber or Lyft, you can make someone's day. Or you could make the day of a coworker, or someone at a local store, or the person delivering your mail. Life at times is difficult, painful, and heartbreaking, but you can still live on the sunny side. You and I have so many things to be grateful for. When you're struggling the most, you need to brighten someone else's day and their smile or laugh will brighten your day. You can do it!

If anyone asks why you're so cheerful, why you're laughing, why you're smiling—tell them about those four lads from Liverpool, England. They are still bringing joy to the world fifty years after their band broke up. You could tell them about a ten-year-old girl from Bowling Green, Kentucky. Or, if you must, you can tell them about me, the Sunshine Man, and my adventures driving on the sunny side with over ten thousand strangers.

Wishing you and yours all the very best,

—Jeff (The Sunshine Man)

PS: I wish my mom and dad were still with us; they would have enjoyed this book. Thanks, Mom and Dad, for everything.

Printed in the USA
CPSIA information can be obtained
at www.ICGtesting.com
LVHW020415280923
759305LV00002B/2

9 798822 915053